D0851627

RULES MATTER: ELECTION LAW REVEALED

Drew Kurlowski
ASSISTANT PROFESSOR
DEPARTMENT OF POLITICS
COASTAL CAROLINA UNIVERSITY

WEST
ACADEMIC
PUBLISHING

The publisher is not engaged in rendering legal or other professional advice, and this publication is not a substitute for the advice of an attorney. If you require legal or other expert advice, you should seek the services of a competent attorney or other professional.

© 2019 LEG, Inc. d/b/a West Academic
    444 Cedar Street, Suite 700
    St. Paul, MN 55101
    1-877-888-1330

West, West Academic Publishing, and West Academic are trademarks of West Publishing Corporation, used under license.

Printed in the United States of America

ISBN: 978-1-68328-073-6

For my family.

Table of Contents

Table of Cases

RULES MATTER: ELECTION LAW REVEALED

CHAPTER 1

Introduction

A. RULES

At an 1826 caucus in Philadelphia, the matter was taken up of whether or not to adjourn from a crowded courtroom to the nearby yard. A voice vote was taken, and when the chair found himself unable to discern between the two factions, a calamity broke out. Reports of the event discussed the 'material injury' of furniture, the ejection of the chairman, who became a 'floor man' when his chair was abruptly taken from under him, and members of the quorum brandishing knives, fighting, and biting each other.[1] Other stories of caucus violence and corruption are not hard to come by. One scholar relates a story of viva voce votes at an 1890s caucus, where whispers of aye defeat boisterous nays. One candidate for nomination in Boston presented his party chairman with a request to see the open ballot box before voting commenced. The written request was torn up, thrown in the fire, and the candidate was escorted out by police. In the final tally, the man lost 510–234, a staggering defeat considering the 300 who were in attendance that day.[2]

While these examples of unruly behavior and outright electoral fraud make for interesting and humorous anecdotes, the reality of the electoral landscape in America is that we have been on a perpetual quest to refine our election procedures since the founding of the nation. We have fought to end the disenfranchisement of large majorities of the populace, and to make voting easier and more accessible for all. We have simultaneously struggled with the integrity of our electoral processes, combating those who would wish to defraud our political systems. Our electoral system today consists not only of a complex set of federal rules, but also of election rules and codes in all 50 states. These diverse sets of rules each have particular and peculiar eccentricities which are the product of each state's unique journey. In some states, the progressive impulse has fashioned open and liberal election laws, where in others, strong party machines

1

fashioned more restrictive rules. Throughout the south, election laws are marked by a history of racial discrimination and disenfranchisement.

The aim of this book is to explain the nature, history, and application of the rules that govern our electoral processes. At its core, the central premise of this book is that *rules matter*. This is to say, the rules which govern our electoral processes have meaningful consequences for our elections. To state it in another way, our rules are not neutral—they determine who votes, who runs for office, and how we cast and count out ballots.

Our laws determine who may vote in our elections. The Constitution did not originally specify who would be allowed to vote, leaving the eligibility of voters up to state laws. Today, the Constitution protects the right to vote for nearly all Americans, but state laws still contain important restrictions on voters, like registration rules and voter identification laws. These rules are not neutral in that they have a clear and meaningful impact on the outcomes of our elections. Changing the makeup of the electorate by making it easier or harder to vote could affect the outcome of an election. Thinking more normatively, we can ask ourselves questions about the importance of participation for democratic governance. Should we make it easier for individuals to register to vote, or harder? How concerned should we be with the integrity of our elections? Are there certain responsibilities attached to voting? Should convicted felons be allowed to vote? Should individuals with intellectual disabilities or other mental health disorders participate in our elections? By setting the parameters of the electorate we are making important choices about our country's relationship with democracy, and which voices will be heard on Election Day.

Our laws determine who may run for office. Again, the Constitution sets very specific qualifications for federal office, limiting the field of potential candidates. State laws do the same for a wide array of statewide and local offices. In many cases these qualifications set a low threshold for eligibility, only speaking to age, residency, and citizenship. Should we have more rigorous qualifications for candidates for public office? Perhaps our meager qualifications are already too strict, disqualifying capable leaders who do not meet citizenship requirements or happen to be too young. In addition to these rules, candidates are bound by term limits in some cases and have to follow specific procedures to have their names placed on the ballot. Conversely, there are no term limits for members of Congress. Do these elected officials become better as they stay in office longer, or should we force them out after only a few terms? While running for office, we restrict the behavior of candidates, especially with regards to campaign finance, setting the bounds for how candidates raise and spend money. Government is not the only player in this process, as parties play an important role by setting rules and procedures for nomination. This constellation of rules structures our elections by limiting the universe of potential choices.

Our laws determine how we cast and count our ballots. When, and in what form do we designate our choices? Things as simple as ballot design have the potential to alter election outcomes by structuring how we vote. Some designs have been shown to increase the chances that a voter casts an invalid ballot, whereas other ballot designs can make casting a vote much easier. We can design simple voting systems that elect simple plurality winners, or more complex systems that allow us to rank order our choices. Even after we vote, sets of rules determine how ballots are counted, or even recounted, ensuring the accuracy of the tabulation of votes. Whether it be the specific procedures of a party nominating contest or the complex process behind the Electoral College, rules control how we determine the winner of a particular election.

In addition to making the argument that these rules matter, this book hopes to explain *how* these rules matter. While the bulk of the upcoming chapters will help to explore and explain different systems of rules across the states, each chapter contains a section dedicated to exploring the potential consequences of these rules. It is important to understand what rules exist, and how they operate in practice, but it is also important to understand the practical implications of these differences. Recent research in the field of political science will help us to illuminate the relationships between rules and outcomes. Should we expect different candidates to run if we change the qualifications for office? Will more people vote if ease registration requirements? We will attempt to explore these questions and grapple with the normative implications of rules throughout this book.

B. OUTLINE

Before beginning our exploration of election rules, let's look at an overview of the topic we will explore.

Chapter 1 introduces the voter as perhaps the most fundamental of all actors in an election. This chapter deals primarily with setting up the right to vote and the requirements and restrictions surrounding the act of voting. The chapter will introduce, briefly, major changes which have expanded the right to vote to non-property owners, non-white males, women, and those aged 18–21. The discussion will then turn to those groups that remain disenfranchised in the American electoral system. The chapter will also cover registration laws in the states, including recent changes like same-day, or election-day registration. The chapter will also introduce, but will not completely cover, how registration affects the ability to participate in partisan primaries. Specifics about these systems will be included in Chapter 4. Finally, the chapter will conclude with a discussion of voter identification laws, their legal basis, and status in the states.

Chapter 2 will introduce laws that affect the candidates. Broadly, these rules cover basic Constitutional requirements for federal office (including what 'natural-born citizen' means), term limits, ballot access, and independent candidacies. The chapter will also contain a discussion of sore-loser laws, petition requirements, and other rules that govern independent candidates.

Chapter 3 will examine the apportionment of U.S. House seats, districting, and gerrymandering. This chapter answers important questions about how we determine the number of House seats a state receives, how often we do this, and how electoral maps are drawn. We will examine state-by-state differences on how this procedure is conducted. While many states allow their state legislature full autonomy in drawing district lines, other states use some form of partisan or independent commission to complete this process. After this discussion, the chapter examines how districts are actually drawn. What characteristics do we value? What constitutes a compact or contiguous district? Do we split towns, or try to maintain communities of interest? This chapter will also look at legal controversies surrounding equal-population, at-large districts, and gerrymandering. What exactly constitutes an unconstitutional gerrymander versus a constitutional gerrymander, and why do these geographic districts matter?

Chapter 4 will introduce the party as an important player in the process and discuss the legal status of parties over time, as well as how they structure the first part of our electoral procedure—nomination. The discussion will proceed from parties as loose associations, to their status as quasi-public entities, akin to public utilities. Part of the focus of this chapter will be on how many early election laws were not state laws themselves, but rather party rules. It was not until the late 19th and early 20th century that states began either giving legal force to party rules or adopting party rules as statutes. This chapter will also focus on nominations in two parts. The first section will discuss the direct primary, which is the system that nominates candidates for most sub-presidential offices. This section will briefly touch on why we use primaries, caucuses, and conventions to nominate (vis-à-vis parties) and how these rules have evolved over time. The second section on nomination will discuss presidential nominating politics. The main goal of this section will be to discuss the rise of the primary system for choosing delegates to the national party conventions. Who are the delegates to the conventions? How do we select these people, and do the rules differ by state? How do we determine how many delegates there are per state? This chapter will demystify these differences by highlighting the role of the parties in the process, explaining how parties determine the number of delegates per state, and discussing the various delegate allocation rules that exist in the states.

Chapter 5 will turn to a discussion of the Electoral College. This institution is one that, while relatively simple to understand, is cloaked in mystery. This chapter will lift the veil on these electors, how they are chosen, and what role they fill in electing the president. This chapter will also discuss the normative implications of the Electoral College through an examination of historic scenarios that threw the College into crisis. Looking back on contested elections, we will learn about the process and procedure that the Electoral College uses to deal with contested electors, unfaithful electors, ties, and other scenarios. Finally, this chapter will introduce some of the more popular possibilities for reform of the Electoral College and discuss their practical implications on presidential elections.

Chapter 6 is a very important chapter, but one that often receives little attention in the classroom. Campaign finance laws are muddled and complex, and often pose a challenge to students of politics. This chapter will begin by briefly introducing the history of campaign finance laws in the United States, before looking at legal developments over the past two decades. The Bipartisan Campaign Reform Act, as well as a number of court cases, have dramatically altered the campaign finance landscape. The chapter will present the legal status of spending, fundraising, and other campaign finance laws, and discuss the normative implications of these rules. One hurdle to understanding campaign finance is in distinguishing various types of spending groups. This chapter will discuss these groups in detail, explaining abilities and restrictions, and how groups can even work together to finance campaigns.

Chapter 7 will examine elections by looking at how we cast, count, and recount votes in the United States. By comparing and contrasting various alternative methods for determining winners we can see how basic majority and plurality rules can lead to different outcomes. The chapter also discusses other vote counting systems in use across the country, including runoff elections, and preferential systems like ranked choice voting. We will then turn to balloting methods, and we will explore how voters in different states cast their ballots, whether by hand or by machine, as well as how election authorities go about counting votes. This chapter will also cover rules regarding recounts—how are they triggered, and how are they conducted.

Hopefully, by the end of this book, you will have a better understanding of what rules exist, how they are different, and why these rules matter for our elections.

---

[1]   Niles, W. Ogden. Niles, H. 1837. Niles' weekly register. Baltimore: H. Niles. P. 85.

[2]   Dallinger, Frederick. 1897. Nominations for Elective Office in the United States. Longmans, Green and Co: New York. p. 119.

Citizens and the Right to Vote

A. THE RIGHT TO VOTE

A reasonable attempt to examine election rules ought to start with the most basic building block of our electoral system—the right to vote. The United States has a contentious history with this right, at once guaranteed by the Constitution, yet historically denied to large swaths of the populace. While the United States has moved through eras of expansion and suppression of the franchise, across the long arc of history, the franchise has expanded to encompass nearly the entirety of the country. While a complete history of all laws is not the purpose of this volume, the following chapter will briefly recount the history of the right to vote, before examining the administrative rules which govern voter eligibility.

1. Sources of American Voting Restrictions

In the earliest days of the United States, and during the colonial era, the franchise was extremely limited. As with many other institutional rules, the first voter-eligibility rules were vestiges of the British system. British law required voters to be male, over the age of 21, and own property. These restrictions entered American institutions by way of colonial, and later state, law. The U.S. Constitution is relatively silent on voter eligibility, beyond later amendments. It makes no reference to any particular eligibility requirements, and moreover only directly speaks to qualifications for those voting in U.S. House elections. The founders envisioned electoral schemes for the office of President and Senator that were centered around state legislatures (the direct election of Senators was not included in the Constitution until 1917, and the Constitution gave states complete authority to devise methods to select electors to the Electoral College), thus the Constitution did not need to make any mention of voter eligibility in these contests. However, members of the House of Representatives were directly elected, and the Constitution specified that eligibility for voting in House races should match state laws for eligibility to vote in state legislative races, specifically lower house elections. This meant that early qualifications for voting would necessarily be promulgated by states themselves, rather than the federal government.

Voting requirements across the states varied widely during this time, but all had a similar flavor. Borne of a desire to limit the franchise to those who were financially independent, most states required voters to own real property or otherwise demonstrate financial independence. Blackstone's *Commentaries* makes this thought clear when he discusses the idea that the wealthy could potentially exert undue influence over those without financial independence.[1] Thus, a property requirement was promoted as a protection against the corruption of elections.

This property requirement carried with it an implicit age requirement. Tradition and English common law set the age of majority at 21. This meant that individuals must meet this age before being able to buy property. While this leaves open the opportunity for some inheritors of property to be under this age, it is not clear in all cases whether or not these property holders would be allowed to vote. Williamson notes in his survey of early voting laws that only Connecticut, New York, North Carolina, Pennsylvania, South Carolina, and Virginia specifically called for voters to be older than 21.[2]

The sources of gender-based restrictions are less clear than financial restrictions. In many cases, laws relating to voting rights did not make any mention of gender. Indeed, the common law sources for property requirements are also silent on gender requirements. Williamson's survey of colonial laws mentions that only Delaware, Pennsylvania, and South Carolina made any explicit effort to limit to the vote to males.[3] It seems, however, that tradition dominated the lack of statutory guidance on the subject in most cases. The prominent counterexample of this is the odd case of New Jersey, where women regularly participated in politics. Judith Klinghoffer and Lois Elkis[4] point out that New Jersey's unique (albeit brief) grant of suffrage generally seen by scholars as the result of haphazard or ambiguous construction of language, rather than by a purposive effort to enfranchise women. If this conventional account is true, it lends credence to the argument that gender-based voting requirements were based more in custom, than in statute. A revision of the New Jersey law in 1807 would finally bring gender into the election code, by specifying that voters be male. Keyssar[5] notes that other states that had disenfranchised women based on tradition, but not statute, would gradually follow suit and introduce specific statutes to codify male-only voting.

This would end the early experiment in voting for women and disenfranchise women for years to come.

Beyond these three restrictions, all proximately derived from the requirement to own property, there were also some other specific restrictions on voting that existed during the colonial era and the days of the early United States. Both Keyssar and Williamson point out that some states, notably Georgia, North Carolina, South Carolina, and Virginia denied the vote to property-owning black males. As discussed in the next section, race-based restrictions would begin to expand in the early half of the nineteenth century. Additionally, many colonies denied the vote to non-protestants—either through a religious requirement or through an outright prohibition on voting by Catholics or Jews.[6] Although these religious tests quickly disappeared after the revolution, South Carolina was a notable exception, maintaining a clause that "The qualification of electors shall be that every free white man, and no other person, who acknowledges the being of a God, and believes in a future state of rewards and punishments. . ."[7] This provision would not be removed from their constitution until 1790,[8] being the last state to do so.[9]

Throughout the colonial era, changes to voting laws were common. The practical effects of these changes varied widely—some restricting voting and some enlarging the right. As Keyssar points out, the net change in voting rights was likely positive, but on only modestly. What the colonial era gave us, however, was a system of voting rules that were codified at the state level. This reality sets into motion the narrative of this book. The history of voting laws in the United States is one where the principal battlegrounds are state constitution and state statute. The movement of the federal government into the fray is a more modern development, and when the federal government does play a role—at least in terms of voting rights—its contribution is generally constitutional, and still in need of state enforcement.

2.   The Early Eighteenth Century

Throughout the early nineteenth century, three principle changes were affected to state laws governing voter eligibility: the elimination of property restrictions, the disenfranchisement of black male voters, and the creation of restrictions on non-citizen voting. Of somewhat lesser impact, this period also saw increased codification of age and gender restrictions that had been customarily enforced (as noted in the previous section). It is important to note that at this time, all of these changes are happening through changes to state law, rather than by any federal intervention. What, then, drove these changes, and how did voting rights change in the early nineteenth century?

A key change to voting laws throughout the first half of the nineteenth century was the gradual erosion of property requirements. While there is no singular reason for these changes, Keyssar and others point out a handful of potential suspects. Understood broadly, landed classes could no longer ignore the growing proportion of the population that could not meet freeholding or property requirements laid out under colonial rule. A growing urban middle class needed to be brought into the electoral fold.[10] Whether convinced by arguments and appeals to rights,[11] or for political or economic expediency,[12] many states began to ease property restrictions. Between 1790 and 1855, the number of states with property requirements would dwindle from ten to three, with those remaining (NY, RI, and SC) being relaxed enough to permit most white males to vote without meeting a property requirement.[13]

Turning our attention to the voting rights of black voters, we see a more disheartening situation unfold. While relatively few states categorically excluded landowning blacks during the founding era, most states adopted exclusionary language between 1790 and 1850. Keyssar makes an important point that every state that entered the union after 1819 barred blacks from voting.[14] New York abolished their property requirement for whites but left it in place for blacks, effectively keeping most blacks in the state disenfranchised.[15]

Non-citizens were another target for disenfranchisement over this early period. Many state constitutions gave the right to vote to inhabitants of the state. It would not be until successive amendments to those constitutions, that many states would limit voting to citizens only by changing the wording of laws from 'inhabitant' to 'citizen'.[16] Federal statute[17] set the requirements for citizenship as a residency period of two years, and then later, five years. These restrictions were combined with residency requirements in many states, which curtailed the voting rights of transient workers and other recent arrivals to jurisdictions.

During this same period, similar changes were being made across many states (or being written in the constitutions of new states) that clarified restrictions on age and gender. While these requirements were likely customarily enforced, examples like the previously mentioned New Jersey case show that the clarifications came quickly to limit ambiguity in language.

Taken in whole, this early period in American history was a mix of expansion and contraction of voting rights. What little expansion that did take place before the civil war was primarily to benefit a growing middle class of white men. It would take two movements in the latter half of the century would begin to enlarge the franchise to blacks and women—federal intervention and the progressive era.

3. Constitutional Change and the Early 20th Century

As mentioned in the previous section, the first half of the nineteenth century saw gains in voting rights for white male voters, however, blacks and women still did not have the right to vote. Two very different paths were taken to secure voting rights for these two groups. For women, a bottom-up approach would eventually lead to a Constitutional amendment that would secure their voting rights. For black Americans, a war would lead to Constitutional Amendments, but those rights would not be honored across large swaths of the country. A fight for civil rights would still need to take place in order to prompt increased federal action.

The years 1848 and 1920 commonly bookend the struggle for women's suffrage. The Seneca Falls Convention, the first meeting of its kind, produced a movement that would finally culminate in the ratification of the Nineteenth Amendment to the Constitution, guaranteeing women the right to vote. In the intervening years, women fought for the right to vote using a state-by-state strategy. By convincing sympathetic states to amend their statutes or constitutions to allow women the right to vote, momentum gradually built for national action. Indeed, across a large portion of the country, women had the right to vote before the ratification of the Nineteenth Amendment in 1920. The underlying motivations for passage of these laws were not universal. Their message was first received in Wyoming, where a scarcity of women and the desire for positive publicity drove the adoption of a bill granting suffrage.[18] Populism won the day in Colorado and Idaho in the 1890s, whereas progressive momentum brought suffrage in many other western states in the early 1910s.[19]

These state-by-state victories won out where legal strategies failed. After the passage of the 14th Amendment, a Missouri woman tested her voting rights on the grounds that male-only voting was a violation of her Constitutional rights. *Minor v. Happersett*[20] would set the precedent that voting was not a privilege or immunity protected by this amendment. Still, even with these state-by-state victories, large areas of the south and east still prohibited women from voting. The last wave of states to grant women the right to vote would include New York, Michigan, Oklahoma, and South Dakota—New York being the most important of these adoptions. The support of the Tammany machine, most likely in light of what seemed to be the inevitability of national women's suffrage, sealed a major victory and cemented the introduction and ratification of the Nineteenth Amendment.[21]

The fight for voting rights for black Americans took a decidedly different path than that for women. Although the Fifteenth Amendment ostensibly protected the voting rights of blacks and former slaves, the Supreme Court narrowly interpreted this guarantee. In *United States v. Reese*,[22] *United States v. Cruikshank*,[23] and *United States v. Harris*,[24] the Court weakened federal protections of voting rights, stating, among other things, that the Fifteenth Amendment did not positively confer suffrage rights, and that any federal protections did not apply to the actions of individuals. This led to a wave of increased disenfranchisement of black voters in southern states. While outright violence was common, the states themselves fashioned many restrictions that were outside federal protections because of their race-neutral language. Restrictions on the vote such as poll taxes (including the cumulative poll tax, which required voters to pay not only one year of poll taxes, but also a cumulative sum for any unpaid years) and literacy tests were written with race-neutral language, applying the restrictions to all voters. These poll taxes were often prohibitively high, and literacy tests, or understanding tests, were so difficult, only the most astute student of politics would be able to pass. If these tests were applied in a racially neutral way, they could have the effect of disenfranchising white and black voters. In order to prevent this, southern states were able to exempt white voters from these rules through the use of grandfather clauses, which exempted individuals whose grandfathers (or some other ancestor) were eligible voters on a certain date (often the year granting black suffrage in the state). This necessarily excluded all blacks, whose ancestors would have been legally barred from voting at that time. The combination of these methods was extremely effective in disenfranchising black voters while keeping many whites on the voting rolls.

Over time, some of these disenfranchisement mechanisms would meet their demise through the action of the courts. In 1915, grandfather clauses were struck down, but the underlying literacy tests remained in force.[25] Oklahoma, the state where this case arose, reacted to the court's decision by offering a 12-day window during which any individual could register to vote (exempting those who had been previously covered under the now-unconstitutional grandfather clause). It would not be until 1939 until this new and more convoluted grandfather clause would be similarly ruled unconstitutional.[26] Another one of the more nefarious ways of disenfranchising black voters was through the all-white Democratic primary. Due to the overwhelming hegemony of the Democratic party throughout the south, primary elections became the only meaningful contest in many states (no competition in general elections would lead to the coronation of a candidate elected in a more competitive Democratic primary). Because of the nature of political parties, understood at the time to be private associations, the Democratic Party could overtly exclude blacks from voting in primary elections.[27] In *Smith v. Allwright,* the Supreme Court found this discrimination was unconstitutional.[28] Again, it would take a second case in 1953[29] for there to be a true remedy to the issue, because of the use of 'pre-primaries' where candidates for the official primary would be selected by informal groups of Democratic partisans. With few exceptions, including these, the first half of the twentieth century saw little improvement in the voting rights for blacks living in the south. However, the coming Civil Rights Movement, and its associated court cases and legislation would spur new hope for voting rights in America.

4.   The Civil Rights Era and the Voting Rights Act

The Civil Rights movement of the 1950s and 1960s brought another wave of litigation and legislation that would change the landscape of voting in America, and particularly, the south. In combating discrimination in the south, Congress passed a series of civil rights laws, including the Civil Rights act or 1957, 1960, and 1964. The first of these created an Assistant Attorney for Civil Rights within the Department of Justice. The Department later created a Civil Rights Division to enforce the measures in the act. While the Acts of 1957 and 1960 were intended to provide statutory enforcement of voting rights, both did little to increase the ability of blacks to register to vote in the south. Even by 1964, registration numbers remained dismally low. The average black registration rate across the five states with the largest black populations (AL, GA, MS, NC, and SC) was 22.5 percent, and only 6.7 percent in Mississippi.[30]

In 1964, the Twenty-fourth Amendment was passed, prohibiting poll taxes, which were still enforced in Alabama, Arkansas, Mississippi, Texas, Virginia at the time. Virginia would continue to enforce a poll tax for state elections until the Supreme Court ruled in *Harper v. Virginia Board of Elections*[31] that the Amendment barred poll taxes in both federal and state elections.

The most influential piece of legislation that would arise during this era was the Voting Rights Act (VRA). This legislation was used to end the vote-denial and vote-dilution techniques that had limited the franchise of black voters. The VRA would not only provide a mechanism for challenging existing discriminatory voting laws, but for *preventing* the implementation of discriminatory laws. Additionally, the VRA, in later amendments, would go on to ban the use of literacy tests and durational residency requirements (beyond 30 days, and for presidential elections) across the country. The VRA has three sections that are particularly important to a discussion of voting rights. Section 2 contains a prohibition on voting laws that result in discrimination on the basis of race, color, or language-minority group membership. Section 5 of the VRA went further and required federal pre-approval (or preclearance) of changes to election laws. This meant that, while Section 2 would require an individual to initiate a lawsuit to compel compliance with the law, Section 5 would prevent potentially discriminatory changes to laws before they took effect. Section 5 also differed from Section 2 in its applicability to the states. Section 4 of the VRA contained a 'coverage formula,' which identified the specific jurisdictions that would be subject to Section 5 preclearance. Whereas Section 2 would apply nationwide, Section 5 would only be in effect for areas that had a history of voter discrimination. Recent court decisions have challenged the coverage formula and left the future of preclearance unclear. Let's look at each of these sections more fully, in order to understand the VRA and its effects.

a. Section 2

Section 2 of the VRA is essentially a statutory enforcement of Fifteenth Amendment protections that applies nationwide, without expiration. While it duplicates protections that already exist constitutionally, the law has been amended to provide stronger protections for claims of vote dilution and has become the centerpiece of more recent litigation on gerrymandering and majority-minority districts (discussed in a later chapter). Section 2 was initially interpreted to be a protection against laws passed with discriminatory intent. Indeed, in a case arising out of an at-large electoral scheme in Mobile, Alabama,[32] the courts found that the city's electoral laws were not in violation of the law because there was no proof of discriminatory *intent* in fashioning the law. Congress later reacted to this decision in their 1982 amendments to the VRA. In what became known as the Dole compromise (after Kansas Senator Bob Dole), Section 2 was amended, and the basis for discrimination claims was changed from intent to results.[33] This had the effect of distinguishing Fourteenth and Fifteenth Amendment claims of purposeful discrimination from VRA claims of discriminatory effects.

This aspect of the VRA became the center of many redistricting claims because the results-based test could be used to test the constitutionality of congressional maps. The law, however, was still unclear as to what might constitute a valid claim of discriminatory vote dilution. The Supreme Court later clarified this concept in *Thornburg v. Gingles,*[34] where the court laid out three preconditions necessary to assert a Section 2 claim of vote dilution. These conditions were that the minority group had to be large enough and compact enough to form a majority, that the minority group was politically cohesive, and that the majority had to vote as a bloc to defeat minority candidates (that is to say, white voters are able to vote as a bloc so as to defeat minority candidates). As mentioned previously, a later chapter will explore racial gerrymandering and the VRA more completely.

Figure 2.1   Map of Section 5 Covered Jurisdictions

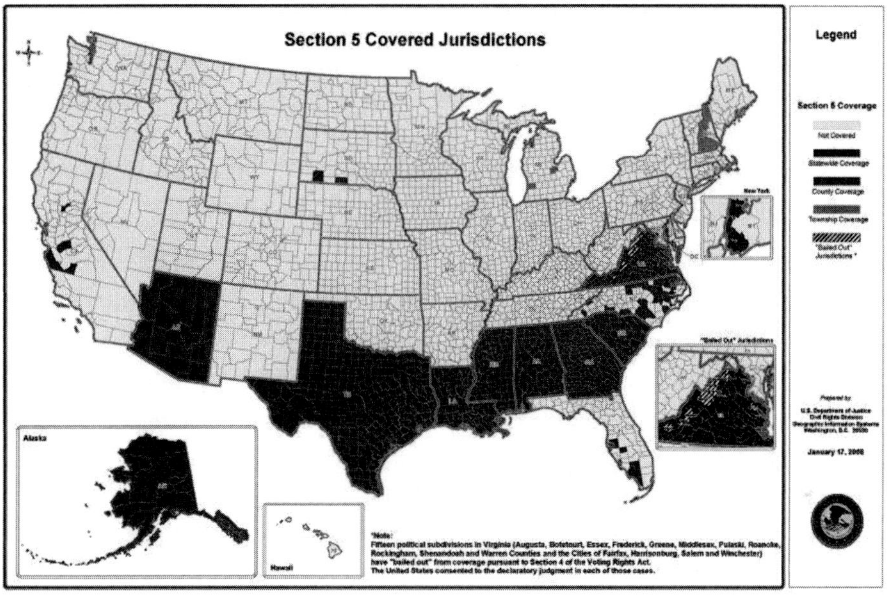

b.   Section 5

Section 5 of the Voting Rights Act is a mechanism for the review of changes to election laws in states covered under the Act. While claims of voter discrimination could be brought to the courts prior to the VRA, they required costly litigation. Additionally, in order to have the standing to bring a suit, a discriminatory law had to already be in place, and have affected an individual voter. Preclearance was designed to interrupt discriminatory laws *before* they were enacted. Under the VRA, covered jurisdictions (see Section 4) were required to submit all changes in their electoral laws to the federal government for approval. The federal government would determine whether the proposed change had a discriminatory purpose or effect in one of two ways. One option was for covered jurisdictions to submit their proposed changes to the District Court for the District of Columbia in order to receive a declaratory judgment that the law is not discriminatory. Alternatively, jurisdictions can submit proposed changes to the

Attorney General. In this case, the Department of Justice's Civil Rights Division will review the proposed change and may either approve the change or object to the change. If no objection is filed within 60 days, the change can also take place. Although these two methods are available to jurisdictions, nearly all requests for preclearance take the administrative route through the Attorney General's office. This is likely due to the time and monetary expense of seeking judicial review.[35]

c. Section 4

Section 4 of the VRA is critical to the operation of Section 5. In this section, the law lays out a formula for determining which political jurisdictions will fall under the scope of the preclearance requirement. This formula is fairly simple, but it has changed over time. The original coverage formula set out in Section 4 of the VRA covered all states or jurisdictions that had used a test or device (such as a literacy or understanding test) to restrict voting rights, and where voter registration or voter turnout was less than 50 percent (using 1964 figures in the original law). Under this formula, Alabama, Georgia, Louisiana, Mississippi, South Carolina, and Virginia were completely covered as states, and a number of counties were covered in Arizona, Hawaii, Idaho, and North Carolina. A Supreme Court decision later held that jurisdictions in partially covered states had to seek preclearance for state laws if those laws would effect changes in the covered jurisdiction.[36] This means that statewide changes to election law, like redistricting changes, would need to pass muster in these partially covered states.

With reauthorization of the law in 1970, this coverage formula was altered to reference 1968 registration and voting statistics. This change resulted in the inclusion of counties in Alaska, Arizona, California, Connecticut, Idaho, Maine, Massachusetts, New Hampshire, New York, and Wyoming. These northeastern states might seem odd, but in 1968, turnout in a number of small towns in New Hampshire fell below the 50 percent threshold, and at that time, the state utilized a literacy test. In fact, Connecticut and Massachusetts were the first two states to pass a reading or writing test for voting in 1855 and 1956, respectively.[37] In California, which also had a literacy test, four counties were targeted because of low turnout, although it seems likely that these counties had low turnout due to other factors. A brief from one of the covered counties, Merced, stated that it was likely that the county's turnout rate dropped below 50 percent (it was calculated at 49.6 percent) because of transient military personnel at a local Air Force base, who were treated as eligible voters.[38] It is worth noting that all of the four covered California counties similarly hosted a military base.[39]

When the 1975 reauthorization of the VRA occurred, the law was expended to encompass 'language minority' groups in addition to racial minority groups. This called for a change to the coverage formula, not only to reference 1972 registration and voting data, but also to include English-only ballots as a test or device when a language minority made up more than five percent of the eligible electorate. With this change, Alaska, Arizona, and Texas came under preclearance requirements. This would be the last expansion of the coverage formula, as well as the last update to the relevant registration and turnout statistics—an important fact for future litigation over the constitutionality of the law.

Another important part of Section 4 is a provision that allows jurisdictions falling under the coverage formula to 'bail out' of coverage or be released from their obligation to preclear changes to voting laws. Under this provision, jurisdictions could be released from coverage if they could prove a 10-year history (originally a five year requirement, before being changed to 10 years in 1970, 15 years in 1975, and then back to 10 years in 1982) of no voting tests or devices, no adverse judgments on voting discrimination cases, and full compliance with preclearance (which included no adverse rulings on changes submitted under preclearance). The aforementioned case of New Hampshire is the only example of a state being able to bail out entirely from the preclearance requirement.

d. *Shelby and the Future of the VRA*

While legal challenges have confronted the VRA since its inception, the courts have regularly upheld the constitutionality of the act. In *South Carolina v. Katzenbach*,[40] and later *City of Rome v. United States*,[41] *and Lopez v. Monterey County*,[42] the Supreme Court affirmed the authority of Congress to maintain preclearance restrictions on covered jurisdictions. The courts affirmed this authority for a number of different reasons, including the "exceptional conditions"[43] of discrimination that existed in the covered areas. This judicial support would begin to wane after the 2006 extension of the law. Soon after the reauthorization, a small water district in Austin, Texas filed suit because of language in the law that limited bail out from preclearance to political jurisdictions that register voters. The water district wanted the courts to find that they could, in fact, be able to apply for bailout even if they did not register voters. If they were not granted this relief, they claimed that the preclearance provision was unconstitutional. In the Supreme Court's Decision, *Northwest Austin Municipal Utility District Number One (NAMUDNO) v. Holder*,[44] the court ruled in favor of the utility district, arguing that NAMUDNO should be able to apply for bailout. While the court did not rule on the constitutionality of preclearance, it did open the door to challenges by noting that "the Act imposes current burdens and must be justified by current needs . . . The statute's coverage formula is based on data that is now more than 35 years old, and there is considerable evidence that it fails to account for current political conditions."[45] This decision foreshadowed events to come, and a challenge that would dramatically change the VRA.

Shelby County, Alabama is a county just south of Birmingham, which, in 2013, sought to challenge the constitutionality of the VRA (the county was ineligible for bailout due to recent preclearance objections to county laws).[46] In *NAMUDNO*, the court was able to avoid the constitutional questions of the VRA because the utility district asked for permission to bail out first, and only questioned the constitutionality of the act as a second prayer for relief. With *Shelby*, the courts could not ignore the constitutional question and had to face it head-on. In their opinion, the court ruled the Section 4 preclearance formula unconstitutional on the grounds that the old coverage formula was no longer sufficiently related to the problem it targeted.[47]

It is worth keeping in mind that the Supreme Court's decision in *Shelby* affected only the Section 4 preclearance formula. The other sections of the VRA remained in effect after the decision. While Section 5 preclearance remained constitutional, in practice, with no coverage formula, no jurisdictions were subject to preclearance procedures (Section 2 rules also remained in effect for the entire country). While Congress could amend the VRA and adopt a new coverage formula, it has not. What does this mean for the future of the VRA?

One potential avenue for the VRA's preclearance requirement to continue to operate is through Section 3 'bail-in' provisions. Rather than a jurisdiction being covered by virtue of Section 4's coverage formula, Section 3 allows courts to prescribe preclearance as a judicial remedy in cases of alleged discrimination. This has happened a number of times in the past, with two prominent examples being the bail-in of the states of Arkansas and New Mexico.

Arkansas offers an example of how bail-in procedures operate, and also how they can be limited by the courts. Arkansas's case saw a number of offenses brought before the courts, but only one where the courts could agree that the state has acted in a discriminatory fashion—majority-vote requirements.[48] Majority-vote requirements are rules that require a winning candidate to capture a majority of the votes in an election, rather than simply a plurality. Litigants in Arkansas had complained that these rules were adopted to suppress the electoral activities of blacks in the state. When the courts analyzed the claim, they were unable to conclude that the statewide majority-vote requirements had been adopted for a discriminatory end. There was clear historical evidence that the state's constitution was amended in response to the election of plurality winners in white-only Democratic primaries. The white-only primary had been effective enough at disenfranchising black voters, and thus, the courts did not find that the majority-vote law was adopted with clear racial bias in mind. The court went on to find that there was a discriminatory intent in the adoption of majority-vote requirements for *local* office, which had only been adopted in the 1970s. The courts, then directly linked their bail-in of the state to this offense, requiring the state to preclear any changes to their majority-vote laws, but leaving them unburdened in other areas of election law.[49]

This example shows not only the difficulty of proving a case of discriminatory election law, but also the latitude that courts have in prescribing a preclearance remedy. In this case, although Arkansas was made subject to preclearance, it was a time-limited restriction and it only applied to majority-vote laws. This means that for the remainder of their electoral laws, Arkansas did not need to seek preclearance. Whether or not bail-in mechanisms are a promising avenue for continuing the use of the preclearance mechanism is unclear. What is clear, however, is that Congress continues to have the power to make changes to the VRA and if they should choose to do so, could implement a new coverage formula that would pass constitutional muster.

B. REGISTERING TO VOTE

Having discussed the right to vote and the general growth of the franchise, it is worth taking time to examine a closely related topic—voter registration. Voter registration is the concept that the state should maintain a record of eligible voters. While today these take the form of an electronic database in many jurisdictions, in its infancy, voter registration rolls were maintained as written lists of qualified voters. Before this, voters would prove their eligibility to vote at the polls on Election Day.[50] Registration provides a way for election officials to know who is and is not eligible to vote in an age where poll workers can no longer be expected to know everyone in the community.

Historical sources go into a great deal of detail trying to disentangle the variation in reasons for adoption of registration laws,[51] but for our purposes, it is sufficient to say that the adoption of voter registration laws took two distinct paths in the United States. In the south, voter registration emerged after the Civil War and Reconstruction as useful methods for disenfranchising black voters. V.O. Key, noted scholar of southern politics, summed up southern registration in the south as "the principal governmental agency for Negro disenfranchisement."[52] In the north, voter registration was ostensibly adopted as a political reform aimed at preventing voter fraud.[53] While voter registration laws were scarce in the early nineteenth century (Massachusetts would adopt the first registration law in 1801[54]) they would blossom through the turn of the century and leave us today with registration laws in every state except North Dakota.

While federal laws regulate many aspects of voter registration, states still have a good degree of latitude in setting their registration practices. Looking across the range of statutes, there are a few important criteria that can distinguish registration processes and practices.

First, as noted before, all states have a voter registration procedure in place with the exception of North Dakota. The burden of that registration falls on the voter in nearly every state, but recent changes have moved that responsibility to the state. In 2015, Oregon passed House Bill 2177, which was an update to the state's "Motor Voter" bill. These motor voter laws were passed across the country in the wake of the adoption of the National Voter Registration Act of 1993. Their purpose was to ease the burden of voter registration by linking it to applications for driver's licenses. While the national law only called for states to offer opportunities for individuals to register, Oregon's new law has taken this a step further by automatically registering any individuals who apply for a driver's license (individuals may opt out of the choose).[55] A number of other states have made strides towards automatic registration in the past few years.[56]

In states without automatic registration, a key rule for voters is a state's voter registration deadline. While these deadlines vary considerably, the VRA prevents states from setting deadlines further than 30 days out from Election Day. Some states have collapsed this window entirely and now allow voters to register to vote at their polling place on Election Day. This procedure is commonly called Election Day registration. This is a separate concept from states which have early voting and allow voters to simultaneously register and vote early, but not on Election Day.

Another distinguishing feature of state registration laws is the relative difficulty of the actual registration act. One recent development has been the adoption of online voter registration systems. These systems allow citizens to register to vote without having to fill out, mail, or return any physical forms or paperwork. Only a handful of states have not adopted online voter registration (AR, ME, MI, MS, MT, NH, NJ, NC, SD, TX, and WY) however there are many states that are already in the process of moving toward easing the burden of registration by adopting automatic registration, or allowing Election Day registration, although there are still a number of states which have not moved toward any of these reforms (only AR, MI, MS, NC, SD and TX lack both an automatic, election day, or online registration process).

C. ABSENTEE VOTING

As noted in earlier sections, residency has been a key requirement in the constellation of rules surrounding the right to vote. However, as early as the Civil War, states have had to contend with the issue of voters who are not able to be physically present to cast a ballot on Election Day. Keyssar notes that many states created measures to allow soldiers to vote while away from their home districts. According to Benton[57] 25 states attempted to allow battlefield voting for soldiers during the Civil War. These attempts were sometimes thwarted by state constitutions which required voters to be present in their districts in order to vote. In some states, these constitutions were amended, effectively relaxing some preexisting voting requirements, but in others, states found a way to work around these laws. In some states, soldiers would mail their ballots back to proxies, who would effectively cast the soldier's ballot for them at his home polling place. This did not mean, to the letter of the law, that the soldier had cast a ballot away from home. In states without restrictions on the place of voting, commissioners or other appointed persons could essentially bring the election to the soldiers, allowing them to cast their ballot in person, on the battlefield. It is not entirely clear that these votes had a measurable impact on election outcomes during the war. Benton cites a handful of small elections and a change to the constitution of Maryland as being credibly influenced by these absentee votes. In terms of the presidential election of 1864, scholars disagree about whether or not the absentee vote swayed the results. While soldiers cast their ballots for Lincoln at high rates, the low number of overall ballots cast needs to also be taken into account. While Nevins[58] suggests that the vote was not a factor in any state's result, William Davis,[59] Shelby Foote,[60] and Frank Zornow[61] all suggest to varying degrees that the soldier vote put Lincoln over the top, especially in close races like Connecticut and New York. What is more important to take away from this early example is how states grappled with the administrative task of allowing voters to cast their ballots away from the polling place. Unfortunately, absentee balloting would quickly disappear across the county in the post-war years and would not return until the twentieth century.[62]

Post-war experiments with absentee voting were rare and were not without administrative difficulties. There were often concerns about the secrecy of absentee ballots,[63] as well as which remote locations would be acceptable for absentee balloting. In some cases, soldiers were allowed to vote absentee, but only if they remained within the borders of their home state.[64] The timing of absentee balloting also varied in early laws (as it still does today). Early laws in Missouri required absentee voters to cast their ballot during voting hours on Election Day, whereas a North Dakota law provided ballots to absentee voters up to thirty days in advance of Election Day.[65] Throughout the early part of the twentieth century, a number of states would begin to adopt absentee voting laws, again spurred in part by the need to allow soldiers to vote when serving during World War I. However, the War Department did not facilitate efforts to allow overseas personnel to vote in the 1918 elections, citing concerns about military efficiency.[66]

Modern absentee voting now takes a number of different forms, from permissive systems that allow voters to declare a permanent absentee status, to more restrictive systems that require voters to declare a particular excuse or reason why they must cast an absentee ballot.

According to the National Conference of State Legislatures, twenty states allow absentee voting but require voters to offer some kind of excuse for why they cannot cast their ballot on Election Day. These excuses can include things like travel, work, or caring for a sick family member. While some states like Virginia require some basic information to support their request (such as the name of their business), and while it is often a felony to provide false information on absentee ballot forms, it is not clear how often these laws are enforced. Some of these states allow individuals to apply for an absentee ballot, receive the ballot, and cast that ballot at the same time at an election office before Election Day. This system is commonly called 'in-person absentee' voting and is very similar to systems that simply allow for early voting. A key distinction between these systems is the need to present an absentee excuse. Many states have dropped the requirement to have a particular excuse and offer what is called 'no-excuse' absentee voting. In these states, any individual may request an absentee ballot without having to provide a specific excuse for why that cannot vote on Election Day. Some of the most permissive states allow voters to place themselves on permanent absentee status, which means they do not have to request an absentee ballot every election, and one is automatically sent to them instead. In some states that offer this, voters must have an excuse such as a permanent disability, but the number of states offering no-excuse permanent absentee voting is rising. Taking this system to its extreme, Colorado, Oregon, and Washington now conduct all of their elections by mail, sending ballots to all registered voters a number of weeks before the election.

It is not clear what effects these different absentee balloting systems have on our elections. Fears of voter fraud have commonly fueled opposition to early and all-mail voting, but ease of access and increased turnout have been cited as positive outcomes. Scholars, however, are not in agreement as to whether or not turnout increases in more permissive systems. One study showed a differential effect of all-mail voting on turnout, identifying minor increases only in sub-federal elections.[67] Other studies[68] have even shown a decrease in turnout with the adoption of all-mail voting or early voting.

What is clear, is that the gradual adoption of absentee balloting laws and the slower proliferation of no-excuse and early voting laws show the overarching trend towards the separation of voting rights and physical location. No longer is the right to vote completely predicated on being able to present oneself at the polling place on Election Day, and if current trends continue, more states may do away with the polling place entirely, allowing citizens to cast their votes from the comfort of their homes.

D. VOTER IDENTIFICATION

Perhaps one of the most contentious issues surrounding the right to vote in recent years has been voter identification. Voter ID laws require voters to provide some sort of documentation to verify their identity. Voter ID laws have existed in some form since South Carolina enacted an identification law in 1950 which allowed poll workers to request additional identification from voters as they saw fit.[69] Since the enactment of this law, many other states have followed, although the requirement to produce photo identification is a relatively recent phenomenon (Indiana's 2006 law being the most prominent example). Today a majority of states have some sort of identification requirement, although there are a number of different ways these requirements can be implemented.

Voter ID laws can be classified in a number of different ways, however, there are essentially two important factors to examine. First, is the type of identification required, if any, and second, is the allowed alternative to producing an ID when voting. States that opt for a voter ID law may require photo identification or some kind of non-photo document. Non-photo identification can consist of documents that are not traditionally thought of as identification documents, like utility bills or bank statements. Additionally, states may require voters to produce this identification every election, or in some cases, only on the first time an individual attempts to vote. The second criteria examines what alternatives are available to an individual that cannot produce an identification document. In some states, voters may simply vote without an ID by signing an affidavit attesting to their identity. In other states, voters without an ID can cast a provisional ballot, but then they are required to return to an elections office to show their ID before a set deadline. Seven states require the strictest combination of these rules—requiring a photo ID every time an individual votes and requiring voters to cast a provisional ballot and return with ID after the election if they do not have identification at the polling place.

Voter identification is an issue that requires a delicate balance between the integrity of elections and the imposition of burdens on voters. While Indiana's photo ID law was challenged in court, a 2008 decision[70] upheld the Constitutionality of the law. Further, while some states previously subject to preclearance (notably Texas in 2012) were unable to get approval for photo id laws, the decision in *Shelby v. Holder*[71] has sparked a number of new voter ID laws in previously covered states. This is not to say that these laws necessarily comport with the VRA, but it does mean that any challenges will have to come through litigation, and not through administrative review.

One successful challenge to voter ID has come in the argument that identification cards are effectively a poll tax. In Georgia, identification cards cost $20, leading to a court decision striking down the photo ID law.[72] In the Indiana case, *Crawford v. Marion County Election Board,* the court noted that the law would not have passed Constitutional muster if the identification cards had not been free.[73] Going even further, the Missouri Supreme Court struck down its state identification law because of the cost of obtaining secondary documentation (the documents necessary to procure an ID, like a copy of a birth certificate).[74] With this exception, so long as states are bearing the cost and administrative burden of setting up these identification programs, the courts have been fairly deferential to the states.

E. DISQUALIFICATION

While the franchise has continued to expand in many ways, there are still two specific disqualifications that restrict the right to vote for many in America. The Voting Rights Act allows states to disqualify voters in cases of "criminal conviction or mental incapacity."[75] Throughout the country, most states opt to incorporate both of these restrictions into their election codes, with only a handful of states remaining silent on the matter. Because these rules take fairly divergent forms, and because of the critically important consequences of denying the right to vote to an individual, it is worthwhile to examine these provisions across the states.

1.   Felon Disenfranchisement

Felon disenfranchisement is the concept that voting rights are taken away from those who are convicted of certain criminal offenses. In addition to any penalties like fines or imprisonment, the Fourteenth Amendment (as well as VRA legislation) gives states the power to restrict voting rights as an additional punishment for a crime. Section 2 of the Fourteenth Amendment, as previously discussed, prohibits the states from abridging the right to vote, but makes a specific exception to this provision for "participation in rebellion, or other crime."[76]

Why should we strip criminals of their right to vote? Drawing on Locke's arguments about the social contract, one appellate judge summarized the argument as "A man who breaks the laws he has authorized his agent to make for his own governance could fairly have been thought to have abandoned the right to participate in further administering the compact."[77] Thus, if an individual cannot be trusted to obey the law, he ought not to have a say in the creation of those laws. While the point of this book is not to consider the normative arguments in favor or against felon disenfranchisement (retributive or deterrent effects, or a lack thereof, might be advanced as arguments on either side of this argument) we can look at the objective structure and impact that these rules have.

Looking at how felon disenfranchisement rules play out in the states today, we see a wide variety of rules that span the entire spectrum, from lifetime disenfranchisement, to being able to vote from a prison cell. In Maine and Vermont, convicted felons retain their right to vote, even when incarcerated. These states sit at the far end of the spectrum of felon disenfranchisement, having no restrictions on the voting rights of criminals. In every other state, however, felons are barred from voting while they are incarcerated, and in some states, the restrictions carry on even after they are released. In 15 states, felons immediately and automatically have their voting rights restored when they are released from prison.[78] In California, Colorado, Connecticut, and New York, felons remain disenfranchised if released on parole (but not if on probation). The remaining thirty states disenfranchise all felons in prison, on probation, and on parole. Twelve of these thirty (AL, AZ, DE, FL, IA, KY, MS, NE, NV, TN, VA, and WY) extend felon disenfranchisement past end of any sentence or probation/parole, either requiring a waiting period or some additional administrative action on the part of the individual to restore their voting rights.[79] Of these twelve, Florida, Kentucky, and Iowa have such strict procedures for restoration of rights that their laws are, in essence, lifetime bans.

What impact do these voting restrictions have on our electorate? According to one recent report, approximately 6.1 million people are barred from voting, or about 2.5 percent of the voting age population. Interestingly, only about 22 percent of these individuals are currently incarcerated, with the majority having fully completed their prison sentence. Florida, a state that effectively bans felons from voting for life, accounts for 27 percent of the total disenfranchised population.[80]

2. Capability

A second criterion for disenfranchisement that is currently allowed under federal and state law, is that of competence or capability to vote. While 11 states have no restrictions on voting based on competence or capability,[81] the rest have some form of law which restricts the right to vote. For the purposes of titling this chapter, 'capability' serves as a stand-in for discussions that span a wide array of mental health disorders or other conditions that might leave an individual unable to vote. Indeed, our discussions on this topic have always been framed by the language we use. A number of states continue to use outdated terms such as 'idiot' or 'insane persons' (more often in constitutions, rather than statutes, as statutes are easier to amend). This suggests that disenfranchisement ought to occur on the basis of a specific diagnosis or illness. This outdated language creates barriers to the enforcement of voting restrictions because of the ambiguous nature of these terms, and their disappearance from medical use.[82]

While some states have updated their statutes to reflect less stigmatizing language, they often focus on mental disability, mental illness, or intellectual disability, which necessarily suggests a relationship between disenfranchisement and a particular medical diagnosis. However, these terms are still not entirely adequate for adjudicating the capability of an individual to vote. Ambiguities in these terms and the conditions they encompass can create legal difficulties when attempting to determine an individual's right to vote. Various illnesses, injuries, or disorders might be unnecessarily encompassed in one term, but not included in another. Consider such divergent conditions as a developmental disorder, a traumatic brain injury, an emotional or mood disorder, or a degenerative disease like Alzheimer's disease. These conditions might not all fit one category of disorders as mentioned, and not all victims of these disorders may be incapable of voting.

Some states have framed these discussions differently, denying the right to vote to those who have been placed under guardianship. In most cases, a judicial determination must be made as to the competence or capacity of an individual, however, there are no clear and universal standards for this kind of judicial finding.[83] Moreover, reasons for a guardianship arrangement may not have a legitimate relationship with an individual's capacity to vote. For example, someone may be placed under guardianship for a physical disability, but this would not otherwise affect their capacity for voting. Thus, in this construct, disenfranchisement is not based on capacity or a specific illness, but on the finding that an individual is not capable of fully caring for themselves.

Two problems with both of these approaches are concerns about equal protection and due process. Equal protection claims may arise by painting with too broad of a brush, as suggested in both cases above. Of equal concern, are due process considerations that need to be taken into account when considering the disenfranchisement of these individuals. To address cases in a more individualized way, half of states have a specific requirement that a court must determine that an individual lacks the specific capability to vote.[84] While this method is perhaps the most likely to avoid equal protection claims, there is still no accepted standard for adjudicating the capacity of an individual to vote. One group of researchers proposed a simple three-part test that would help ascertain whether or not an individual understood voting and was capable of expressing a choice.[85] It is unclear, however, whether or not a test such as this would pass muster under VRA restrictions on literacy tests. The American Bar Association has suggested that rather than attempt to judge competence, an individual might only need to express "with or without accommodation, a specific desire to participate in the voting process."[86] Under this standard, a court could make case-by-case determinations to disenfranchise individuals if that court had convincing evidence that someone had no way of communicating their desire to vote.

While these less restrictive standards are surely a victory for voting rights, they need to be backed up by support from both election administrators, providing accessible methods of voting, and caregivers, in respecting the voting rights of those in their care. Recent studies have uncovered the disenfranchisement of groups of individuals by those who are charged with their care. In one case, a number of individuals were disallowed from voting by healthcare professionals at Philadelphia nursing homes. Although the state has no statutes with regards to competency, staff were noted to have prevented residents from voting based on their own claims of incompetence.[87]

F. THESE RULES MATTER

Rules that govern the citizens right to vote, as well as the process by which they register and present themselves for voting, are some of the most central to our democracy. The composition of the electorate, and by extension, the choices they make, are governed by the rules laid out in this chapter. If these rules differentially impact certain groups of voters, we might see important changes in the outcomes of our elections. Looking back at our history, we can see the way barriers to voting have disenfranchised large portions of the populace, often to the electoral advantage of a more privileged group. Beyond this broad look, what can political science tell us about how these rules affect our elections?

One avenue of research might look at registration, for instance. If registration is a mandatory prerequisite to voting, it could be considered the most important barrier to voting. If one declines to register, they are necessarily prohibited from voting. We might assume, then, that easing voter registration laws would increase voter turnout. Political science research, however, tells us a different story. A string of research has shown that these gains in voter turnout, when found, are modest at best. If the purpose of this book is to argue that rules matter, this might be an inauspicious start to the volume. However, perhaps we can explain why easing registration laws seems to have little impact on voter turnout. One reason for the lack of a relationship might be because those who are already registered to vote are the most likely to vote. That is to say, individuals that are not registered are unlikely to vote even if they become registered. Perhaps there is a portion of the population that would never vote, regardless of how registration rules were structured. As mentioned previously, North Dakota is the only state without voter registration, so this offers us a natural experiment to test whether or not voter registration acts as a significant barrier to entry. A study in the 1990s determined that turnout in North Dakota actually lagged behind other states, suggesting that other variables were more important for voter turnout.[88]

This is not to say that registration does not matter. It still presents a real hurdle to voting, and we can see from our past that it can be used to disenfranchise large swaths of the population. Thus, perhaps it is not the existence of registration that is the key variable, it is in the form with which registration takes. One need only think back to our discussion of poll taxes and literacy tests—enormous barriers to registration for large swaths of voters. To be sure, the elimination of these barriers has increased turnout, but it is less clear what gains are being made from current law changes. Online voter registration, for example, has been difficult to examine because of the wide array of forms that it takes in the states. A recent study showed no significant changes, with the exception of young voters, highlighting the differential effect that rules can have on different segments of the population.[89] The important point to take away from this discussion is that registration laws can have a tremendous impact on voter turnout, as they have in the past, however, as they are constructed today, it is difficult to realize meaningful gains in voter turnout by relaxing registration rules further.

Investigating another avenue, conventional wisdom tells us that liberalizing (or opening) our absentee ballot laws should make voting easier. If we have made voting easier, we would expect turnout to go up. Research has shown, however, that this relationship is not as simple as it seems. One study showed that voters who are most likely to vote absentee are those who are highly educated and politically active. If this group already has a high turnout rate, then absentee voting may not drive higher turnout. On the positive side, this same study showed that turnout did drive higher among persons with disabilities. The takeaway seems to be that, absentee balloting can increase voter turnout in groups that have concrete barriers to access the ballot on Election Day. However, for those already unlikely to vote, absentee voting may do little to help.[90]

Perhaps the story of why these rules matter cannot be told in isolation. Examining registration, voter identification, and absentee voting, it is possible we might have to look for special combinations of rules in order to see meaningful change. This highlights the importance of understanding rules. There are so many potential variables in the electoral landscape that the most interesting effects might only be seen when rules begin to interact with each other. One recent study made precisely this point, suggesting that in order to understand how rules matter we must look at the entire electoral landscape rather than attempting to look at rules in isolation.[91]

G. CHAPTER 2 DISCUSSION QUESTIONS

1. Consider the various strategies that groups have used to gain their right to vote. While some groups pursued legal strategies, others looked to direct democracy. Were these strategies uniquely suited to these groups or could the right to vote have been won with varying tactics?

2. The debate over voter identification is often couched as a contest between the right to vote and electoral security. Do either of these concerns outweigh the other? What arguments can be made that the right to vote is more important than preventing voter fraud? What about arguments in the reverse? Is there a balanced approach that could be taken to appease both sides of the debate?

3. Consider the quote from the appellate judge in the section on felon disenfranchisement. Do you agree that committing a crime means one has forfeited their right to vote within the context of the social contract? Should criminals, who have abandoned the social contract by committing a crime, be

readmitted to the contract once they have paid any fines and served any term of incarceration? Are criminals rehabilitated by their prison sentences to the point that they should regain the right to vote, or should they be perpetually restricted from participating in the electoral process?

4.   The question of whether or not certain individuals with intellectual disabilities should be allowed to vote is a difficult one. As mentioned in the chapter, one potential solution is to craft some sort of test to determine whether or not an individual understands the election process and is capable of making a choice. While this solution seems intuitively appealing, recall back to how literacy tests were used to disenfranchise voters. Who would determine who would take the test? Do you think these tests would pass Constitutional muster? How would you go about solving this problem?

---

[1]   Blackstone, William. 1765. *Commentaries on the laws of England.* Clarendon Press: Oxford.

[2]   Williamson, Chilton. 1960. *American suffrage: from property to democracy, 1760–1860.* Princeton: Princeton University Press p. 15.

[3]   Williamson, Chilton. 1960. *American suffrage: from property to democracy, 1760–1860.* Princeton: Princeton University Press p. 15.

[4]   Klinghoffer, Judith Apter and Lois Elkis. 2012. " 'The Petticoat Electors': Women's Suffrage in New Jersey, 1776–1807" *Journal of the Early Republic* 12(2): 159–193.

[5]   Keyssar, Alexander. 2009. *The Right to Vote: The Contested History of Democracy in the United States.* New York: Basic Books. p. 44.

[6]   Williamson, Chilton. 1960. American suffrage: from property to democracy, 1760–1860. Princeton: Princeton University Press. p. 15–16.

[7]   Constitution of South Carolina 1778, Section XIII.

[8]   Constitution of South Carolina 1790.

[9]   Williamson, Chilton. 1960. *American suffrage: from property to democracy, 1760–1860.* Princeton: Princeton University Press p. 115.

[10]   Keyssar, Alexander. 2009. *The Right to Vote: The Contested History of Democracy in the United States.* New York: Basic Books. p. 37.

[11]   Keyssar, Alexander. 2009. *The Right to Vote: The Contested History of Democracy in the United States.* New York: Basic Books. p. 36.

[12]   Keyssar, Alexander. 2009. *The Right to Vote: The Contested History of Democracy in the United States.* New York: Basic Books. p. 37.

[13]   Keyssar, Alexander. 2009. *The Right to Vote: The Contested History of Democracy in the United States.* New York: Basic Books. Table A.3.

[14]   Keyssar, Alexander. 2009. *The Right to Vote: The Contested History of Democracy in the United States.* New York: Basic Books. Table p. 44.

[15]   Keyssar, Alexander. 2009. *The Right to Vote: The Contested History of Democracy in the United States.* New York: Basic Books. Table A.5.

[16]   Rosberg, Gerald. 1977. "Aliens and Equal Protection: Why not the right to vote?" *Michigan Law Review* 75:5/6: 1092–1139. pp. 1097–1098.

[17]   1 Stat. 103, 1 Stat. 414.

[18]   Larson, T. A. 1956. "Woman Suffrage in Wyoming." *The Pacific Northwest Quarterly.* 56(2): 57–66.

[19]   Mead, Rebecca J. 2004. *How the Vote Was Won: Woman Suffrage in the Western United States, 1868–1913.* New York University Press: New York.

20 88 U.S. 162 (1875).

21 McDonagh, E., & Price, H. 1985. "Woman Suffrage in the Progressive Era: Patterns of Opposition and Support in Referenda Voting, 1910–1918." *American Political Science Review*. 79(2): 415–435.

22 92 U.S. 214 (1876).

23 92 U.S. 542 (1876).

24 106 U.S. 629 (1883).

25 *Guinn v. United States*, 238 U.S. 347 (1915).

26 *Lane v. Wilson*, 307 U.S. 268 (1939).

27 Key, V. O. 1945. *Southern Politics in State and Nation*. Alfred A. Knopf: New York. p. 539.

28 321 U.S. 649 (1944).

29 *Terry v. Adams*, 345 U.S. 461 (1953).

30 Davidson, Chandler. 1994. "The Recent Evolution of Voting Rights Law Affecting Racial and Language Minorities in Quiet Revolution in the South" In *The impact of the Voting Rights Act 1956–1990* ed. Chandler Davidson and Bernard Grofman. Princeton: Princeton University Press.

31 383 U.S. 663 (1966).

32 *Mobile v. Bolden*, 446 U.S. 55 (1980).

33 Boyd, Thomas M.; Markman, Stephen J. (1983). "The 1982 Amendments to the Voting Rights Act: A Legislative History". *Washington and Lee Law Review*. 40(4): 1347–1428.

34 *Thornburg v. Gingles*, 478 U.S. 30 (1986).

35 Canon, David T. 2005. "Race Redistricting and the Courts." In *Redistricting in the New Millennium*. ed. Peter F. Galderisi. Lanham: Lexington Books. p. 89.

36 *Lopez v. Monterey County*, 525 U.S. 266 (1999).

37 Crawford, F.G. 1923. "The New York State Literacy Test." *The American Political Science Review*. 17(2): 260–263.

38 Brief of Merced County, California, as Amicus Curiae, pg. 11, *Shelby County v. Holder*, 570 U.S. 529 (2013).

39 Lemoore Naval Air Station, Kings County; Castle Air Force Base, Merced County; Fort Ord, Camp Roberts, Monterey County Beale Air Force Base, Yuba County; Brief of Merced County, California, as Amicus Curiae, n. 15, *Shelby County v. Holder*, 570 U.S. 529 (2013).

40 383 U.S. 301 (1966).

41 446 U.S. 156 (1980).

42 525 U.S. 266 (1999).

43 383 U.S. 301 (1966) at 334.

44 557 U.S. 193 (2009).

45 557 U.S. 193 (2009) at 203.

46 *Shelby County v. Holder*, 570 U.S. 529 (2013).

47 *Shelby County v. Holder*, 570 U.S. 529 (2013) at 9.

48 *Jeffers v. Clinton*, 740 F. Supp. 585 (E.D. Ark. 1990).

49 *Jeffers v. Clinton*, 740 F. Supp. 585 (E.D. Ark. 1990) at 601.

50 Keyssar, Alexander. 2009. *The Right to Vote: The Contested History of Democracy in the United States*. New York: Basic Books. p. 151.

51 Harris, Joseph P. 1929. *Registration of voters in the United States*. Brookings: Washington.

52 Key, V. O. 1949. *Southern Politics in State and Nation*. Alfred A. Knopf: New York. p. 560.

53 Burnham, Walter Dean. 1970. Critical Elections and the Mainsprings of American Politics. Norton: New York. p. 81.

54 Harris, Joseph P. 1929. *Registration of voters in the United States*. Brookings: Washington.

55 Oregon Revised Statutes 247.017.

56 According to the Brennan Center at NYU, AK, CA, CO, DC, GA, IL, MD, NJ, OR, RI, VT, WA, and WV have adopted some automatic voter registration law, although not all of these states have implemented those changes.

57 Beaton, Josiah. *Voting in the Field: A Forgotten Chapter of the Civil War.* Boston: Plimpton Press, 1915.

58 Nevins, Allan. 1971. *The War for the Union: The organized war to victory, 1864–1865.* Scribner: New York. p. 138.

59 Davis, William C. 1999. *Lincoln's Men: How President Lincoln Became Father to an Army and a Nation.* New York: Free Press.

60 Foote, Shelby. *The Civil War: A Narrative.* New York: Random House. pp. 1958–74.

61 Zornow, William Frank. 1954. *Lincoln & the Party Divided.* Norman: University of Oklahoma Press.

62 Benton, Josiah H. 1915. *Voting in the Field: A Forgotten Chapter of the Civil War.* Boston: Privately Printed.

63 Orman, Ray P. 1914. "Absent Voters." *American Political Science Review.* 12(3): 461–469. p. 467.

64 Keyssar, Alexander. 2009. *The Right to Vote: The Contested History of Democracy in the United States.* New York: Basic Books.

65 Orman, Ray P. 1918. "Military Absent-Voting Laws." *American Political Science Review.* 8(3): 442–445. p.444.

66 Martin, Boyd A. 1945. "The Service Vote in the Elections in 1944." *The American Political Science Review.* 39(4): 720–732. p. 722.

67 Gronke and Miller. 2012. "Voting by Mail and Turnout in Oregon: Revisiting Southwell and Burchett." *American Politics Research.* 40(6): 976–997.

68 See Kousser, T., & Mullin, M. 2007. "Does voting by mail increase participation? Using matching to analyze a natural experiment." *Political Analysis,* 15(4): 428–445. As well as Burden, Barry C., David T. Canon, Kenneth R. Mayer, and Donald P. Moynihan. 2013. "Election Laws, Mobilization, and Turnout: The Unanticipated Consequences of Election Reform." *American Journal of Political Science.* 58(1): 95–109.

69 1950 S.C. Act 858 § 8–2.

70 *Crawford v. Marion County Election Board,* 553 U.S. 181 (2008).

71 570 U.S. 529 (2013).

72 *Common Cause/Ga. v. Billups,* 406 F. Supp. 2d 1326.

73 553 U.S. at 198.

74 *Weinschenk v. State,* 203 S.W.3d 201, 206 (Mo. 2006).

75 52 U.S. Code § 20507 (a) 3 (b).

76 U.S. Constitution Amendment XIV, § 2.

77 380 F.2d 445 (2d Cir. 1967) at 451.

78 According to the National Conference of State Legislatures, this group includes DC, HI, IL, IN, MD, MA, MI, MT, NH, ND, OH, OR, PA, RI, and UT.

79 Chung, Jung. 2016 Felony Disenfranchisement: A Primer. Sentencing Project.

80 This data was all sourced from The Sentencing Projects 2016 Report, "6 Million Lost Voters: State-Level Estimates of Felony Disenfranchisement, 2016" Christopher Uggen, Ryan Larson, and Sarah Shannon. 2016.

81 According to a recent report by an advocacy group, these states fall under this category: CO, ID, IL, IN, KS, ME, MI, NH, NC, PA, and VT. Bazelon Center for Mental Health Law, Autistic Self-Advocacy Network, National Disability Rights Network, and Schulte, Roth & Zabel LLP, VOTE. It's Your Right: A Guide to the Voting Rights of People with Mental Disabilities; Washington DC and New York, NY 2016.

82 According to a recent report by an advocacy group, AK, AZ, KY, MN, MS, MT, and OH, fall into this group. Only KY, MS, and OH still use the language 'Idiot,' in their constitutions, all have changed the language in their voting statutes. Bazelon Center for Mental Health Law, Autistic Self-Advocacy Network, National Disability Rights Network, and Schulte, Roth & Zabel LLP, VOTE. It's Your Right: A Guide to the Voting Rights of People with Mental Disabilities; Washington DC and New York, NY 2016.

83 According to a recent report by an advocacy group, ten states fall under this category: AL, LA, MA, MN, MO, SC, SD, TN, UT, and VA. Bazelon Center for Mental Health Law, Autistic Self-Advocacy Network,

National Disability Rights Network, and Schulte, Roth & Zabel LLP, VOTE. It's Your Right: A Guide to the Voting Rights of People with Mental Disabilities; Washington DC and New York, NY 2016.

84   According to a recent report by an advocacy group, these states fall under this category: AK, AZ, AR, CA, CT, DE, FL, GA, HI, IA, KY, MD, NV, NJ, NM, NY, ND, OH, OK, OR, TX, WA, WV, WI, WY. Bazelon Center for Mental Health Law, Autistic Self-Advocacy Network, National Disability Rights Network, and Schulte, Roth & Zabel LLP, VOTE. It's Your Right: A Guide to the Voting Rights of People with Mental Disabilities; Washington DC and New York, NY 2016.

85   Appelbaum, Paul S., Richard J., Bonnie, and Jason H. Karlawish. 2005. "The capacity to vote of persons with Alzheimer's disease." *American Journal of Psychiatry*. 162: 2094–2100.

86   AMERICAN BAR ASSOCIATION ADOPTED BY THE HOUSE OF DELEGATES August 13–14, 2007 RECOMMENDATION.

87   4 Jason H. T. Karlawish et al., Identifying the Barriers and Challenges to Voting by Residents in Nursing Homes and Assisted Living Settings, J. Aging & Soc. Pol'y, vol. 20 issue 1, at 65, 72 (2008).

88   Highton, Benjamin. 1997. "Easy registration and voter turnout." *Journal of Politics* 59(2): 565–75.

89   Yu, Jinhai. 2016. *Does State Online Voter Registration Increase Voter Turnout?* Unpublished Manuscript.

90   Karp. Jeffrey A. And Susan A. Banducci. 2001. "Absentee Voting, Mobilization, and Participation." *American Politics Research*. 29(2): 183–195.

91   Burden, Barry C, David T. Canon, Kenneth R. Mayer and Donald P. Moynihan. 2014. Election Laws, Mobilization, and Turnout: The Unanticipated Consequences of Election Reform. American Journal of Political Science. 58:1 95–109.

CHAPTER 3

The Candidates

A. CONSTITUTIONAL QUALIFICATIONS FOR OFFICE

Having examined the right to vote, and the qualifications and procedures that govern the electorate, it is worthwhile to spend some time examining candidates for office. Considered broadly, we can think of the limitations on candidate eligibility as being derived from either a qualification or a disqualification. While this may not seem like a clear distinction, the rules regarding eligibility for office distinguish between criteria that an individual must meet, qualifications, and criteria that would render an individual ineligible for office, disqualifications. The Constitution contains few qualifications for federal office, the most important being those that are based on age, residency, and citizenship. Individuals seeking federal office must meet these criteria in order to take office. While states have the authority to set qualifications for their own offices, only a smattering of additional qualifications beyond these three are actually imposed on state elected officials. In addition to these qualifications, a number of disqualifications exist. While House and Senate candidates are not term-limited, these restrictions exist for candidates for the presidency and many state offices. Having served two terms, an individual is disqualified from being elected president again. Similarly, some states might criminal disqualifications, however, none exist at the federal level beyond the disqualification for the commission of treason. These qualifications and disqualifications are important because they limit the pool of potential candidates, altering the choices that we are presented with.

In addition to meeting any qualifications, candidates for offices must deal with the issue of ballot access. Each state, as part of its Constitutional authority to regulate the time, place, and manner of elections, has rules that govern how individuals petition to have their name placed on the official ballot. These rules have differed across time, across states, and even differ within states, depending on if a candidate identifies with a major or minor party, or choose to remain unaffiliated. Major and minor party candidates often have streamlined paths to the ballot, needing only to win their party's internal nominating contest. Individuals who choose to run as independents must complete other requirements in order to have their name placed on the general election ballot. Write-in candidates, who run for office without placing their name on the ballot, must sometimes deal with other administrative hurdles to ensure that election authorities properly count ballots cast in their favor.

This chapter will discuss the origins and application of the basic Constitutional qualifications for office, as well as discuss some interesting additional qualifications and disqualifications before examining the topic of ballot access, independent candidacies, and write in candidacies.

1. Age

Qualifications based on age are one of the simplest regulations governing elected office in the United States. These qualifications are nearly universal, existing for all federal offices and most all state and local offices. The Federalist 62 and 64 discuss these qualifications at the federal level as being important as a proxy for virtue, character, or ability. Referring to the difference in age requirements between the House and Senate, Madison notes that since the Senate requires "greater extent of information and stability of character", that a candidate, "should have reached a period of life most likely to supply these advantages."[1]

The Constitution lists three specific age requirements for federal offices. Article I section 2 states that members of the House of Representatives should be 25 years of age, Section 3 of that same article sets the age for Senators at 30, and Article II, Section 1 sets the age of 35 for the office of the president and vice president. While it is not explicitly clear from the Constitution, it seems apparent from Congressional example that these ages must be met by the time a newly elected member of Congress is sworn in, rather than at the time of the election. One notable example, Rush Holt Sr. was the youngest person to be elected Senator. Unfortunately, he would not actually turn 30 until midway through his first year in office. The Senate delayed accepting his credentials until two days after his June 19th birthday.[2] No president has yet tested this assumption, so it is unclear if it also applies to the presidency.

Beyond these restrictions for federal office, many states have adopted their own age requirements for office. While Vermont is silent on the issue of age, this is an exception to the rule. Some states link their requirements for office to the requirements for voters (usually this is done by simply requiring the candidate to be a qualified voter), meaning the age of 18 would be the requirement for office. A majority of the states, however, have set an age of 21 or higher as a minimum for most office. In general, age restrictions range from 18, in a number of states, to 31, which is the minimum age in Oklahoma for statewide offices.[3]

2. Residency

Residency is a second basic qualification for federal office. When the Constitution defines the term for presidential qualification, it uses this term, residency, however, when it discusses Senate and House qualifications it uses the term inhabitance. Speaking to presidential qualifications, the Constitution requires that an individual has been a resident within the United States for a period of at least 14 years. Qualifications for the Senate and House only mention being an inhabitant of a state at the time of the election. While these seem simple clauses, they deserve some investigation as to their purpose and scope.

Qualifications for the Senate and House were debated at much more length and concerns were made clear during the Constitutional Convention about the potential for "Rich men of neighboring states [to] employ with success the means of corruption in some particular district and thereby get into the public Councils after having failed in their own State." (Farrand 218). It was equally clear that the Convention did not want to exclude those who were temporarily residing in Washington while serving in public office (ibid 218). What results is a restriction that does not have strict components like duration or property ownership, but does require some connection to a home constituency. As with all Senate and House qualifications, those bodies are the final arbiter of what constitutes residency, and they have had to make judgments over time as to the eligibility of some members. In practical interpretation, members of the Senate and House are generally expected to maintain some sort of home in the state that they represent. Before moving on, it is worth noting that there is no qualification that House members be residents of the districts that they represent—merely an "Inhabitant of that State" (Const. Art 1 § 2 Cl. 2).

3. Citizenship

Citizenship is a third class of constitutional qualifications for federal office. The Constitution specifies that the President, Vice President, and Members of Congress must all be citizens of the United States, however, the specific nature of these citizenship requirements vary. Those seeking the office of the presidency (or vice presidency) must be natural born citizens. This is an important term, and we will discuss it further in the next section, but before doing so, we should look briefly at citizenship qualifications for the House and Senate.

The Constitution provides that Representatives and Senators be citizens of the United States, each for a specific length of time—Representatives for at least seven years, and Senators for at least nine years. In the debates of the Constitutional Convention, the framers mandated citizenship for federal offices because of the potential for agents of foreign governments to find their way into the government of the United States. Terms of citizenship such as these were seen as a favorable compromise between requiring birthright citizenship (as was the case the presidency) and no citizenship requirement at all.[4]

At the state level, nearly every state has an explicit citizenship requirement for state offices as well as for their state legislature, with most fashioned in the style of federal laws. In states that do not have citizenship requirements, these states often require candidates to be a qualified elector, meaning a qualified voter, which would carry with it its own citizenship requirement.

a.   *Natural Born Citizens*

The citizenship clause for the office of the president makes an additional qualification—that one must be a *natural born* citizen. This creates some difficulty because the phrase is not clearly defined anywhere in the Constitution. There is, however, a good amount of case law (although the Supreme Court has not weighed in on the matter) that can provide some guidance on what the clause means. A recent report by Jack Maskell of the Congressional Research Service gives a good account of this legal history, summarizing a distinction between two types of citizenship—natural born citizens, and naturalized citizens.[5] The first category receives their citizenship at birth, or perhaps, by virtue of their birth. This stands in contrast to non-citizens who are subsequently naturalized and receive their citizenship after their birth.

The citizenship clause of the Fourteenth Amendment states that "All persons born . . . in the United States, are citizens of the United States." This gives us some guidance on a subset of people who could be considered 'natural born'—those born within the United States. This rule has been interpreted to apply to anyone born on U.S. soil, regardless of the citizenship of his or her parents.[6] In a recent case that addressed the eligibility of President Obama, an Indiana court interpreted federal law, stating "Based on the language of Article II, Section 1, Clause 4 and the guidance provided by *Wong Kim Ark*,[7] we conclude that persons born within the borders of the United States are "natural born Citizens" for Article II, Section 1 purposes, regardless of the citizenship of their parents."[8]

There are also paths for natural born citizenship for those born outside of the United States. Federal law gives more specific guidance on the matter, with 8 U.S.C. § 1401 clarifying that individuals born outside of the United States, to at least one parent who is a citizen, qualify for birthright citizenship. This section of federal law does make some qualifications based on the length of time that one of the qualifying parents must reside in the United States (for instance, if the person has one parent of U.S. citizenship, the parent must have been "physically present in the United States. . . for a continuous period of one year at any time prior to the birth of such person."[9] This seems to make clear that any individual born in the United States, or outside the United States to at least one parent of U.S. citizenship, would qualify for citizenship at birth, and thus, be a *natural born* citizen.

B. ADDITIONAL QUALIFICATIONS AND DISQUALIFICATIONS

Age, residency, and citizenship are not the only qualifications for political offices, but they are the only ones for federal office. The Supreme Court, in cases including *Burton v. United States*,[10] *U.S. Term Limits, Inc. v. Thornton*,[11] and *Powell v. McCormack*,[12] have repeatedly found that the qualifications for House and Senate that are set out in Article I of the Constitution are the exclusive qualifications for those offices, and that no additional qualification may be added. This, however, does not speak to potential disqualifications, of which there are a mere few for federal office. Additionally, these limits on qualifications do not apply to the states, allowing them to individual set their own qualifications and disqualifications, which are usually more expansive than federal rules.

1. Criminal Disqualification

Criminal history is one potential qualification for candidates for office. At the federal level, there are no explicit restrictions on felon status. Recall again, that the Constitution lists the exclusive qualifications for Congress. There is, however, a disqualification for candidates for House and Senate in the Fourteenth Amendment. This language specifically disqualifies those who have taken an oath to support the Constitution, and then subsequently engaged in certain treasonous behavior. Additionally, 18 U.S. Code § 2381 specifically states that those convicted of treason are "incapable of holding any office under the United States." It is not entirely clear if this statute constitutes an impermissible or unconstitutional additional qualification on candidates for the House or Senate, but does create a clear disqualification for other federal offices.

An explicit disqualification for criminal behavior might not be the only avenue through which to disqualify a Member of Congress or candidate for Congress. For instance, would an individual retain their inhabitance (one of the constitutional requirements for office) if they were incarcerated in a prison in a state other than the state they represent? Interestingly, one report by the Congressional Research Service looked specifically at the question of congressional disqualification for out-of-state incarceration. According to their analysis, the fact that the individual would be held in another state involuntarily would likely bolster their case that they remain an inhabitant of their home state while in an out-of-state prison.[13] However, the report makes the point that Congress is the judge of the qualifications for their body. It would likely remain up to the specific chamber as to whether or not someone in this situation would meet the qualifications for office.

Looking beyond the federal case, many states, which are able to set their own qualifications for office, summarily exclude felons or other persons who have been convicted of a crime. In some cases, this prohibition is explicitly set out. Alabama, Arkansas, Delaware, Indiana, and Pennsylvania all explicitly ban convicted felons from holding office and provide no mechanism for restoration of the right to run.[14] In a number of states, a convicted felon's right to run is restored after a particular length of time—15 years in the case of South Carolina.[15] Some states, such as Montana, are more lenient and simply require that an individual complete their sentence,[16] whereas New York's constitution makes no mention of criminal backgrounds in relation to qualifications for office.[17] Most common, however, is not a disqualification for criminal offenses, but a link between eligibility to vote and eligibility to run. In these states, a candidate for office must be a qualified elector for the position they seek. If a state disenfranchises voters for felony convictions, they would not be an eligible elector for that office and would fail in that qualification for office.

2.   Religious Disqualifications

Although the U.S. Constitution contains a prohibition on religious tests for officeholders,[18] the early American nation was no stranger to religious (or at least theist) restrictions on holding office. With the Constitutional restriction on religious tests applying only to federal officeholders, some state constitutions were written with provisions which, while not necessarily denying public office to certain religions, would ban those who did not believe in a god.[19] As of 2018, seven states' constitutions still contained some religious test on officeholders. Four of these states make outright restrictions on those who deny a supreme being or a god. The constitution of Arkansas states "No person who denies the being of a God shall hold any office in the civil departments of this State."[20] Similar language exists in Mississippi—"No person who denies the existence of a Supreme Being shall hold any office in this state."[21] North Carolina's list of candidate disqualifications includes "First, any person who shall deny the being of Almighty God"[22] and South Carolina's states "No person who denies the existence of a Supreme Being shall hold any office under this Constitution."[23] Interestingly Tennessee's constitution, which originally included a restriction that included belief in both testaments of the Bible,[24] was changed to only include belief in god or "or a future state of rewards and punishments."[25] In an interesting contradiction, Maryland's constitution states that, while no religious tests can be imposed, "a declaration of belief in the existence of God" can be required.[26] Texas similarly mentions that there can be no religious tests for office and that no individual "can be excluded from holding office on account of his religious sentiments, provided he acknowledge the existence of a Supreme Being."[27] The Supreme Court has applied Article VI to state offices in *Torasco v. Watkins,*[28] meaning that these provisions, if tested, would not pass constitutional muster. Moreover, some states have acknowledged the unconstitutionality of the provisions but have not taken steps to purge the text (North Carolina's Attorney General drafted an opinion as to the unconstitutionality of the provision in 1972[29]).

3. Impeachment

Another Constitutional disqualification for federal office is one surrounding impeachment. Article I of the Constitution provides for a process for the impeachment and removal of public officials. The House of Representatives has the sole power to impeach an official (essentially to make a formal charge or allegation of misconduct.[30] Article I, Section 3, clause 6, provides that the Senate shall have the power to try impeachments, and provides for a procedure for doing so. This section also states that punishment for impeachment shall include "removal from office, and disqualification to hold and enjoy any office of honor, trust, or profit under the United States."[31] This clause creates an additional disqualification, barring anyone from holding federal office, who had been impeached and removed from office. This clause has never been tested, and it is unclear if the presidency, or a congressional seat, would qualify under this definition of an "office of honor, trust, or profit." Further, it is unclear whether or not this disqualification comes as an automatic punishment, or if the disqualification must be provided for as a specific part of the punishment.[32]

4. Dual Office Holding and Resign-to-Run Laws

Dual office restrictions prevent one individual from holding multiple offices at one time. Article I of the Constitution explicitly restricts "Officers of the United States" from serving in the House or Senate. This essentially restricts executive or judicial officers from simultaneously holding legislative office. It also restricts members of the House or Senate from being appointed to any newly created position or any position whose salary had been increased during the tenure of the Member of Congress to prevent Representatives or Senators from creating new jobs for themselves or authorizing pay increases for a position and then taking that position.[33] Interestingly, this Constitutional provision does not prohibit a number of activities, such as holding state office as well as Congressional office, holding executive and judicial office, holding federal or judicial office while *running* for Congress. An entirely different law, known as the Hatch Act, however, does prevent many officials in the executive branch from actively campaigning for partisan office.[34]

While these federal laws do not restrict dual office holding between state and federal office, many states prohibit this behavior in their own laws. Oregon's prohibition speaks directly to its purpose as a method of separation of powers, by stating that "No person charged with official duties under one of the branches of government, shall exercise any of the functions of another."[35] Some states take this restriction even further by prohibiting elected officials from even seeking office while they hold another. These laws require elected official to resign from their currently held position before being able to run for another office. These resign-to-run laws do not restrict an incumbent from contesting election for the position they currently hold. These laws exist presumably to reduce the possibility of an elected official using their position to gain an advantage in that election, or perhaps to prevent officials from shirking their responsibilities while running for office. Currently, only. Only Arizona, Florida, Georgia, Hawaii, and Texas currently have these laws in effect.

5. Term Limits

Term limits are rules that limit the number of terms that an elected official can serve in a given office. Essentially, term limits constitute an additional qualification for office, or perhaps even more precisely, a disqualification for office. When an elected official has served the maximum number of terms allowed by a term limit law, they are effectively disqualified from running again.

Term limits, while a matter of discussion for the founders during the Constitutional Convention as well as the ratification debates, did not have a place in the original Constitutional structure of the country. While Washington himself set the early precedent of two terms in office, his high-minded rationale for rotation in office would be continued for less virtuous reasons. From Jefferson to Jackson, the spoils system began to develop in the U.S. Civil Service, necessitating rotation in office.[36] However, as it grew with the spoils system, the importance of rotation in office would likewise begin to wane as a result of increasing distaste with the spoils system.[37] In addition, the idea of a legislative career became more normalized with the increasing professionalism and institutionalization of the House. Over the course of the late nineteenth century, the percentage of new members to the House of Representatives began a precipitous decline. The elections of 1882 marked the last time the House would see membership turnover at a rate higher than 50 percent.[38]

At the presidential level, term limits were, until the third term of Franklin Roosevelt, a matter of tradition. As discussed earlier, although term limits did not find their way into the Constitution, they did have supporters. Early supporters like Washington and Jefferson expressed this support through example, limiting themselves to two terms. The first president to attempt to seek a third term was Ulysses S. Grant. Although he did not seek a consecutive third term in 1876, he threw his hat into the ring for the Republican nomination in 1880. Grant would lead in the first round of balloting at that 1880 convention, but opposition would congeal around dark-horse nominee James Garfield in the 36th round of voting, denying Grant the opportunity to seek a third term.[39] Teddy Roosevelt failed to win the support of the Republican Party in 1912 and ran as the nominee of the Progressive Party. While this would not have been a third election for Roosevelt (he had ascended to the presidency after the assassination of William McKinley, and only been elected to the presidency once in 1904), he would have been the first president to serve more than eight years. Finally, Woodrow Wilson sought his party's nomination for a third term in 1920 but failed to gain any support, receiving only two votes during the convention balloting.[40] The Twenty-second Amendment would finally limit presidents to being elected to two terms. The amendment also limited those who served more than two years of another president's term from being elected more than once. In effect, this seems to create a two-term limit, with a maximum time of service of ten years (assuming one could serve up to the two-year limit of another president's term, and then be elected twice).

One interesting thought about the Twenty-second Amendment is that its language specifically mentions being *elected* no more than two times. This is in contrast to language in Article II, and the Twelfth Amendment, which discusses eligibility for the office. Some scholars have argued that the Twenty-second Amendment's restriction on election might not constitute a restriction on eligibility for the office of the presidency (in the same way that citizenship or age is set in the Constitution as a restriction on eligibility).[41] This raises the question of whether or not a former president, who had served two full terms, could be elected as a vice-president, and then ascend to the presidency—perhaps even through some machinations or a prearranged agreement.

States have had a similar history with term limits, but unlike their absence from Congress, states began to revisit state legislative term limits in the 1980s, with gradual adoption occurring in a number of states over the 1980s and 1990s.[42] Today, 15 states have legislative term limits of some variety. In some cases, these limits are constructed as to limit the number of years a state legislator can serve within a given window, while others are absolute limits on a set number of terms. Governors in the states face limits as well, with various limits ranging from absolute limits of two terms to schemes that merely limit consecutive terms. Today, 36 states impose gubernatorial term limits.

6. State-Imposed Federal Qualifications

One point of conflict between the power of the states and the federal government has come to light a number of times in recent history. Can the states, under their Constitutional power to regulate the time place and manner of elections, impose additional restrictions or qualifications on candidates for federal office? In attempting to decide this question, we must make an important distinction between restrictions on presidential candidates, and restrictions on congressional candidates. This is because of the unique way in which states participate in the election of a president. While states directly elect members of Congress, states do not, in fact, elect presidential nominees. Rather, they elect electors, who will later cast their ballot for the president.

As mentioned in the previous section, members of Congress are not term-limited. In the early 1990s, some states attempted to enact term limit statutes of their own. While these states did not have the authority to set qualifications for Congress, they could set qualifications for ballot access. To enact their own term limits, these states (23 according to one count) barred candidates from filing for office if they had previously served some number of terms.[43] In mid-1995, this wave of term limit provisions came to an abrupt halt when the Supreme Court issued their decision in *U.S. Term Limits, Inc. v. Thornton*[44] which was a challenge to term limit laws in Arkansas. The court held, in a 5–4 decision, that these states could not impose any qualifications on candidates for Congress other than the exclusive qualification listed in the Constitution.

There have been cases where states have attempted to enact additional qualifications for office that are not in conflict with the exclusive qualifications that the Constitution lays out. In the wake of the discredited 'birther' movement, which questioned the natural-born citizenship of President Obama, a number of states attempted to pass legislation requiring candidates to submit their birth certificates, or some other proof of citizenship in order to have their names placed on the ballot. Because a birth certificate is directly related to one of the exclusive Constitutional qualifications, citizenship, it might not be seen by the courts as the addition of a new qualification. In other words, a birth certificate requirement would not necessarily be adding an additional qualification to candidates for office, but would merely be requiring candidates to prove that they meet one of the exclusive Constitutional qualifications.

Alternatively, what if an additional state-imposed qualification does not directly relate to an exclusive Constitutional qualification? One recent example of this can be found in state attempts to require presidential candidates to disclose their tax returns. In the wake of President Trump's refusal to release tax information, a number of states have considered compelling disclosure of tax returns as a prerequisite to ballot access. While none have passed as of yet, it is unclear if these laws would be seen as unconstitutional additional qualifications on the office, or as permissible requirements for ballot access.

C. BALLOT ACCESS AND INDEPENDENT CANDIDACIES

In addition to meeting Constitutional qualifications and not being otherwise disqualified, candidates must meet certain requirements in order to have their name placed on the ballot. States are able to set these rules under their Constitutional authority to regulate the time, place, and manner of elections. Ballot access requirements are dependent upon the office sought, and the party affiliation (or lack thereof) of the candidate.

American elections are ruled in many ways by our two-party system. Parties structure our choices because of the preferential treatment they receive in navigating ballot access laws. While third-party candidates may find it difficult to navigate the electoral landscape, independent candidates often have a more difficult time. In many cases, third party candidates are still entitled to access to the general election ballot by virtue of their party's status within the state. The same is not true for independent candidates. Candidates for major party office need to meet ballot access requirements to be placed on the primary ballot, but winners of the primaries are placed on general election ballots automatically. Third-party candidates will also need to meet some filing requirement, but then usually are placed on the ballot automatically by virtue of being the winning candidate from their party. Independent candidates, however, generally do not contest primary elections, and meet their respective filing requirements in order to be automatically placed on the general election ballot.

This general overview glosses over the vast differences in how states handle ballot access, and the difficulty of the obstacles that candidates face. To give an example of one particularly odd scenario, we can look at Hawaii's ballot access laws. In Hawaii, all candidates are required to file for the primary elections by compiling signatures and paying filing fees regardless of party affiliation.[45] All candidates then contest the primary, with nonpartisan candidates listed in their own separate section, but still on the same ballot. While recognized party candidates need only receive the most votes amongst their fellow partisans, nonpartisan candidates face a different standard. For independent candidates to qualify for the general election ballot, they must receive either 10 percent of the total vote or a number of votes equal to the qualifying partisan candidate who receives the fewest number of votes.[46] For example, a third-party candidate may qualify for the general election being the top vote-getter in their party, even if they receive less than 10 percent of the total vote. However, an independent (who cannot qualify by being a winning party candidate) must either get 10 percent of the overall vote, or match the vote total of this third-party candidate who qualifies with less than 10 percent.

Ballot access laws are extremely diverse across the states, and even across offices and parties within states. While this makes an exhaustive catalog of rules extremely difficult, we can look at an overview of the typical bounds of these rules to get a sense for their application in the states.

1. Getting on the Ballot

If a candidate has met all qualifications for office, they must then secure access to the ballot. States, in the interest of winnowing competition to only the most competitive candidates, can impose barriers to access to the ballot. These ballot access requirements generally take the form of filing fees and signature requirements. While the former are generally straightforward monetary fees paid to the state (and sometimes distributed to the parties), the later come in a number of designs and widely varying levels of restriction.

When thinking about ballot access we are generally referring to a subset of ballots within the larger framework of elections. In order to see the whole array of ballot access, we must consider different elections—primary and general, different parties—major, minor, and independent, and different offices. Generally speaking, states treat major party candidates, minor party candidates, independent candidates, and write-in candidates differently (the following section will discuss independent candidates, and Chapter 5 will discuss the distinctions in nominating procedures between major and minor party candidates more fully). Ballot access requirements usually apply to party candidates when they are seeking their party's nomination in a primary election. Once a candidate wins their party's primary, they are automatically granted access to the general election ballot and do not need to clear any more ballot access hurdles. Independent candidates or third-party candidates that do not contest a primary may be subject to ballot access limitations for the general election. Additionally, due to their nature as a winnowing mechanism, requirements generally change with the level of the office sought, with stricter requirements for higher offices.

While states have a wide degree of latitude in setting ballot access requirements, the courts have determined that there are some limitations to state authority. In a case arising out of Texas, the Supreme Court found that the state's filing fees were exorbitantly high, and a violation of the Equal Protection clause of the Fourteenth Amendment.[47] Moreover, the courts have held that states must provide an alternate path to the ballot for indigent candidates who are unable to pay filing fees.[48]

Today, filing fees and signature requirements run a spectrum from trivially low to substantial. In Tennessee, candidates for federal and statewide office must gather a total of 25 voters from anywhere within the state.[49] In most other states with a signature requirement, candidates for Congress must gather signatures equaling a fixed percentage of the voters in the district, or state, depending on the office sought. Filing fees vary widely as well. Maryland levies a modest fee of $100 for candidates for House and $290 for candidates for the Senate.[50] Contrast this with Florida, on the other hand, which levies a filing fee of 6 percent of the office sought. This fee is divided into a ballot fee, an election assessment, and a party assessment.[51] At the current Congressional salary of $174,000, these fees total $10,440. Sometimes these signature limits and filing fees can be particularly difficult, especially for independent candidates. In Georgia and Illinois, for example, independent candidates for the U.S. House must gather signatures totaling 5 percent of the voters in the district.[52] By comparison, major party candidates in Illinois need only collect signatures totaling .5 percent.[53] While this may seem at first glance to be the kind of impermissible barrier to ballot access, the Court specifically upheld Georgia's 5 percent requirement in 1971.[54]

2. Timing

One interesting consideration, perhaps especially for independent candidates, is a state's filing deadline. As mentioned in the previous section, major and minor party candidates, as well as independent and write-in candidates are often treated differently in terms of ballot access. In particular, each must generally fulfill some administrative requirement with respect to their nomination by a predetermined deadline. Major party candidates must file for candidacy in their party's primary election by a certain date, likewise, minor parties have a deadline by which candidates must either file for their party's primary (if one is held) or the party must notify the state that it has nominated a candidate through a convention. In addition to party candidates, independents and write-in candidates are subject to a deadline to file paperwork in states that require petitions, filing fees, or declarations of write-in candidacies. While it may not seem surprising or perhaps even interesting that these deadlines exist, they may play an important part in the strategic decision of a candidate to run for office. As these dates do not always align with major party deadlines, a potential candidate may have more or less information about their field of competition based on those deadlines. For example, if independent candidates are required to file on the same day that major party candidates file for their primary, an independent might not know the entire field of party candidates. If the independent filing date is between the major party filing date and the primary date, an independent candidate might know the field of potential major party candidates, but would not know the eventual nominees. For independent candidates, their desire to run may be based upon the outcome of a party primary. Therefore, if an independent or write-in filing date is before (or even on) the party primary date, they are prevented from having full information about the field of candidates. In previous court cases *Williams v.*

Rhodes[55] and *Anderson v. Celebrezze*[56], the court struck down extremely early third party and independent filing deadlines as unconstitutional burdens. The court, however, did not set a specific standard, and a number of states including Mississippi, California, Idaho, and Utah, still have independent filing deadlines as early as March. In all four of these states, the independent deadline is the same as the major party deadline. While no states currently have independent filing dates before major party deadlines (which would be a significant barrier, and perhaps one that would be subject to Constitutional challenge), only 18 have independent filing dates after the major party primaries.

3. Write-in Candidates

Sometimes, candidates do not appear on the ballot even though they plan to contest the election. In most states, voters can cast their vote for a candidate not appearing on the ballot by writing their name in a blank space provided for that purpose. While this may seem like a simple act, a number of rules frame the way write-in votes can be cast and counted.

While many voters have the option of writing in any candidate, some states do not allow the practice. According to a report from the National Association of Secretaries of State, five states completely disallow write-in voting (HI, LA, NV, OK, and SD).[57] The Constitutionality of Hawaii's ban was upheld in 1992 in *Burdick v. Takushi*,[58] cementing the ability of states to prohibit write-in candidacies. To complicate the matter, Arkansas,[59] New Mexico,[60] and South Carolina[61] all allow write-in votes for some offices, but not for presidential contests. Arkansas and South Carolina do this through an explicit ban, while New Mexico effectively bars presidential write-ins through a combination of statutes which do not provide an avenue for a write-in candidate to nominate presidential electors. Other states and localities can set laws to restrict write-ins to specific races. This means that there are some cases where a state may allow write-in votes in the general election but bar them in primary races.

The states that do allow for write-in votes generally have a process by which candidates declare an intention to be a write-in candidate. Only a handful of states allow write-in votes for any candidate, without pre-registration.[62]

4. Sore Loser Laws

Sore loser laws are laws that are designed to prevent general election candidacies of individuals who lost their respective primary elections. In all states with the exception of Connecticut, Iowa, and New York,[63] if a candidate contests a partisan primary election, they are excluded from running in the general election as a member of a different party, or as an independent candidate. Generally, these laws take one of a number of forms. A state may explicitly bar anyone who has lost a primary election from appearing on the general election ballot. Alternatively, some states merely prohibit losers of partisan primaries, or in some cases, anyone who participates in a primary, from appearing on the ballot as independents. As mentioned earlier, ballot access is generally contingent on winning a party primary (for anyone who is not running as an independent). Thus, states are able to force candidates into choosing to run as a candidate for party nomination or as an independent, prohibiting the choice of both. Regardless of form, these laws have the practical effect of prohibiting independent candidacies from losing partisan candidates. It is worth noting that not all states prohibit candidates from filing for the primary elections of multiple parties. In these states, candidates who lost one party primary but won another could still appear on the ballot. This, however, does not resemble a sore-loser candidacy in the traditional sense, as the candidate still has to win one of these party nominations.[64]

D. THESE RULES MATTER

Speaking in the broadest of terms, electoral rules that restrict the potential pool of candidates have a limiting effect on our democratic processes in a number of ways. By simple virtue of their winnowing effect, voters are necessarily left with fewer choices because of the obstacles of candidacy restrictions. The effects of ballot access laws, for instance, have been widely studied, and a good deal of research has shown that petition requirements and filing fees limit contestation rates in elections. One study of congressional elections showed that states without ballot access requirements saw a dramatic reduction in the number of uncontested seats.[65] Research on state legislative races yielded similar results.[66] In addition to this line of research on contestation rates, some scholars have studied whether or not these rules lead to any systematic biases in the types of choices we are presented with. If electoral rules systematically bias our electoral procedures against certain types of candidates, then these rules become more than a mere nuisance, and have tremendous impact on the outcomes of our elections. One study examined third-party gubernatorial candidates and found that restrictive ballot access laws had a particularly limiting effect on the number of these candidates in races.[67] In addition to limiting third party and independent candidates, restrictions on candidates may affect the nature of major party candidates. One study by Burden, Jones, and Kang suggested that the appearance of sore loser laws might increase partisan polarization by forcing primary candidates to adopt more extreme positions in order to cater to more ideologically extreme primary electorates. When primary elections and their polarized electorates nominate extreme candidates, moderate candidates do not make the general election ballot. Sore loser laws then prevent these moderates from gaining access to the general election ballot as independents. By excluding these more moderate candidates from the general election, we necessarily restrict the choices of the electorate to more extreme candidates.[68]

E. CHAPTER 3 DISCUSSION QUESTIONS

1.   What biases, if any, do you think exist in our elected officials because of constitutional restrictions on candidates? Do you think that age restrictions on candidates should be removed? What about restrictions on citizenship, and in particular, the requirement that presidential candidates be natural-born citizens? Are the founder's concerns about foreign influence still important enough today to warrant the exclusion of citizens who are not natural-born?

2.   Sore loser laws prevent candidates who have lost a party primary from running in a general election. In 2006, Joe Lieberman lost Connecticut's Democratic primary, but because the state did not have a sore loser law, he ran as an independent and won. The usual argument for sore loser laws is that a sore loser might fracture a party's vote and play the role of a spoiler candidate. In this case, a plurality of the state favored the sore loser candidate. Do sore loser laws protect parties from spoilers, or do they unfairly limit the choices of the electorate?

3.   Many of the rules discussed in this chapter advantage the major parties. In particular, ballot access is much easier for candidates of the major parties. Proponents of this would say that we do not want our ballots crowded with too many inconsequential minor party and independent candidates. Others might suggest that these restrictive laws are, in fact, the reason that third parties perform poorly in elections. Which of these arguments sounds most plausible to you?

---

[1]   Madison, James. *Federalist* No. 62, in *The Federalist Papers,* ed. Clinton Rossiter. New York: New American Library, p. 376.

[2]   United States Congress. Biographical Directory of the United States Congress 1774–Present.

[3]   OK Const. Art. VI § 3.

[4]   See Federalist 62 for a discussion of this point.

[5]   Congressional Research Service. 2016. "Qualifications for President and the "Natural Born" Citizenship Eligibility Requirement."

[6]   *United States v. Wong Kim Ark*, 169 U.S. 649 (1898).

[7]   *United States v. Wong Kim Ark*, 169 U.S. 649.

[8]   *Ankeny v. Governor of the State of Indiana*, 916 N.E.2d 678, 688 (2009).

[9]   8 U.S.C. § 1401(e).

[10] *Burton v. United States*, 196 U.S. 283 (1905) *Burton v. United States*, 202 U.S. 344 (1906).

[11] 514 U.S. 779 (1995).

[12] 395 U.S. 486 (1969).

[13] Congressional Research Service. 2002. "Congressional Candidacy, Incarceration, and the Constitution's Inhabitancy Question.".

[14] Alabama. Code § 36–2–1, Arkansas Code § 16–90–112(b) Delaware Constitution A. II § 21, Indiana Code § 3–8–1–5, Pennsylvania Constitution A. II, § 7.

[15] South Carolina Constitution A. VI § 1.

[16] Montana Constitution A. IV, § 4.

[17] New York Constitution A. III § 7.

[18] U.S. Const. Art. VI cl. 3.

[19] See Kabala, James S. 2016. *Church-State Relations in the Early American Republic, 1787–1846*. New York: Routledge. For a more complete discussion.

[20] Arkansas Constitution Article 19 § 1.

[21] Mississippi Constitution Article 14 § 265.

[22] North Carolina Constitution Article 6 § 8.

[23] South Carolina Constitution Article 17 § 4.

[24] Kabala, James S. 2016. *Church-State Relations in the Early American Republic, 1787–1846*. New York: Routledge.

[25] Tennessee Constitution Article IX § 2.

[26] Maryland Constitution, Declaration of Rights, Article 37.

[27] Texas Constitution Article 1 § 4.

[28] 367 U.S. 488 (1961).

[29] 41 N.C.A.G. 727 (1972).

[30] U.S. Constitution Article I, Section 2.

[31] U.S. Constitution Article I, Section 3.

[32] Congressional Research Service. 2015. "Qualifications of Members of Congress."

[33] U.S. Constitution Article I, Section 6, Clause 2.

[34] 5 U.S. Code § 7323(a)3.

[35] Oregon Constitution. Article II, § 10.

[36] Maranto, Robert and David Schultz. 1991. "A short history of the United States Civil Service." Lanham: University Press of America.

[37] Petracca M.P. 1996. "A History of Rotation in Office." in Grofman B. ed. *Legislative Term Limits: Public Choice Perspectives*. Studies in Public Choice, vol 10. Norwell, MA: Kluwer Academic Publishers.

[38] Polsby, Nelson. 1968. "The institutionalization of the US House of Representatives". *American Political Science Review* 62: 145.

[39] Republican Party. "Proceedings of the Republican National Convention, held at Chicago, Illinois, Wednesday, Thursday, Friday, Saturday, Monday, and Tuesday, June 2d, 3d, 4th, 5th, 7th and 8th, 1880. Resulting in the following nominations: for President, James A. Garfield, of Ohio. For Vice-President, Chester A. Arthur, of New York. Compiled by Eugene Davis." Chicago: Jno. B. Jeffery Printing and Publishing House.

[40] Democratic Party. "Official report of the proceedings of the Democratic national convention, held in San Francisco, California, June 28, 29, 30, July 1, 2, 3, 5, and 6, 1920, resulting in the nomination of Hon. James M. Cox (of Ohio) for president and Hon. Franklin D. Roosevelt (of New York) for vice-president." Compiled by Edward B. Hoffman. Indianapolis: Bookwalter-Ball Printing.

[41] Peabody, Bruce G.; Gant, Scott E. 1999. "The Twice and Future President: Constitutional Interstices and the Twenty-Second Amendment". *Minnesota Law Review*. 83(3): 565–635.

[42] Squire, Peverill, and Keith E. Hamm. 2005. *101 Chambers: Congress, State Legislatures, and the Future of Legislative Studies*. Columbus: Ohio State University Press. p. 64.

[43] Lopez, Edward J. 2002. "Congressional voting on term limits." *Public Choice*. 112: 405–431. p. 407.

44 514 U.S. 779 (1995).

45 HRS § 12–5—Signatures; HRS § 12–6—Fees.

46 HRS § 12–41.

47 *Bullock v. Carter*, 405 U.S. 134 (1972).

48 *Lubin v. Panish*, 415 U.S. 709 (1974).

49 Tennessee Code 2–5–101.

50 Maryland Statutes 5–401.

51 Florida Statutes 99.092.

52 O.C.G.A. 21–2–170; 10 ILCS 5/10–2; 10 ILCS 5/10–3.

53 10 ILCS 5/7–10, 7–10(b)(k).

54 *Jenness v. Fortson*, 403 U.S. 431 (1971).

55 393 U.S. 23 (1968).

56 460 U.S. 780 (1983).

57 National Association of Secretaries of State. 2016. "State Laws Regarding Presidential Ballot Access for the General Election."

58 504 U.S. 428 (1992).

59 Ark. Code Ann. § 7–5–205.

60 New Mexico Statutes 1–15–3.

61 South Carolina Code of Laws 7–13–360.

62 https://www.washingtonpost.com/graphics/politics/2016-election/write-in-votes/.

63 Burden, Barry C. Bradley M. Jones, and Michael S. Kang. 2014. "Sore Loser Laws and Congressional Polarization." *Legislative Studies Quarterly*. 39(3): 299–325.

64 Kang, Michael S. 2010 "Sore Loser Laws and Democratic Contestation." *Georgetown Law Review*. 99: 1013–1075 offers a complete listing of all statutory combinations as well as a complete listing of different state statutes.

65 Ansolabehere, Stephen, and Alan Gerber. 1996. "The effects of filing fees and petition requirements on U.S. House elections." *Legislative Studies Quarterly*. 21: 249–64.

66 Stratmann, Thomas. 2005. "Ballot access restrictions and candidate entry in elections." *European Journal of Political Economy*. 21: 59–71.

67 Lern, Steve B., and Conor M. Dowling. 2006. "Picking their spots: Minor party candidates in gubernatorial election." *Political Research Quarterly*. 59: 471–80.

68 Burden, Barry C. Bradley M. Jones, and Michael S. Kang. 2014. "Sore Loser Laws and Congressional Polarization." *Legislative Studies Quarterly*. 39:3 299–325.

Apportionment, Districting, and Gerrymandering

A. DEFINING CONCEPTS

The crafting of legislative boundaries for the United States House of Representatives is a complex process. The Constitution lays out a general framework, but much of the specific processes are contained in federal statutes or state law. Speaking broadly, three steps must take place in order to determine legislative boundaries—an enumeration of the population, an apportionment of seats, and the drawing of legislative districts. In other words, we must first count the population, then divide up the total number of seats between the states, and finally divide the states into geographic boundaries. Let's look at each of these processes individually and bring some clarity to this process.

The first of these three steps, the enumeration of the population, is a simple count of the number of people living in the country, and within each of the individual states. In order to allocate the 435 House seats to the states, the Constitution provides that representatives be apportioned according to their population. In order to do this, we must know the size of the country and the size of each of the individual states in order to calculate each state's proportion of the total population. To determine the size of the country, a census, or a count of the population, is conducted every ten years by the federal government. The census also provides population breakdowns for each state. These numbers provide the necessary information to divide the House across the individual states.

The second of the three steps in this process is the apportionment of seats. Apportionment simply means to create appropriate shares, or portions, of House seats for each state. This process involves a mathematical formula that divides the total number of seats in the House among each of the states in proportion with their share of the nation's population. Proportions of seats align with the proportion of the population in each state, and while slight variations in population arise, efforts are taken to attempt to keep these variations at a minimum.

The third step in setting legislative boundaries is the process of dividing a state into geographic districts of equal size. We call this procedure districting, or redistricting. Once we know the population of a state and its seat allocation, we must craft geographic boundaries that comply with various Constitutional and statutory guidelines. Each state maintains its own procedures for this process, with different rules, participants, and considerations playing a role.

This chapter will walk through each of these three processes and discuss the history and evolution of the rules which govern enumeration, apportionment, and districting. We will also discuss the more recent history of gerrymandering, the drawing of district boundaries for political advantage.

B. ENUMERATION OF THE POPULATION

The first step in crafting legislative districts is the enumeration of the population of the United States and of the states individually. Article I, Section 2 of the Constitution provides for a decennial census (a census taken once every ten years). The census has been conducted since 1790, counting households and individuals throughout the country.

Before the modern United States Census Bureau was formed in 1902, the census lacked a permanent administrative home in the federal government. The first censuses were conducted by U.S. marshals and their appointed assistants. These marshals were officers of the court that were appointed in every judicial district by the Judiciary Act of 1789. In 1790, a Census Act was passed directing these marshals to appoint assistants to help them to count the inhabitants in their respective districts.[1] These 'enumerators,' as they were called, were to visit each household in their judicial district, collecting the names of the heads of household, and the number of persons in those households. Census reports could then be tabulated in order to determine the number of people living in a judicial district and be summed up to the state and national level.

An important consideration in enumerating the population is the determination of which people would be counted for purposes of representation. Would representation just be based on the number of votes in a state, or the number of adult males, or on all inhabitants of a state? According to Article I, apportionment would be based on a count of all persons, excluding 'Indians not taxed' and counting slaves as three-fifths of one person. This Constitutional rule meant that while voting rights were still extremely limited, disenfranchised groups like free blacks, women, and minors, were all still counted fully for the purposes of apportionment. The three-fifths rule, which would remain in force until the adoption of the Fourteenth Amendment, offered an unsatisfying solution to the disagreement over the counting of slaves for representation. While southern states, who stood to benefit from increased representation (via increased population), advocated for the full counting of slaves, northern interests contended that only free inhabitants should be counted for the purposes of representation. The compromise position would count slaves partially for purposes of representation.

The three-fifths rule, and the population advantage that it gave to southern states, may have had an important impact on the outcomes of early elections because of the way apportionment interacts with presidential election mechanisms. Because a state's electoral votes are linked to the size of their congressional delegation, the three-fifths rule provided an advantage to southern states in the Electoral College. It is possible that this added influence may have had an impact on presidential election outcomes. Historians Garry Wills and Paul Finkelman have argued that the 1800 and 1824 elections could have seen different outcomes without the rule.[2]

Change came to the process of taking the census each decade. Questions changed, forms standardized, and manual tabulation became more difficult with the increasing size of the country. U.S. marshals and their assistants continued to enumerate the census until 1880, when the census began to hire their own enumerators and their office saw the introduction of new technology that greatly sped up census calculations.[3] While much was to change at the census offices, of more importance to electoral rules, was the adoption of the Fourteenth Amendment, which altered apportionment math by providing for the full weighting of newly freed slaves in population calculations.

Section 1 of the Fourteenth Amendment is likely known to all students of American government, but Section 2 is more relevant to our discussion on apportionment and redistricting. This second section was a restatement of Article I Section 2 of the Constitution, providing for the apportionment of representatives according to population and giving full weight to all persons (this Amendment left in place the exclusion of non-taxed Indians). While one would assume that the immediate effect of this would be an increase in the number of seats in the former slave states of the south, this did not take place. Scholars point to three likely reasons for this unexpected outcome—large population growth in other areas of the country, the death of many southerners in the Civil War, and a dramatic undercount of the population in the region. Population growth in other areas of the country outpaced southern population growth, negating any relative gains in representation, while Civil War deaths and population undercounts reduced absolute southern population counts.[4]

Another overlooked part of the Fourteenth Amendment is a penalty for denying the right to vote to citizens. Although we now know that gains in representation did not come to fruition for the south, there were worries at the time (echoing the Constitutional Convention) that southern states might reap the benefits of increased population, while continuing to deny the right to vote to newly freed slaves. To counter this possibility, provision was inserted into the Fourteenth Amendment that set a penalty in case of the abridgment of voting rights in a state—a reduction in apportionment to the same degree that any number of citizens were denied the right to vote. While the provision could have provided penalties for the disenfranchisement of newly freed slaves in the post-reconstruction era, the penalty was never enforced on any state by the courts.[5]

After the Fourteenth Amendment, no further Constitutional changes to the enumeration process would take place, and with just a few exceptions, no statutory changes have been made to significantly alter the process. Technological advances, however, have driven a more accurate census. Today, the Census takes count of all persons inhabiting a state for the purposes of apportionment. This means that population counts include individuals who are might not otherwise be able to vote. Citizens and non-citizens alike are counted, as well as individuals under the age of 18. This process captures the whole population of a state for representation, not just those who are able to vote. When the census cannot gather information about a specific household, they are now able to use statistical techniques to make fairly accurate guesses about the occupancy, or size of a household based on data collected from similar households. This technique is called 'hot deck imputation' and has been the subject of litigation in the past.[6] By using procedures like this, census counts are becoming more accurate. In the 1970 count, the Census began to incorporate overseas military personnel into state population counts, assigning them to their home state for enumeration.[7] However, Americans who might be overseas for other reasons are not included in population counts.

Once a complete accounting of the population is complete, the process can proceed to the next stage, the apportionment of seats.

C. APPORTIONMENT OF SEATS

Apportionment is the second step in crafting our legislative boundaries. After we have completed our count, we must mathematically divide the total number of House seats across the states according to their population. There are two primary concerns with this process. One concern is setting the size of House, in terms of seats. Another concern is how to mathematically divide this number. One way of tackling this problem would be to set a specific population per seat and determine the size of the House based on the population of the individual states. This would mean that the size of the House would change as the population of the country changed. A second way of approaching the problem would be to arbitrarily set the size of the chamber and divide those seats across the states. We have taken both approaches to apportionment at different times in the country's history. Let's look at how these processes work and the math behind apportionment.

The apportioning of seats presents an interesting mathematical problem. In only very rare circumstances would a distribution of seats among states yield a neat and tidy division (one without remainders). It would be improbable for a number of states to have populations that are all equally divisible by a number appropriate for the size of a legislature. Moreover, in order to compute this division, one needs to arrive at either a total number of seats or desired population per representative. These interesting mathematical problems have yielded even more interesting solutions at different points in the history of the country.

At its most basic, two methods can be used to distribute seats to states. In the first method, the size of the legislature can be set, and a rate of population per representative can be obtained by dividing the total population of the country by the number of seats in the legislature. The quotient of this simple division can be used to determine the number of seats awarded to a state by dividing the total state population by the resulting population per representative. A problem arises when this division leaves a remainder, or a fraction of a seat (which, again, barring unlikely mathematical circumstances, will happen in every state). With these remainders, what is a fair procedure for allocating seats? Again, in the most basic example, one course of action would be to round up, down, or to the nearest whole number. Doing this, however, would likely violate the size of the legislature set in the first stage of calculation. Looking at the table below, we can see that with the desired legislature size of 105, rounding up, rounding down, or rounding to the nearest number, all violate the desired legislature size.

Alexander Hamilton proposed a solution for this problem by first rounding down to the nearest whole number of seats, then awarding the remaining seats to states in order of the size of their remainder. In practice, this calculation would look something like the example below:

TABLE 4.1   HAMILTON APPORTIONMENT PLAN

Legislature Size - 105

Population Total - 51748

Population Per Seat - 492.84

State	Population	State population / Population per seat	Round Down	Round Up	Round Nearest	Remainder	Allocation of Remaining Seats (Hamilton)	Total Seats
A	7644	15.51	15	16	16	0.51	0	15
B	10465	21.23	21	22	21	0.23	0	21
C	14236	28.89	28	29	29	0.89	1	29
D	7008	14.22	14	15	14	0.22	0	14
E	4330	8.79	8	9	9	0.79	1	9
F	2355	4.78	4	5	5	0.78	1	5
G	5710	11.59	11	12	12	0.59	1	12
Total	51748		Total Seats	Total Seats	Total Seats			Total Seats
			101	108	106			105

In this example, the legislature is set at 105 seats and the total population is 51,748. This yields a population per seat of 492.84. By simply dividing the state population by the population per seat, we get an allocation of seats. However, rounding down and dropping our remainder only apportions 101 seats. Similarly problematic, rounding up would apportion too many seats, 108, and rounding to the nearest would apportion one too many, 106. Hamilton's method rounds down (apportioning 101 seats), and then awards the remaining four seats to the states with the largest remainders—States C, E, F, and G. State A, which would have rounded up to 16 seats, is not awarded an extra seat, leaving a legislature of the desired size, 105 seats.

George Washington vetoed this Hamiltonian plan—the first presidential veto. In place of the Hamiltonian plan, an alternative plan proposed by Thomas Jefferson was instituted. In this plan, rather than fixing the divisor as the population per seat, Jefferson proposed choosing a new divisor that would yield the appropriate number of seats when the quotients were rounded down. In other words, instead of determining the number of seats per state by dividing a state's population by an exact number of people per seat (necessarily resulting in the incorrect number of seats being apportioned, and some distribution being done according to remainders), Jefferson suggested changing the number of people per seat until the resulting division yielded the correct number of seats. This meant that there would be no need for the second round of allocation based on remainders, however, it required a trial-and-error process. The example below shows what that process would look like:

TABLE 4.2 JEFFERSON'S APPORTIONMENT PLAN

Legislature Size - 105

Population Total - 51748

**Population per seat -
492.84**

		Trial and Error		
State	**Population**	**State Population / 475, Rounded Down**	**State Population / 476, Rounded Down**	**State Population / 475.7, Rounded Down**
A	7644	16	16.0	16
B	10465	22	21.0	21
C	14236	29	29.0	29
D	7008	14	14.0	14
E	4330	9	9.0	9
F	2355	4	4.0	4
G	5710	12	11.0	12
Total	51748	106	104	105

In this example, choosing a divisor of 492.84 (the population per seat) yields too few seats (101—see Table 4.1 Seats per state, rounded down). Adjusting downwards (smaller divisors yield larger quotients), a divisor of 475 yields 106 seats. Being too many seats, we can then continue our trial-and-error process by selecting 476 (which yields too few seats—104). By selecting a number between these two—475.7, we find our desired result of 105 seats. Comparing these methods, we can see that State F loses a seat in the Jeffersonian model, and State A gains a seat. This highlights a critical feature of the Jeffersonian plan—mathematically, it benefits larger states.

In no short order, the Jefferson plan was challenged, this time by Daniel Webster, who proposed a method whereby state seats would simply be rounded to the nearest number. As you can recall from the first table, this sounds much like the Hamilton plan, where states would be allocated extra seats in the order of their remainders. However, if you recall from that example, State A had a remainder above .5 but did not receive an extra seat. This would mean that simply rounding to the nearest whole number would result in an incorrect number of seats. The Webster plan solves this by altering the divisor to a number which results in the appropriate number of states with remainders above .5. This trial-and-error process is similar to the Jefferson plan, but instead of seeking an appropriate divisor to yield the correct number of seats when rounding down, the Webster plan seeks an appropriate divisor to yield the correct number of seats when rounding to the nearest whole number. Looking at Table 4.3, we can see that changing the divisor to 495 changes the remainders so that only four states receive extra seats. This yields the correct number of seats in the legislature. The Hamilton plan is presented for comparison:

TABLE 4.3 WEBSTER AND HAMILTON PLANS

Legislature Size - 105
Population Total - 51748
Population Per Seat – 492.84
Experimental Divisor - 495

State	Population	Webster Plan			Hamilton Plan				
		State Pop / Pop per seat, Rounded To Nearest	State pop / Experimental Divisor	State Pop / Experimental Divisor, Rounded To Nearest	State pop / Pop per Seat	Rounded Down	Remainder	Extra Seat Allocation	Hamilton Total
A	7644	16.0	15.4	15	15.51	15	0.51		15
B	10465	21.0	21.1	21	21.23	21	0.23		21
C	14236	29.0	28.8	29	28.89	28	0.89	1	29
D	7008	14.0	14.2	14	14.22	14	0.22		14
E	4330	9.0	8.7	9	8.79	8	0.79	1	9
F	2355	5.0	4.8	5	4.78	4	0.78	1	5
G	5710	12.0	11.5	12	11.59	11	0.59	1	12
Total	51748	106 (1 too many)		105		101		4 Extra	105

The Hamilton plan would eventually be favored in Congress and remain in effect throughout the rest of the nineteenth century, and into the early twentieth century, although it was not without its flaws. Sometimes, a change in the size of the House or the addition of a new state might change the various remainders that are calculated. In some instances, these remainders slipped below .5, meaning a state might lose a seat due to recalculation. However, chamber sizes could also be changed to make sure that states did not lose seats. Similarly, a legislature size could be chosen that would ensure that the Hamilton and Webster plans were in agreement. This would limit consternation and debate over apportionment methods.

Today, Congress uses a procedure called the Method of Equal Proportions, or the Huntington-Hill method. This method is similar to the previous methods but creates a new cut-point for rounding—the geometric mean. A geometric mean is simply the *n*th root of the product of *n* numbers (the cubed root of the product of three numbers, or the 5th root of the product of five numbers, and so on). In the Huntington-Hill method, we take the number of seats awarded and round both up and down. Next, we calculate the geometric mean of these two numbers. This result becomes the new cut-point for the awarding of additional seats.

TABLE 4.4   METHOD OF EQUAL PROPORTIONS

Legislature Size - 105
Population Total - 51748
Population per seat - 492.84

State	Population	State Pop / Pop Per Seat	Round Down	Round Up	Geometric Mean (new cutoff)	Extra Seats (if remainder> geometric mean)	Total Seats
A	7644	15.510	15	16	15.49	0	15
B	10465	21.234	21	22	21.49	0	21
C	14236	28.886	28	29	28.50	1	29
D	7008	14.220	14	15	14.49	0	14
E	4330	8.786	8	9	8.49	1	9
F	2355	4.778	4	5	4.47	1	5
G	5710	11.586	11	12	11.49	1	12
Total	51748						105

In this example, our calculation of seats matches the Hamilton and Webster methods. However, by examining the geometric means, we can see a pattern—geometric means decrease as the number of seats gets lower. This means the cutoff for extra seats is lower for smaller states. State F only needs a remainder of .47 to receive an extra seat, while State C needs a remainder greater than .5. This plan gives a slight advantage to small states, and in its initial use in the 1940 apportionment, Michigan (a larger state) lost a seat to Arkansas (a smaller state). This method has been used since that apportionment and has repeatedly favored smaller states. For instance, Indiana lost a seat to New Mexico in 1980, and Massachusetts lost a seat to Oklahoma in 1990. These differences highlight the importance of these rules—especially to those states that stood to gain or lose seats in apportionment.

D. DISTRICTING

Having set the number of representatives for each state, the next question becomes how those representatives shall be elected within the state. Today, seats in the House of Representatives are elected from single-member geographic districts in the state. When a state has only one representative, the district is essentially an at-large district. This system for the distribution of representatives within a state has not always been set in this way. While the apportionment of the states was dealt with by the Constitution, there was little federal oversight over districting in the early years of the Republic. Until 1842, states determined their own systems for electing representatives, with many using at-large systems initially, and converting to district schemes with time. Virginia was the first to use a single-member district system in 1800, with other states like Vermont and North Carolina following suit in 1802.[8] A number of states even proposed Constitutional amendments to mandate election by district, but none would come to fruition. By the time the Congress established election by district[9] in 1842, 22 of the 31 states used a district system.[10] Congress would go on to later mandate that districts ought to have an equal number of inhabitants,[11] and be a contiguous and compact territory.[12] Although Congress had now mandated this new scheme for the states, it was unclear whether or not it had the Constitutional authority to do so, and whether or not any state ever felt compelled to comply, with one scholar having noted "except in so far as the laws . . . may have had a moral influence, their effect has been nil."[13] Indeed, in 1929, when the Permanent Apportionment Act was passed (the previously mentioned act which set the size of the House at 435 seats), none of these previously adopted standards were included.[14] This means that with only a few exceptions, states have wide latitude in determining not only who can draw district lines, but the criteria they take into consideration when crafting districts. To get a better understanding of the districting process we can look at who has the authority to draw districts, and how they draw them.

1. State Procedures

Across the country, different individuals are tasked with districting. State laws determine what body will have the authority to craft legislative districts, and sometimes this authority is different for Congressional districts and state legislative districts.

TABLE 4.5 DISTRICTING RESPONSIBILITY
FOR STATE LEGISLATIVE DISTRICTS[15]

State Legislatures

With Gubernatorial Veto

Alabama		Massachusetts		New York	AC	Virginia
Delaware		Maine	AC	Oklahoma	BC	Vermont
Georgia		Michigan		Oregon		Wisconsin
Iowa	AC	Minnesota		Rhode Island	AC	West Virginia
Illinois	BC	North Dakota		South Carolina		Wyoming
Indiana		Nebraska		South Dakota		
Kansas		New Hampshire		Tennessee		
Kentucky		New Mexico		Texas	BC	
Louisiana		Nevada		Utah		

No Gubernatorial Veto

Connecticut	BC
Florida	
Maryland	
Mississippi	BC
North Carolina	

Political Commissions

Arkansas

Colorado

Hawaii

Missouri

New Jersey

Ohio

Pennsylvania

Independent Commissions

Alaska

Arizona

California

Idaho

Montana

Washington

TABLE 4.6   DISTRICTING RESPONSIBILITY
FOR CONGRESSIONAL DISTRICTS[16]

State Legislatures

With Gubernatorial Veto

Alabama		Massachusetts		New York	AC	Virginia
Delaware		Maine	AC	Oklahoma	BC	Vermont
Georgia		Michigan		Oregon		Wisconsin
Iowa	AC	Minnesota		Rhode Island	AC	West Virginia
Illinois	BC	North Dakota		South Carolina		Wyoming
Indiana		Nebraska		South Dakota		
Kansas		New Hampshire		Tennessee		
Kentucky		New Mexico		Texas	BC	
Louisiana		Nevada		Utah		

No Gubernatorial Veto

Connecticut	BC
North Carolina	

Political Commissions

Hawaii

New Jersey

Independent Commissions

Arizona

California

Idaho

Washington

Arizona

California

At-Large (One Representative)

Alaska

Delaware

Montana

North Dakota

South Dakota

Vermont

Wyoming

In a vast majority of the states, state legislatures are tasked with the process for drawing district lines—not only for Congress, but also for their own state legislative districts. In many cases, the state legislature acts alone, but in a few cases, the legislature is assisted by an advisory commission (designated as AC in the following tables) which will create districts and then submit them for legislative approval. Often, districts are drawn and passed in the same way simple legislation is passed. This means districts must garner a majority vote in each chamber of the state legislature, as well as receiving the approval of the state's governor. In a few states, governors are precluded from having the ability to veto districting plans, but this setup is rare. In some cases, states provide for the use of a backup commission (BC) that will create districts if the legislature is unable to agree on a districting plan.

Other states have taken the power to craft districts out of the hands of the legislatures and put it in the hands of special redistricting commissions. These commissions all have varying membership and different procedures for how members are selected, but they can be categorized based on their political independence. In some states, the members of the redistricting commission are political or partisan leaders in the state. These states have been designated as having political commissions in the tables below. A number of other states have attempted to limit political considerations from the process by disallowing elected officials, lobbyists, and other party officials from participation in drawing district lines. These states, rather than forming political commissions, have independent commissions to draw district maps.

2. Districting Considerations

Now that we know a little about who handles redistricting in the states, we should spend some time looking at what considerations go into crafting district boundaries. Although it has not always been a consideration in district boundaries, population equality (a topic that will be discussed at length in the next section on gerrymandering), is one of the baseline criteria for redistricting. After the court ruled that redistricting claims were justiciable in *Baker v. Carr*,[17] they tackled the question of district size. In *Wesberry v. Sanders*,[18] the court mandated that congressional districts ought to be as nearly equal in population as possible. A less restrictive standard was later applied to state legislative districts in *Reynolds v. Sims*.[19]

Besides the size of a district, a number of other criteria exist that are either contained in state constitution or statute, or are at least informally considered. One of the most prominent of these is contiguity, which means that all points in a district are contained within a single boundary. You would never need to leave the district to travel to another point within the district. Surprisingly, perhaps, there is no Constitutional mandate, nor any federal law that mandates that districts be contiguous, although many states have their own rules which require contiguity in state legislative or Congressional districts.[20] One of the few exceptions to the vast majority of districts which are drawn contiguously are island districts, or districts where separation occurs due to water. While there is a physical separation of land, these districts are generally thought of as still being contiguous. The New York 12th district is an example of this.

FIGURE 4.1 MAP OF NEW YORK 12TH DISTRICT (SOURCE: OPENSTREETMAP)

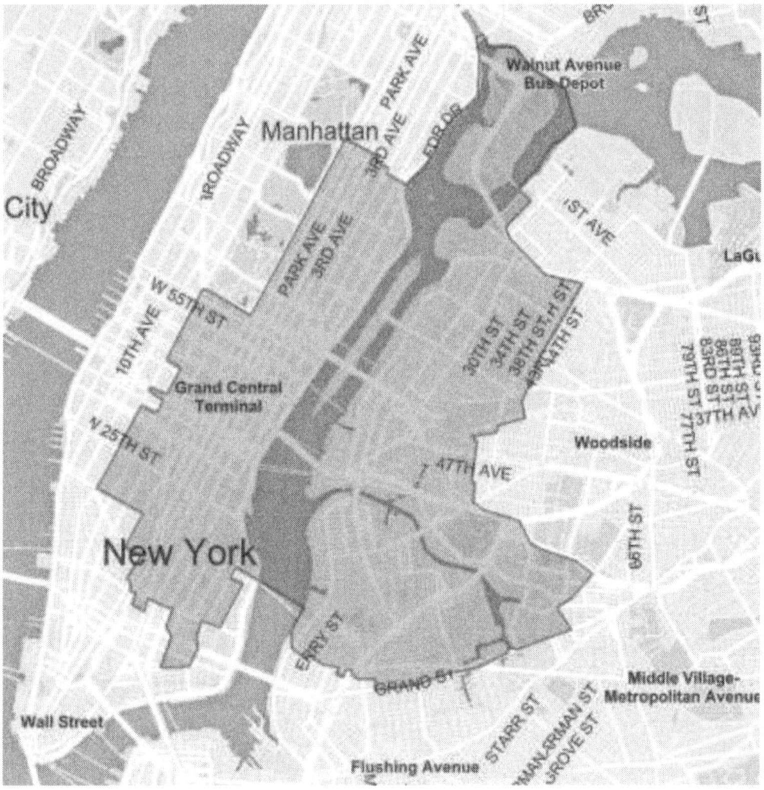

Another important criterion for districting is that districts be compact. Again, there are no federal requirements that Congressional districts meet a certain definition of compact, but many states operationalize some definition of compactness for their district. Thinking generally, the most compact potential district would be a circle. Researchers have attempted to mathematically quantify compactness in a number of ways, like the Polsby-Popper ratio,[21] a ratio of the area of the district to a circle with the same perimeter as the district. This method is used by Arizona's redistricting commission,[22] however, these formulas have not seen common use in districting procedures. Indeed, a number of states have districts, like the Maryland 3rd district, which cannot by any stretch of the imagination be seen as compact.

FIGURE 4.2 MAP OF MARYLAND 3RD DISTRICT (SOURCE: OPENSTREETMAP)

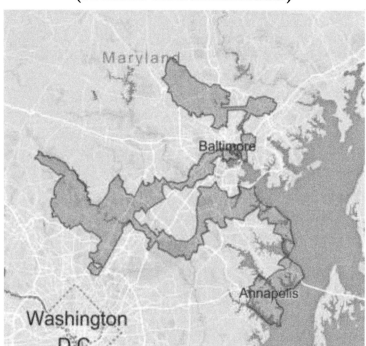

In addition to compactness and contiguity, redistricting authorities may take a number of other criteria into consideration, such as the preservation of certain political boundaries like cities, or counties. There may also be the desire to preserve demographic boundaries, or communities of interest, as they are commonly called. In some locations, district lines have been drawn to enhance or diminish the relative political power of certain groups. When lines are drawn for the benefit of a particular group, the practice is called gerrymandering. Let's look more at how this practice has affected districting.

E. GERRYMANDERING

Gerrymandering, or the drawing of district lines for political advantage, has taken many forms and has been regulated to various degrees over the course of

American history. From the earliest districts, which often bore little resemblance to each other in terms of size, to today's districts of very nearly equal population, various groups have attempted to draw district lines, to gain a political advantage. In some cases, as previously mentioned, these groups attempted to gain an advantage by not drawing districts at all. Examining this trend, we can see three distinct eras of gerrymandering and regulation—one based on population equality, a second on racial gerrymandering, and a third centered on political gerrymanders. In the first case, we see examples of over-representation in sparsely populated areas and under-representation in urban population centers. In the second case, gerrymandering techniques have been used to dilute the vote of minority groups, in particular, black voters in the south. Finally, the third case looks at how political control of the districting process has led to systematic advantages for political parties.

Gerrymandering often involves the use of one of two tactics in order to craft districts with desired characteristics. The first of these techniques is called cracking. Cracking is the process of taking a group of voters with a shared characteristic and drawing districts in such a way as to split up their voting power. By drawing a district through the middle of such a group (whether a racial minority or voters of a particular party) their combined voting strength is then split into two districts, diluting their influence. Packing, on the other hand, is a gerrymandering technique that takes this same group of voters and places them into one district, or into the fewest number of districts as possible. Since a candidate need only garner a plurality of votes in a district, packing a district with voters contributes to wasted votes, meaning more votes than are necessary to elect a candidate. If a group had the numerical strength to contest multiple races (if they were spread across districts), packing could reduce competition by concentrating that group's vote into the fewest number of districts possible.

The broad takeaway of gerrymandering is that these techniques operate to distort election outcomes in favor of a certain group. If efficiently gerrymandered, a majority group can capture more seats than they would otherwise win given their relative strength. If, for example, a majority had 60 percent of the votes in an election, we might expect them to win roughly 60 percent of the seats in the legislature. A gerrymandered map might allow this majority to transform their 60 percent vote into 70 or even 80 percent of the seats. This skews the proportion of representation in the legislative body, and in some cases, runs afoul of the Constitution.

1. One Person One Vote

The earliest examples of gerrymandering tended to deal with districts of unequal population, and efforts to combat this revolved around the premise of 'one person, one vote.' Early efforts to equalize the size of districts, however, were not very successful. In Illinois, the failure to redraw Congressional districts for over 40 years had led to widespread malapportionment. Rather than districts of equal (or even roughly equal) size, the Congressional districts in the state ranged in size from 112,000 to 900,000 people.[23] Individuals from three districts had filed suit that their Constitutional rights had been violated. Voters in districts with fewer voters had much more voting power than their neighbors in larger districts. The Supreme Court, however, decided that this malapportionment was a nonjusticiable political question that was better remedied by the state legislature.[24]

Malapportionment was not limited to Illinois, as many states failed to redistrict and allowed growing urbanization to distort the size of state legislative and Congressional districts.[25] One interesting case of malapportionment arose through a unique system in Georgia. Each of Georgia's 159 counties was placed into one of three different classifications—urban, town, or rural. This classification dictated apportionment to the state legislature, with the largest eight counties receiving three representatives, the middle 30 counties receiving two representatives, and the smallest 121 counties each received one representative. In addition, this classification governed statewide primary elections, creating a system that resembled the Electoral College. Based on this classification, the counties received six, four, or two votes, respectively, and these votes would be awarded in a winner-take-all fashion for statewide primaries. Both of these situations greatly advantaged rural counties, which would be able to wield significantly more power than urban counties.

In the 1960s, the Supreme Court had another chance at tackling malapportionment, when a case arose out of Tennessee. Under similar circumstances as the Illinois example in *Colegrove*, Tennessee had failed to redraw their state legislative districts, causing widespread malapportionment. In *Baker v. Carr*,[26] the court reversed its decision in *Colegrove*, creating a new test for political questions, and creating an avenue for Fourteenth Amendment Equal Protection claims when districts violated the principle of one person, one vote. Georgia's county system would be similarly challenged the next year in *Gray v. Sanders*,[27] Congressional districts would be required to be of equal size in *Wesberry v. Sanders*,[28] and *Reynolds v. Sims*[29] would mandate that state senate districts also be of roughly equal size.

All of this litigation, however, left open the question of *how* equal these districts needed to be. Two standards are now used to determine if population equality has been met. One standard is used for state legislative districts, and one for Congressional districts. *Wesberry v. Sanders* set the Congressional bar high, requiring districts to be "as nearly [equal] as practicable."[30] What does this standard of equality mean in practice? In the congressional case, the court has been hesitant to suggest that any population deviation would be small enough to be trivial in the eyes of the law. One particular case arose out of New Jersey, where proposed districts had a population variation of less than one percent. The majority opinion by Justice William Brennan said that "there are no *de minimis*[31] population variations . . . which meet the standard of Article I, Section 2."[32] This decision essentially laid out a standard of absolute equality in the population size of districts within a state. It is important to note that these deviations apply to within-state deviations. Given the mathematics of apportionment that was explained in the previous section, each state will have its own ideal or equal district size. These need not be the same across states, just within states.

For state legislatures, the courts have been much more lenient in their standards for district equality. While there are a number of cases that came before the courts with regard to population equality in legislative districts, the case that explicitly laid out the current standard was one arising out of Wyoming, which ruled that "Our decisions have established, as a general matter, that an apportionment plan with a maximum population deviation under 10% falls within this category of minor deviations."[33] Under this standard, the maximum deviation is calculated as the difference between the deviations of the largest and smallest districts. To calculate this, an ideal district size must first be calculated. This is simply the total population divided by the number of districts. Deviations from this ideal are then calculated by dividing the actual district size by the ideal size. The maximum deviation is the difference between the largest and smallest districts' deviations. If the largest district in a state was four percent larger than the ideal size, and the smallest was five percent smaller than the ideal size, then the maximum deviation would be nine percent and would pass constitutional muster under this standard.

2. Racial Gerrymandering

Gerrymandering in order to dilute the influence of racial minorities, or negative racial gerrymandering, has been a feature of the American political landscape since Reconstruction. Early gerrymanders in the south were combined efforts to disenfranchise radical Republicans as well as black voters and were very successful in their effects.[34] One of the most egregious cases of this negative racial gerrymandering came out of Tuskegee, Alabama. In order to effectively disenfranchise the black majority in the city, the state legislature altered the boundaries of the city, taking it from a simple square to a 28-sided figure that nearly completely moved all black voters outside the city limits. The change was challenged by Charles Gomillion, a professor from the Tuskegee Institute, which is a historically black college in the city.

FIGURE 4.3 MAP OF TUSKEGEE, ALABAMA GERRYMANDERING (SOURCE: 364 U.S. 339 (1960))

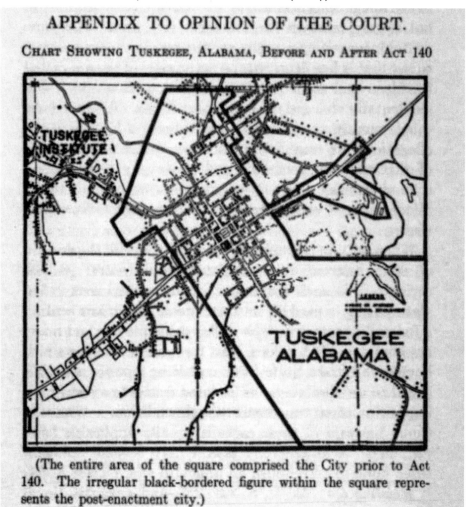

(The entire area of the square comprised the City prior to Act 140. The irregular black-bordered figure within the square represents the post-enactment city.)

In *Gomillion v. Lightfoot*,[35] the court found that the alteration of the city's boundaries constituted an infringement on the citizens Fifteenth Amendment protections. This ruling, however, would be limited in a later case, *Mobile v. Bolden,* where the courts decided that discriminatory results were not enough to claim racial discrimination in voting, and that discriminatory intent would be necessary to establish this claim.

In addition to gerrymandering, some states have resorted to methods including the creation of at-large districts and even the elimination of election for some offices. It was, however, the creation of at-large districts that provided an avenue to combat the dilution of the black vote. In a case arising out of Mississippi, the creation of new at-large districts became a battleground for the application of the preclearance requirement of the Voting Rights Act. In order to disenfranchise black voters, an at-large system elects multiple candidates from a larger geography than an individual district. The hope in this change is that, while a minority group may comprise a majority of the voters in a district, white voters would comprise a majority of the voters in an expanded at-large district. Thus, the majority could easily elect an entire slate of officials rather than have to surrender seats to a majority-minority voting district. Mississippi had enacted an at-large system for the election of their county supervisors. Arguing that this change did not affect the right to vote, Mississippi did not seek preclearance. The Supreme Court disagreed with Mississippi's argument, casting a wide net for the types of changes that would require preclearance in the future.[36]

As mentioned in an earlier chapter, one of the most important cases to arise out of racial gerrymandering claims was *Thornburg v. Gingles,*[37] which was a Section 2 VRA vote dilution challenge of multi-member state legislative districts in North Carolina. The key takeaway from this case, as previously mentioned was the three-prong test for vote dilution. Plaintiffs must provide evidence of the compactness and cohesiveness of a minority voting group, as well as evidence of racial bloc voting in order to bring a claim of vote dilution. To prevent claims of vote dilution and to maintain compliance with the VRA, some states began to create majority-minority districts. One problem with *Thornburg* was that its conditions were not well expanded in the decision. A particular problem with regard to this new positive racial gerrymandering was the idea of compactness, and specifically, how geographically compact a minority group needed to be. Indeed, in cases *Shaw v. Reno*[38] and *Miller v. Johnson,*[39] the court overturned (as unconstitutional racial gerrymanders) majority-minority districts that had been drawn at the request of the Department of Justice in its enforcement of the VRA. These districts had been so bizarrely drawn that the court said that race had to be the only motivating factor in their design. This highlights the tension between enforcement of Section 2 VRA claims and current case law on racial gerrymandering. The courts allowed North

Carolina to resolve this tension when, in 2001, the court failed to overturn a bizarrely drawn district on the grounds that it could have been drawn for political purposes (to capture Democratic voters) just as likely as it may have been drawn on racial grounds.[40]

3.   Political Gerrymandering

Rather than draw district lines to dilute or enhance the influence of racial minorities, maps can also be drawn to dilute or enhance the influence of certain parties. Using the same techniques of cracking and packing, districts can be drawn for a number of different partisan ends. As mentioned earlier, state procedures for redistricting often place the power to draw district lines in the hands of the state legislature. If one party dominates the legislature, this may give that party the opportunity to draw politically advantageous districts. If done correctly, partisan gerrymandering can magnify the power of one party by allowing them to capture more seats with fewer votes. Winning more seats, however, is not the only consideration that partisans might make when setting districts. In addition to wanting to capture a large number of seats, partisans should also be expected to want to protect the seats they already control. This might contribute to a gerrymander in which districts are drawn to protect sitting incumbents (if not incumbent legislators, at least the incumbent party). Assuming a finite number of party voters, this can lead to a tension between the desire for more districts (meaning spreading party voters out over a larger number of districts) versus safer districts (meaning concentrating party voters over a smaller number of districts).

Unlike gerrymanders, which have violated the principles of equal protection, or racial gerrymanders, the courts have been less inclined to engage in cases of partisan gerrymandering. In 1986, the Supreme Court heard a case arising out of an Indiana redistricting plan.[41] The Democratic Party contended that the Republican redistricting plan had unconstitutionally diluted the votes of Democrats in the state. While the court ruled that the political gerrymander was justiciable, they could not agree on a standard to adjudicate the claims of the Indiana Democrats. Thus, while the case opened the judicial door to political gerrymanders, the courts did not have a standard by which to evaluate redistricting plans.

More recently, a 2004 challenge was made to the districts drawn by Republicans in the Pennsylvania state legislature. *Vieth v. Jubelirer*[42] came before the Supreme Court after a group of Democratic voters challenged the Congressional maps of the state. The court was again split in their decision in *Vieth,* with two groups taking opposite sides on the question of the justiciability of partisan gerrymanders. Justice Kennedy provided the swing vote to nonjusticiable plurality opinion in a concurring opinion. His concurring opinion, however, argued that he might be persuaded in the future if "a standard might emerge."

During the 2010 redistricting cycle, Wisconsin created a redistricting plan which demonstrated high levels of partisan gerrymandering. In the 2012 elections, Republicans received 48.6% of the statewide vote but were able to capture 60.6% of the seats in the Wisconsin State Assembly. In 2014, the Republicans did even better. Having taken Kennedy's desire to see a standard emerge for measuring partisan gerrymanders, political scientists developed a number of metrics in order to measure to capture this concept. One of these measures is called the efficiency gap. When looking at the votes in any given election, some votes are 'wasted,' meaning they were either more votes than what the winner needed to claim victory (more than half of the votes) or they were cast for a losing candidate, and thus did not work towards electing any candidate. In a single member district system contested between two candidates, 50 percent of the votes are always 'wasted' according to this definition. As such, this figure by itself is not very enlightening. However, what is pertinent to the concept of political gerrymandering, is a comparison between how many votes each party wastes over a number of different districts. If each party were to waste a similar number of votes, then the difference, or gap, would be zero. However, if one party is able to waste fewer votes than the other party, this is evidence of an advantage for the party that has wasted fewer votes. Thinking back to our concepts of packing and cracking, a packed district would mean that a party wastes many votes because they have more votes than needed to obtain a majority. Similarly, if a party is cracked so that they fall just short of a majority, they waste a large number of votes in their loss. For the advantaged party, they should not waste votes in districts where they win, and in districts they lose (districts that are packed full of the other party's supporters), they waste few votes on their losing candidate because they make up a small portion of the population of the district. Thus, efficiency gap is the difference between the wasted votes of the two parties. If one party wastes fewer votes, they are advantaged by the districting plan. The authors of one study suggested that a party wasting more than 7 percent of its vote should be considered vastly disadvantaged.[43]

The efficiency gap measures for the 2012, 2014, and 2016 elections in Wisconsin made it clear that the Republicans were seeing a large advantage due to gerrymandering. A group of Democratic voters brought their case to the Supreme Court (*Gill v. Whitford*[44]) with the hopes that the new metrics would sway a majority of the justices. However, rather than decide on the merits of the new evidence presented, the court unanimously remanded the case on the grounds that the plaintiffs lacked standing. While the decision leaves open the possibility that the plaintiffs can find a way to assert their standing, it is unclear what will happen next.

While some of the cases presented here offer clear evidence that parties can manipulate the districting process to their electoral advantage, there is some recent evidence that gerrymandering may not be the only cause of more polarized districts. Two recent studies have found evidence that voters may be sorting themselves geographically, creating what seem to be more polarized districts, even if the districts were not politically gerrymandered. Evidence for this has come from the finding that counties (whose borders do not change, unlike districts) have become more polarized.[45] This trend has also been seen between redistricting cycles within districts.[46] This seems to suggest that we may be moving ourselves to be next to others with whom we agree, politically. This might mean that partisan gerrymandering may not be as much to blame as our own desire to 'flock together.

F. THESE RULES MATTER

One problem with all of this discussion of districting and gerrymandering is that it is exceedingly difficult to meet *every* criterion. Indeed, many positive criteria can be in conflict, making it difficult to combine population equality with compactness, for example. Likewise, creating compact and contiguous districts might make us run afoul of minority voting rights, potentially diluting minority strength due simply to patterns of settlement. This complex constellation of variables confounds political science in our efforts to discover how these rules matter.

One of the most important questions that political science might ask, and an important one for understanding why rules matter, is how does the creation of majority-minority districts affect the quality of representation for minority groups? While scholarship has been clear about increases in the quality of descriptive representation for minorities (this is to say, that elected legislators share the racial or ethnic characteristics of their constituents), it is less clear what these districts have done or substantive representation, or the representation of the policy interests of a group. Research has suggested that, indeed, the makeup of a constituency is positively correlated with the votes of legislators on civil rights issues.[47] However, there may be a potential unintended consequence of this enhanced substantive representation. If minority voters are drawn into majority-minority districts from surrounding districts, those surrounding districts become 'whiter' or 'bleached.' One study suggested that in these surrounding districts, there was evidence that representatives had paid less substantive attention to issues of race, complicating this issue further.[48] Other scholars have argued that minority interests are thus better served through smaller minority populations being able to exert pressure over a larger number of districts, rather than making up larger proportions of a smaller number of districts.[49]

Looking at partisan gerrymanders, evidence has repeatedly shown the power of parties to increase their seat share through partisan gerrymandering.[50] Some studies have gone further to suggest that this gerrymandering is also to fault for increasing political polarization,[51] however evidence for this conclusion is mixed.[52]

Another facet of political science revolves around apportionment, districting, and gerrymandering, has come in efforts to try to quantify different characteristics of districts, or to come up with unique or novel ways to redistrict. As mentioned in the chapter, this research has often found its way to the courts, with measures of compactness being used as evidence of gerrymandering. Additionally, recent attempts to quantify partisan gerrymandering have been at the core of attempts to combat overly gerrymandered maps in Maryland, Pennsylvania, and Wisconsin. Further, while research on the topic has not yielded conclusive findings, researchers have been attempting to study the way in which redistricting rules and processes yield different outcomes. One recent study find evidence that state legislatures draw less competitive districts than commissions.[53] Other studies have confirmed this, showing that taking redistricting power out of the hands of legislatures may increase competition.[54] This suggests that we might be well served to remember to not only examine rules but the actors that play a role in the process.[55]

G. CHAPTER 4 DISCUSSION QUESTIONS

1. The Supreme Court has, up to now, been somewhat unwilling to engage with cases of political gerrymandering. Some might say that, 'to the victor go the spoils,' but others would say that this constitutes an abuse of power. Do majority parties have an obligation to be 'fair' to minority parties? Is there a threshold at which the majority might have so thoroughly compromised the election system that it fails to be properly democratic?

2. The districting procedure in many states is led by state legislators. This essentially means that these legislators get to 'pick their constituents.' Do you think that individuals who stand to benefit from advantageously drawn districts ought to have a say in those districts? Why or why not? Does a commission solve

this problem? How would that commission need to be assembled in order to insulate it from political considerations?

3.   While partisan gerrymanders are commonly thought of as reducing the power of minority parties in favor of the majority party, the majority party must have enough voters to 'spread around' to other districts to be competitive. This means that their margin of victory will necessarily be reduced across all districts. If a redistricting plan were to not stretch the seat margin as far, this would leave more voters to create safer seats. As a legislator, do you think you would prefer more seats in a legislature, or safer seats? Is the creation of safe districts as nefarious as the idea of taking more seats in a legislature? Consider what would happen in a wave election to the redistricting plan that spread voters thinner in order to capture more seats. What would happen if those seats had larger margins?

4.   One of the cases discussed in this chapter linked racial gerrymanders with partisan gerrymanders by noting that the two are indistinguishable if the racial minority votes as a partisan bloc. Does this decision strengthen the ability to create majority-minority districts and allow minorities to elect candidates of choice? Or does it provide potential cover for racial gerrymanders against minorities to be hidden as constitutional partisan gerrymanders?

---

[1]   Wright, Carroll D. and William C. Hunt. 1900. *The History and Growth of the United States Census.* Washington: Government Printing Office.

[2]   Wills, Garry. 2003. *"Negro President": Jefferson and the Slave Power* Boston: Houghton Mifflin. Finkelman, Paul. 2013. "How The Proslavery Constitution Led To The Civil War." *Rutgers Law Journal.* 43(3): 405.

[3]   Anderson, Margo J. 1989. *The American Census: A Social History.* Yale: New Haven.

[4]   Anderson, Margo J. 1989. *The American Census: A Social History.* Yale: New Haven.

[5]   Bonfield, Arthur Earl. 1960. "Right to Vote and Judicial Enforcement of Section Two of the Fourteenth Amendment." *Cornell Law Review.* 46(1): 108–137.

[6]   Cohn, D'Vera. 2011. "Imputation: Adding People to the Census." Pew Research. Utah Challenged this imputation method in *Utah v. Evans*, 536 U.S. 452 (2002) but the court upheld the technique.

[7]   *Franklin v. Massachusetts*, 505 U.S. 788 (1992).

[8]   Ames, Herman Vandenburg. 1897. "Proposed Amendments to the Constitution of the United States during the First Century of its History." *Annual Report of the American Historical Association.* Vol. 2.

[9]   5 Stat. 491.

[10]   Schmeckebier, Laurence F. 1941. *Congressional Apportionment.* Washington: Brookings. Reprint 1976 Westport CT: Greenwood.

[11]   17 Stat. 492.

[12]   26 Stat. 736.

[13]   Schmeckebier, Laurence F. 1941. *Congressional Apportionment.* Brookings: Washington D.C. Reprint 1976 Greenwood: Westport CT. p. 135.

[14]   46 Stat. 21.

[15]   Levitt, Justin. 2010. *A Citizen's Guide to Redistricting.* New York: Brennan Center for Justice.

[16]   Levitt, Justin. 2010. *A Citizen's Guide to Redistricting.* New York: Brennan Center for Justice.

[17]   369 U.S. 186 (1962).

[18] 376 U.S. 1 (1964).

[19] 377 U.S. 533 (1964).

[20] Levitt, Justin. 2010. *A Citizen's Guide to Redistricting*. New York: Brennan Center for Justice.

[21] See Polsby, Daniel D. and Popper, Robert D., "The Third Criterion: Compactness as a Procedural Safeguard Against Partisan Gerrymandering," Yale Law & Policy Review, 9 301–353 (1991).

[22] Levitt, Justin. 2011. "Redistricting and the West: The Legal Context," in R*eapportionment and Redistricting in the West* ed. Gary F. Moncrief. Lanham: Lexington.

[23] *Colegrove v. Green*, 328 U.S. 549 (1946) at 569.

[24] *Colegrove v. Green*, 328 U.S. 549 (1946) at 556.

[25] See the Appendix of Smith, Douglas J. 2014. *On Democracy's Doorstep: The Inside Story of How the Supreme Court Brought One Person, One Vote to the United States*. New York: Hill and Wang. for a complete listing of the size of districts across the country in 1960, before the courts began to tackle the problem.

[26] *Baker v. Carr*, 369 U.S. 186 (1962).

[27] 372 U.S. 368 (1963).

[28] 376 U.S. 1 (1964).

[29] 377 U.S. 533 (1964).

[30] 376 U.S. 1 (1964) at 8.

[31] De minimis is a term which denotes something small enough to be trivial. This means that no population variation would meet the standard of Article I, Section 2.

[32] *Karcher v. Daggett*, 462 U.S. 725 (1983) at 734.

[33] *Brown v. Thomson*, 462 U.S. 835 (1983), at 842.

[34] Kousser, J. Morgan. 1991. "The Voting Rights Act and the Two Reconstructions." in *Toward a usable past: liberty under state constitutions*. Athens: University of Georgia Press. pp. 213–270.

[35] 364 U.S. 339 (1960).

[36] *Allen v. State Bd. of Elections*, 393 U.S. 544 (1969).

[37] 478 U.S. 30 (1986).

[38] 509 U.S. 630 (1993).

[39] 515 U.S. 900 (1995).

[40] *Easley v. Cromartie*, 532 U.S. 234 (2001).

[41] *Davis v. Bandemer*, 478 U.S. 109 (1986).

[42] 541 U.S. 267 (2004).

[43] Stephanopoulos, Nicholas and Eric McGhee. 2014. "Partisan Gerrymandering and the Efficiency Gap". *University of Chicago Law Review*. 82: 831–900.

[44] *Gill v. Whitford*, 138 S.Ct. 1916 (2018).

[45] Bishop, Bill. 2009. *The Big Sort: Why the Clustering of Like-Minded America is Tearing Us Apart*. Boston: Mariner Books.

[46] McCarty, Nolan, Keith Poole, and Howard Rosenthal. 2009. "Does Gerrymandering Cause Polarization?" *American Journal of Political Science* 53 (3): 666–80.

[47] Cameron Charles, David Epstein, and Sharyn O'Halloran. 1996. "Do majority-minority districts maximize substantive black representation in Congress?" *American Political Science Review*. 90(4): 794–812.

[48] Overby, L. Marvin, and Kenneth M. Cosgrove. 1996. "Unintended Consequences? Racial Redistricting and the Representation of Minority Interests," *The Journal of Politics*. 58:2. 540–550.

[49] Lublin David. 1999. Racial redistricting and African-American representation: a critique of "Do Majority-Minority Districts Maximize Substantive Black Representation in Congress?" *American Political Science Review*. 93(1): 183–92.

[50] In the 1980s: Abramowitz, Alan. "1983. Partisan redistricting and the 1982 congressional elections." *Journal of Politics*. 45(3): 767–70. In the 2000s: Hirsch, Sam. 2003. "The United States House of Unrepresentatives: what went wrong in the latest round of congressional redistricting". *Election Law Journal*. 2(2): 179–216.

[51] Fiorina, Morris, Samuel Abrams, and Jeremy Pope. 2005. *Culture War? The Myth of a Polarized America.* New York: Pearson Longman.

[52] McCarty Nolan, Keith Poole, and Howard Rosenthal. 2009. "Does Gerrymandering Cause Polarization?" *American Journal of Political Science.* 53: 666–80.

[53] Grainger Corbett A. 2010. "Redistricting and Polarization: Who Draws the Lines in California?" *Journal of Law & Economics.* 53: 545–67.

[54] Carson Jamie, and Michael Crespin. 2004. "The effect of state redistricting methods on electoral competition in United States House of Representatives races." *State Politics and Policy Quarterly.* 4(4): 455–69 Carson Jamie, and Michael Crespin. 2014. "Reevaluating the Effects of Redistricting on Electoral Competition, 1972–1912." *State Politics and Policy Quarterly.* 14(2): 165–177.

[55] Winburn, Jonathan. 2008. *The Realities of Redistricting: Following the Rules and Limiting Gerrymandering in State Legislative Redistricting.* Lanham: Lexington Books.

CHAPTER 5

Parties and Nominating Contests

A. PARTY NOMINATION

In the most basic of terms, we can conceptualize candidate nomination as the process by which parties select candidates to run for public office. In the past, these procedures have been different for various levels of office, and for different geographic areas. Today, nomination rules fall into two categories, those for the nomination of presidential candidates, and procedures for all sub-presidential offices (although sometimes state procedures vary for candidates seeking Congressional seats and state offices). While presidential nomination still centers on the quadrennial party conventions, the processes and procedures leading up to that meeting have changed dramatically. Similarly, direct nomination for sub-presidential office has changed dramatically, bearing little resemblance to the smoke-filled back rooms of convention nomination. These changes and reforms have been slow to develop, and parties and states still routinely tinker with their nominating processes. In order to examine these processes, we must look to their source—political parties.

The development of primaries is inextricably linked to the history of parties. Nomination for office has taken many forms since the founding, and we must consider the history of parties in order to understand how these nominating contests began to see government regulation. This relationship between nomination and parties exists because the regulation of nomination *requires* the regulation of parties. Parties, especially in their early forms, were private organizations. As such, their choice of a nominee for office was largely seen as an internal affair. Thus, regulating nominations was almost impossible without the regulation of parties. It would take a breakdown of early nomination systems and the subsequent increase in regulation of parties before modern primaries would emerge.

B. EARLY NOMINATING PROCEDURES

The earliest nominating procedures in America were not the affairs of mass-participation that we see today. As mentioned earlier, it is important to delineate between presidential nominating procedures—dominated by national parties and institutions, and sub-presidential nominations, which were often state or local affairs. While Dallinger[1] gives one of the best renditions of nominations in the late eighteenth and early nineteenth centuries, for the purposes of this inquiry it is easiest to merely take note of general trends. In the cases of both presidential and sub-presidential nomination, early systems rarely provided systematic rules and were often affairs of self-nomination or nomination by small caucuses.[2] It would not be until after the Era of Good Feelings that we would see a more modern national convention system emerge for presidential nomination, and not until the twentieth century before the direct primary would be used for sub-presidential nominations.

A large part of the flavor of nomination contests comes from the state of political parties in the early nineteenth century. Being largely unorganized and unregulated, parties lacked the structure and authority to dictate formal methods for candidate nomination. As many early political commentators noted, sub-presidential nomination was rarely a product of the democratic will.[3] Local, district, and state caucuses would regularly handle the bulk of sub-presidential nominating responsibilities, whereas the party caucuses in the state legislatures would often nominate for statewide offices, or even for the U.S. Senate (as state legislatures had the responsibility of electing Senators before the Seventeenth Amendment in 1913).[4] Local caucuses, or meetings of self-professed party members, would often be raucous events which were rife with corruption.[5] Leon Epstein,[6] a scholar of political parties, notes that little could be done to stop these abuses. The earliest parties in America were loose private associations that saw no government regulation. Thus, there was no government authority to regulate their internal nominating procedures. Early nomination saw no government oversight and suffered from a vast array of problems. V.O. Key perhaps summarized this problem the best, by stating "it was no more illegal to commit fraud in the party caucus or primary than it would be to do so in the election of officers of a drinking club."[7]

Presidential nominating procedures were less informal than sub-presidential caucuses. Early Congressional Caucuses (See Thompson 1902) gave way to a mixture of procedures, including state legislative caucuses and state party conventions. However, after the elections of 1828, the national party convention began to supplant other methods.[8] Early party conventions themselves differ little from the conventions of today, however, demands for reform and popular participation would dramatically change delegate selection procedures and fundamentally alter the nature of modern presidential nomination.

C. SUB-PRESIDENTIAL NOMINATION

Modern sub-presidential nominations can best be described as direct primaries. This terminology is used to contrast early methods (and modern presidential nominating methods) that used indirect selection through conventions and delegates. As mentioned in the previous section, this system arose out of the need to regulate early nominating caucuses, and to stem rampant corruption. The shift to direct primaries, which began as early as the 1860s, would not gain full steam until the early twentieth century.

1.   Adopting the Direct Primary

There are two broad narratives of the adoption of the direct primary. One narrative stems from an early line of scholarship by Charles Merriam and later joined by Louise Overacker. These scholars assert that the progressive impulse and the desire for reform pushed parties into a position where they had to reform their nominating systems. This led to government control over party primaries and the adoption of direct primary laws across the country.[9] Recent work by Alan Ware has challenged this assertion on the grounds that reformers were in no position to demand reform of the parties. Ware argues that parties in power of state legislatures had their own reasons for adopting the direct primary, specifically, reasserting control through legal means.[10] Regardless of the source of the impulse, it is clear from both narratives that control was a driving factor in the adoption of the primaries.

Between the turn of the century and 1915, nearly every state would adopt a direct primary law.[11] While these laws took different forms in the states, at their core they called for primary elections to be held for public offices and afforded these races with legal protections against electoral misconduct. In the beginning, some of these primary laws only covered cities and larger municipalities. The logic of this being that regulation was less necessary in rural areas where voters were most likely to know each other.[12] With time these laws would begin to supersede party bylaws and bring government power to an area which had been previously unregulated. In this sense, sub-presidential nominations gained a new legitimacy and parties became increasingly regulated entities.[13]

2.   Party Enrollment

One key feature of the direct primary reforms were regulations on participation. Many direct primary laws had features that limited participation in primaries to members of the parties. This is an interesting feature because parties in the United States lack many of the formal membership procedures that exist in parties in other nations. Thus, early primaries relied on public declarations of party membership and necessitated diligent poll workers to handle challenges to the membership of potential voters.[14] While these procedures may have been effective in geographies with limited populations, they may not have been as useful in larger towns and cities.

In order to affect any restrictions on participation in primaries, a state must have some procedure for maintaining records of party membership. As mentioned earlier, all states, with the exception of North Dakota, have a procedure for voter registration. According to one recent count, 31 states have some procedure allowing for party registration. Alabama, Georgia, Hawaii, Illinois, Indiana, Michigan, Minnesota, Mississippi, Missouri, Montana, North Dakota, Ohio, South Carolina, Tennessee, Texas, Vermont, Virginia, Washington, and Wisconsin did not have any procedures for capturing party preference.[15] While not all of the states that record party preference actually use it to restrict access to primary elections, it is a necessary administrative hurdle before enacting any sort of restrictive primary system.

Today's primaries exhibit a wide array of procedures for handling participation in primaries. Political scientists and observers commonly group primary laws into two categories—open and closed. In open primary states, voters can generally vote in the primaries of either party without regard for their party membership. In some states, this is because there is no record of party affiliation. However, in some states like Arkansas, the state can capture party affiliation on registration forms but still operate an open primary. In all cases, voters are limited to choosing only one of these primaries. On the other end of this spectrum are closed primaries, in which only party members may participate. This simplified spectrum hides much of the variation in states, and completely neglects new primary forms that have emerged in recent years. To examine these systems more broadly, we can classify primaries as purely open, semi-open, semi-closed, purely closed, or nonpartisan.

On one end of the spectrum, we find purely-open primaries. In these states, voters may vote in either primary of their choosing, and they make this choice privately. This is to say, they are not required to make a public declaration, and no record of their choice is made. In Wisconsin, primary ballots contain all candidates for both parties, and while voters may only vote for candidates of one party, no declaration must be made to obtain the correct party ballot.[16]

In other states, voters are still given an open choice of party ballots, but they must either make some kind of public declaration, or some record is made of their choice. In Illinois, voters must ask poll workers for the ballot of one of the parties. While the specific law states that poll workers must announce this party choice in a "distinct tone of voice, sufficiently loud to be heard by all persons in the polling place"[17] this does not seem to always be the case in practice. This rule likely stems from the aforementioned 'closed primary' systems wherein challenges could be made to the party identification of voters. In a different case, South Carolina allows voters to vote in either party primary, but presidential primaries are held on different days, meaning that a record exists of an individual's choice of ballot (while this bifurcation does not apply in sub-presidential primaries, it is worth noting that this kind of distinction is possible).

Semi-Closed primaries are the first classification of primaries that require some kind of party registration (or party enrollment). In this class of states, voters register as a member of a party when they register to vote. Voters are then only allowed to vote in the primary of their registered party. This class receives a distinction of semi-closed because of a special type of party registration— unaffiliated or independent. In these states, voters who are registered as unaffiliated or independent may vote in either of the two-party primaries without having to become registered partisans.

On the opposite end of the spectrum from purely-open primaries, we have purely-closed primaries. These function in the same way as semi-closed primaries in that the states conduct some sort of party enrollment and limit voting to registered partisans. However, purely-closed primaries do not allow participation of unaffiliated or independent voters. While these voters may be allowed to change their registration and vote in the party primary, they may not carry their unaffiliated status throughout the voting process.

At this point, we may want to try to classify primaries into these various categories, but this task is not as easy as it may seem. A number of additional rules govern party enrollment, and thus change the character of these primary contests. For example, states can set more or less restrictive deadlines for changing party affiliation. In New York, voters must make any changes to their party affiliation months in advance of the primaries, whereas New Hampshire allows *independent* voters to change their party identification on Election Day (and further, it allows them to immediately disaffiliate with a party as they exit the polling place). Iowa's election code states that it runs a closed primary, however, all voters can alter their party identification at the polling place on Election Day. This begs the question—does Iowa really have a closed primary? By the letter of the law, Iowa does restrict its primaries to registered partisans. However, their lax registration requirements mean that this restriction is essentially toothless.

In a small handful of states, primaries defy classification under this scheme. Alaska, California, and Washington have all used a system called a blanket primary at some point in the past, which allowed voters to vote in the primary elections of either party, and even switch between parties when voting for different offices. Recalling our earlier discussion on open primaries, states may allow voters to choose between either ballot, but require voters to vote in only one of the party primaries. The blanket primary allowed voters to vote in the Republican primary for one office, and a Democratic primary for a separate office (although voters could not vote in both party primaries for a single office). These systems are no longer in effect because the Supreme Court ruled that they violated parties' freedom of association rights under the First Amendment. This case, *California Democratic Party v. Jones,*[18] led to administrative changes to rules in these states to avoid Constitutional issues. Alaska reverted to a traditional primary, whereas California and Washington decided to drop party labels from their ballots and combine all candidates into a single non-partisan primary. In this non-partisan system, all candidates for an office appear on a single ballot, candidates are allowed to list their party preference, and the top two candidates proceed to the general election. At first glance, this may seem to be another unconstitutional abridgment of a party's freedom of association, however, a key distinction comes in the fact that the top two candidates, even two from the same party, move on to the general election. Thus, as the Supreme Court ruled in *Washington State Grange v. Washington State Republican Party,*[19] the primary no longer selects *party* nominees and therefore is not in conflict with a party's associational rights.

Louisiana has a similar system to California and Washington, but conducts their 'primary' on the general election day, and does not necessarily require a second round of voting. Under Louisiana's rules, all candidates appear on the same ballot, in a fashion similar to California and Washington, but rather than sending the top two finishers to a general election, Louisiana can immediately elect any finisher who garners a majority of the vote. If no candidate reaches the majority threshold, a runoff election is held one month later.

3.   The Legal Status of Minor Parties

Many of the primary laws discussed in this chapter apply to both of our major parties—the Democratic Party and the Republican Party. However, there are many third parties that also nominate candidates. States regulate the status of these third parties by granting them official party status. In order to gain this status, states generally require some signals of viability, however, laws differ across the states as to what constitutes this signal. Some states allow third parties to be granted official status by submitting petitions signed by a certain percentage of the electorate. In other states, third parties must run their candidates as independents (gaining ballot access through petition as mentioned in Chapter 3), gaining official party status when one of their petition-nominated candidates receives a certain vote threshold in a general election. Recently, North Carolina began to recognize parties that were able to place a presidential candidate on the ballot of at least 35 others states.

Once these third parties demonstrate their viability, they become parties with regulated nomination procedures, just like the two major parties. However, in most states, third parties are not treated the same as the two major parties. Many states have two separate categories of recognized political parties. Major political parties are generally those which hold the support of a large group of citizens in the state. Nevada, which registers voters by party, requires a party to have at least 10 percent of those party registrations in order to be classified as a major party.[20]

In almost every state, as previously mentioned, state law requires the major parties to nominate their candidates for office by a primary election. In some states, minor parties are allowed to select nominees for office through alternative methods. Minnesota, for example, requires minor party candidates to continue to petition for ballot access. Indiana allows minor parties to nominate via convention, and Florida gives these minor parties to nominate in any fashion they see fit.[21]

D. PRESIDENTIAL NOMINATION

Presidential nominating procedures[22] are complex, multi-stage procedures, unlike the relatively simple direct nominations for sub-presidential offices. Today's presidential nominating system is a complicated marriage of caucuses, primaries, party officials, and national conventions.

1. The Process

While caucuses and primaries are the most visible aspect of presidential nominations, it is important to keep in mind that these contests are actually just one step in the nomination process. Rather than being a direct primary in the sense of sub-presidential nominations, presidential primaries and caucuses are indirect nomination methods. The formal mechanism for the selection of presidential nominees is still the quadrennial party convention. As alluded to earlier, recent changes to this process have taken some of the power out of the hands of the parties and placed it in the hands of elected delegates to the conventions. The votes of these delegates are those that actually nominate our presidential candidates. This indirect method has many interesting features to explore, including the allocation of delegate pools to the states, the subsequent allocation of delegate slots to candidates, and the often-unrelated process of filling delegate slots with actual delegates. In a sense, part of this process is similar to the apportionment process that was discussed earlier—we must determine a way to distribute a number of convention delegates across the states. Once this process is completed, we must determine how many delegates will be awarded to each candidate by holding caucuses and primaries in each state. Finally, we must select an actual person to attend the convention and fill these delegate slots. The rules that govern this process are different in every state, between the parties, and sometimes even within states. While it would be nearly impossible to discuss every permutation of rules, this section will briefly discuss the more common ways in which presidential nomination is carried out.

2. Allocating Delegates

At the start of the nomination process, delegates must be allocated to the states by the parties. Each party does this separately, and there is generally no relationship between the number of delegates assigned by each party. In a generic sense, population size and party loyalty are the two factors that both parties use to determine how many delegates each state will receive—however, similarities between the parties end here.

For Democrats, we must do some math to figure out how many delegates to award to a state. To take some measure of population into account, the Democratic Party calculates the average number of electoral votes that a state has over the last three elections (averaging takes into account reapportionment changes) and divides this by 538 to determine the state's proportion of electoral votes. A measure of party loyalty is taken by adding together the state's popular vote for the Democratic presidential candidate over the previous three elections and dividing that by the total Democratic popular vote over the last three elections to determine a state's contribution to the overall Democratic popular vote. These two resulting proportions are averaged, and a state receives a number of delegates equal to this proportion of the total delegate pool. In the most recent 2016 elections, Democrats had a pool of 3,200 total delegates.

States also receive 10 percent of this base delegate calculation as "pledged party leader or elected official" or pledged PLEO delegates. These are party leaders in the state, but they are distinct from superdelegates (discussed later) because there is a fixed number allotted to each state, and they are pledged to support the winner of the primary or caucus, rather than being free to vote as they choose.

On top of this baseline number of delegates, the Democratic Party awards bonus delegates to states that delay their primaries and cluster with neighboring states. These bonuses arise out of a desire to limit frontloading, or the movement of primaries to earlier dates on the calendar. These bonuses are calculated based off of the original baseline number of delegates, and not the total which includes pledged PLEO delegates.

To show an example of Democratic delegate math, we can take Maryland as an example. Maryland has had 10 electoral votes for the previous three elections, so their average electoral vote total is 10. Dividing this by 538 gives us a proportion of .0186. According to official state returns, Maryland cast 1,334,493 ballots for the Democratic presidential candidate in 2004, 1,629,467 in 2008, and 1,677,844 in 2012 (MD State Board of Elections). This yields a total Democratic vote of 4,641,804 votes. According to FEC election returns, the total Democratic vote across these three years was 194,442,758 votes (2004—59,028,444; 2008—69,498,516; 2012—65,915,795; FEC Federal Elections Series 2004–2012). Dividing these two numbers gives us a proportion of 0.0239. We can now average these two proportions, .0186 and .0239 to get the base proportion of delegates for Maryland, 0.02125. With 3,200 total delegates, Maryland should receive 68 delegates. On top of this, Maryland receives bonus delegates by virtue of holding their primary in a later state, and by clustering their primaries with Delaware and Pennsylvania. They receive a 10 percent bonus for timing, and a 15 percent bonus for clustering, adding 17 additional delegates to their total. They will also receive their 15 percent pledged PLEO allocation (based off the original calculation of 68 delegates) adding 15 delegates for a total of 95 pledged delegates. Again, this total does not take into account superdelegates, which will be discussed in another section.

The Republican Party takes a different (and simpler) stance towards delegate allocation. In order to take state population into account, all states are awarded a baseline number of delegates that is equal to five delegates per Senator, three delegates per Representative, and three spots for party leaders. Thus, all states receive a baseline of 10 delegates, plus three per Representative, and another three for party officials. In order to take party affection into account, bonus delegates are awarded in states that elect Republicans. Each state is awarded a number of additional delegates if they voted for the Republican presidential candidate in the previous election year. In addition, states receive bonus delegates for each Republican Senator, for having a Republican majority in their U.S. House delegation, for having a Republican Governor, and for having Republican majorities in either or both of their state legislative chambers. Thus, a state can receive up to six additional delegates, plus a percentage of delegates based on their previous electoral vote.

To give an example of this Republican math, let's take a look at South Carolina. In 2016, South Carolina had two Senate seats and seven House seats. This gives the state 10 delegates for their Senate seats, 21 for their House seats, and again, three for party officials. From this baseline of 34, we must look at the actual composition of the State's elected officials. In 2016, South Carolina had a Republican Governor (Nikki Haley), two Republican Senators (Lindsey Graham and Tim Scott), a Republican majority in their House delegation, and Republican majorities in both chambers of the state legislature. This awards the state an additional six delegates. In addition to this, South Carolina awarded their 10 Electoral Votes for Mitt Romney in 2012. Thus, South Carolina is allocated 34 delegates, plus six for elected officials, and another 10 for their voting history, for a total of 50 Republican delegates.

For two states with relatively similar populations, an observer might wonder why these delegate totals are so different—it is important to keep in mind that absolute delegate totals are only meaningful when taken in the context of the total number of delegate slots. For recent history, the Democratic Party has had a much larger pool of delegates, making all Republican allocations look much smaller than Democratic allocations.

Now that we understand the basic math behind the allocation of delegates to the states, we should take a look at what happens on Election Day.

3. Primaries and Caucuses

Once delegates are allocated, states and parties must use some mechanism to determine the preference of the people. Today, all states use some form of a primary or caucus to gauge the sentiment of the people. As mentioned previously, these contests are not a direct nomination of candidates, but a metric used for the awarding of delegates in a later step of the nomination process. Primaries and caucuses share a purpose, but differ widely in the way they are conducted—and sometimes in the results they produce.

Primaries are the easier of the two systems to understand. Just as with subpresidential direct primaries, an election is held wherein voters cast ballots at polling places that are open throughout Election Day. As previously mentioned, some states and parties have rules on party affiliation and participation in these primaries, and generally, turnout is much lower than in general elections.

Caucuses, however, are much more complicated affairs, and specific procedures can vary between parties and across states. Because of this variation, we will only consider two generic processes. Common to these two processes is the idea that a caucus is a meeting of voters within a voting precinct. These caucuses commonly take place in school classrooms, cafeterias, gyms, and churches, at designated times on Election Day.

In Iowa, the Republican caucuses begin with speeches from representatives of the candidates. After taking the time to consider what they have heard, the caucus attendees cast ballots and votes are tallied. In this sense, the Republican caucuses look much like primary elections, but with considerably less participation. Rather than having the day to vote at one's leisure, caucus-goers must make a point to attend the (often) evening meetings.

On the Democratic side of things, the Iowa caucuses are very different affairs. Attendees are asked to physically group together with other supporters of candidates, and counts are taken of the size of the respective groups. Depending on the size of these groups, a candidate without much support may be forced to bow out of the race, and that candidate's supporters have the opportunity to realign themselves with a different candidate. During this time, supporters of the remaining candidates might take the time to engage with, debate, and attempt to win over supporters of other candidates. After a set period of time, the group again takes different sides of the room and counts are taken to determine the vote.

In the end, both primaries and caucuses result in a final vote count for each of the primary candidates. Unlike a direct primary, this tally must now be used to award a state's delegates in order to complete the presidential nominating process.

4. Awarding Delegates

Perhaps the most important feature of presidential nominating procedures is the awarding of delegates to candidates. As mentioned in the previous section, each state receives a pool of delegates from each party, based on population and party strength. After a caucus or primary, these delegates must then be awarded to the candidates for nomination. The math behind this process varies across states, parties, and can be even be dictated by the timing of the primary or caucus. In all cases, these delegates are either awarded in a winner-take-all style or distributed proportionately, depending on rules.

For a good deal of the post-reform nominating era, the two parties have taken very different approaches to the awarding of delegates. The Republican Party has largely taken a hands-off approach, letting state parties set rules, whereas the Democratic Party has taken a heavier hand in prescribing methods to award delegates to primary and caucus winners. For Democrats, this heavier hand has meant a history of proportional allocation of delegates to candidates, rather than the more frequent winner-take-all affairs in the Republican Party. This is not to say that these are the only two ways to allocate delegates, and in many cases, states have developed very creative and unique ways to award their delegates to the winners of the primaries and caucuses.

In order to understand how states award delegates, we must first revisit the allocation of delegates to the states. In the previous section, we understood how parties calculated a total number of delegates that a state would be allocated. This simple understanding hides an important distinction underlying these delegates—they are not all bundled together.

On the Democratic side of things, the delegates awarded to the states are separated into three distinct groups—district delegates, at-large delegates, and pledged PLEO delegates. Thankfully, we can split up our calculated total delegates into these three groups fairly easily. The Democratic plan calls for 25 percent of the baseline delegates to be allocated as at-large delegates, and the remaining fraction to be allocated as district delegates. Recalling our calculation from the previous section, pledged PLEO delegates make up the additional 15 percent that is calculated after we arrived at our base delegate calculation. The Democratic Party requires one additional step, allocating district delegates to the individual districts. Unlike the Republican process, the Democratic Party allocates district delegates through a formula that takes into account party loyalty. States may select one of four different formulas that break down the total number of district delegates to the individual districts in a manner similar to the way the total number of delegates are awarded to the states. Often, states choose to apportion these delegates based on the Congressional district's recent vote totals in presidential and gubernatorial races. In practice, this means that rather than have an equal number of district delegates, more delegates are awarded to districts that tend to vote more Democratic.

The Republican Party makes a similar distinction between at-large, and district delegates. The 10 base delegates awarded by virtue of Senate seats, the three party delegates, and all bonus delegates are categorized as at-large delegates. Conversely, all delegates awarded by virtue of House representation are considered district delegates and are awarded to the individual Congressional districts evenly. This district-delegate math is much simpler than the procedures for the Democratic Party, and do not take party loyalty into account.

Understanding these delegate distinctions allows us to understand the nuance of procedures to award delegates to contest winners. As mentioned earlier, delegates are generally awarded in one of two ways, a winner-take-all style, or a proportional style. As mentioned previously, the Democratic Party mandates a proportional method of awarding delegates. While there is some variation between states (Montana, for instance, splits the state into two geographic districts rather than use its single at-large district (Montana Democratic Party. 2015. Montana Delegate Selection Plan for the 2016 Democratic National Convention.), the general method is that candidates receive a proportion of at-large delegates based on the percentage of the vote they receive in the state's caucus or primary. Vote totals are calculated in each district, as well as statewide in order to calculate these proportions. This math is relatively straightforward in primary states, but can be confusing in caucus states. Again, some states may have multi-level caucuses, but the will of those caucus attendees are translated into some proportional awarding of both the individual district-level delegates, and the at-large and PLEO delegates. In tabulating these proportions, the Democratic Party utilizes minimum threshold levels (15 percent) that a candidate must reach in order to qualify for delegates. If candidates do not reach this threshold, they are not awarded any delegates, regardless of their vote count.

The Republican Party sees much more variation in how delegates are awarded across the states and has generally left these details up to the states themselves. Only recently has the party pulled back some authority, requiring specific procedures for states with early primaries. The simplest method of awarding delegates is the winner-take-all method. While relatively few states (notably Florida and Ohio in 2016) use this method, it makes these states large prizes for candidates who can capture a plurality of votes in these states. In a larger group of states, a proportional system is in place, but distinct from the Democratic proportionality plan, states may opt to distribute delegates on the basis of statewide results, or a combination of statewide and district results. These states can also specify a minimum threshold, but the specific level is not mandated by the party. Finally, in the largest group of states, there is a hybrid system of delegate allocation that may mean winner-take-all district delegates and a proportional statewide allocation, the reverse, or a proportional allocation of all delegates, with a trigger to award all delegates to a candidate receiving 50% (or some higher threshold) of the vote.

The impact of these rules is that candidate strategy must reflect the specific way a state awards its delegates. Proportional states become important targets for candidates who are running behind in the race. Similarly, winner-take-all states can be lucrative prizes for those candidates who can capture a majority (or plurality, in some cases) of the vote. The distinction between the parties has faded in recent years, but one only has to consider recent elections when the majority of Republican primaries were winner-take-all. This distinction has led to party primaries with a distinct flavor over the past few election cycles. With winner-take-all primaries, one candidate could swiftly amass a majority of the convention delegates relatively early in the process (one might think back to John McCain's early primary victories in 2008). Conversely, proportional primaries allow the entire field of candidates a chance to slowly accumulate delegates. In a proportional system, we may expect races to drag on late into the primary season as second- and possibly third-place candidates remain viable into April and May. Thinking back to the longer primary seasons of 2008 and 2016, we can see how second-place candidates Hillary Clinton and Bernie Sanders were able to draw out the primary season much longer than they would have under a winner-take-all format.

Considering these implications, we can imagine that an astute party might attempt to change or alter their rules in order to craft a primary season that better reflects their desires for candidate nomination. Does a party desire a fast coronation of a favorite candidate? Is there a large field that needs to be slowly winnowed? While we can only infer intent, the recent changes to the Republican primary system may indeed reflect a desire to draw out the primary season by barring winner-take-all contests early in the year.

5.   A Note on Timing

Before continuing on to the convention, we should pause to briefly discuss the timing of presidential primaries. During an election year, primaries and caucuses are spread across the first half of the year. Starting as early as January, and sometimes continuing into June, each individual state sets a date for their presidential primary. While some states run their presidential primary or caucus concurrently with their primaries for other offices, some states set their presidential nominating for a different (usually earlier) date. As states have control over their election calendar, many have attempted to rush to the front of the line and schedule their primary early in the year. This concept of moving nominating contests to the earliest possible dates is called frontloading.

Frontloading has received a good deal of academic attention in order to uncover the reasons states might want to frontload, the degree to which the phenomenon has taken place, and what effects this rush to the front of the line has had on the process of nominating presidential candidates.[23] What seems to be settled, is the idea that early nomination contests influence the nomination process much more than later contests. We are not only able to infer this advantage (or at least the perception of an advantage) from individual state behavior, but also from more coordinated party behavior. This is, perhaps, most evident in the attempt to create an early Democratic 'Super Tuesday' primary in the south. Super Tuesday was designed to pool a number of southern states' primaries on one day, early in the primary season. The goal of this experiment was to temper the liberalism of primaries in other regions with more conservative voices in the south in an effort to give momentum to more centrist candidates.[24] In this sense, the party was hoping to alter the outcome of the primaries by having conservative states exert more influence early in the nomination process. Of course, all of this assumed that when these conservative states voted for a particular candidate, the candidate would receive a boost in momentum going into later races. Interestingly, Super Tuesday would not yield a conservative southern Democrat in 1988, and after the nomination of Bill Clinton, there would be an incumbent southern Democrat running for the White House until 2004.

The reality of frontloading is that, while individual states may benefit from moving earlier in the calendar if multiple states move toward the front of the calendar, it is difficult to say if any single state can still gain an advantage. This movement also has the potential to frustrate the parties. If a number of states are all attempting to jockey for an early position, this is likely to cause consternation for the parties. To exacerbate this, it is important to remember that states determine their own primary date. This limits the ability of parties to control the primary calendar, and when party and state preferences do not align, state preferences are likely to win out. Minority parties in state legislatures are doubly frustrated by this process due to the procedural reality that partisan majorities in state legislatures are often setting these dates.

All of this is not to say that the national parties exert no influence over the calendar, but that they must be creative with their method of control. Since the reforms of McGovern-Fraser, the Democratic Party has attempted to create a primary window. At first, this was merely trying to contain primaries within the calendar year, but more recently this has narrowed further from March until June.[25] It would not be until 1996 that either party would attempt to truly limit the primary window—by incentivizing late primaries and penalizing early ones.[26]

Examining the intersection of delegate allocation and the nomination calendar, we find that states have a pressure point that national parties can push. Control over delegate allocation is important leverage for the national parties over states. Parties have been able to use delegate penalties as a way to force states to comply with party rules in delegate allocation procedures, the procedures for awarding delegates to candidates, and even the timing of primaries. If states do not comply with party rules, parties are able to reduce the number of delegates awarded to the state, reducing their relative voting power. While some legal scholars have argued that these incentives and penalties are ineffectual,[27] both parties have tied the primary calendar to delegate allocation.

Both parties now have delegate penalties for states that move their primaries too early in the primary season (while exempting traditional early-contest states like Iowa, New Hampshire, South Carolina, and recently, Nevada). In previous election years, some states (for example, Florida in 2008) have flaunted this rule and held early primaries regardless of penalties. As mentioned earlier, the Democratic Party has added incentives to these penalties. The party recently created a system of incentives for states to hold their primaries later in the calendar year. These incentives are the bonus delegates that were mentioned in the previous section.

6. Selecting Delegates and Superdelegates

Delegate selection is often the final process before the convention. By this point, we understand how many delegates a state will receive, and often, how many delegates will be awarded to the individual candidates, but we may not know the people who will actually fill these slots. Both parties offer guidance, but delegate selection processes are generally left to the states. In most cases, delegates are selected (following procedures for proportionality) at state or local party conventions. These party meetings take place throughout the country and delegates filter up from precinct meetings, to county or district conventions, and finally to statewide party conventions. In other states, candidates may be able to select slates of candidates (although this is not a common practice) or delegates may be selected on the actual primary or caucus ballots themselves.

Before we discuss the party convention, we must examine one more important delegate type. Superdelegates are a special form of delegates that exist within the Democratic Party. As mentioned earlier, some states receive additional delegates as pledged PLEO delegates. Recall that PLEO stood for 'party leaders and elected officials.' While the delegates we discussed earlier are pledged to the winners of contests in the states, superdelegates are another group of party leaders and elected officials that are not bound to any election result. While lower level officials generally fill pledged PLEO slots, there are roughly 700 individuals that hold higher offices and are allowed to attend the convention and vote for candidates of their own choosing.

Looking at the most recent set of Democratic Party rules, superdelegates are elected official and leaders from one of five categories.

First, are the members of the Democratic National Committee—this group includes the elected chairpersons of the DNC itself, chairpersons of each state and territorial Democratic party, and leaders of various other democratic groups like the Young Democrats of America, the College Democrats, and the Federation of Democratic Women. These positions are spelled out in the Democratic Party Charter and Bylaws (Article III, Section 2). Second, are the president and vice president of the United States, if those offices are currently held by Democrats. Third, are all Democratic members of the U.S. House and Senate. Fourth, all Democratic governors are included. Fifth, and finally, a group including all former presidents, vice presidents, Congressional leaders, and former DNC chairpersons.

Superdelegates perform an important role for the Democratic Party, in that they are supposed to represent the interests of the party, rather than the people. In a sense, pledged delegates and superdelegates represent two competing interests in candidate nomination. Should regular party voters determine presidential nominees, or should this choice be left to party leadership? In the years since the McGovern-Fraser Commission, the Democratic Party has struggled with this question, regularly changing the proportion of these two groups in an effort to find a combination that leads to nationally competitive nominees. This search continues in the wake of the divisive 2016 primaries, as new reforms to reduce the impact of superdelegates have been proposed within the party.

7. The Convention

Once all of our delegate selection mechanisms are complete, it is time for the quadrennial party convention. Once the site of heated nomination fights, modern party conventions play perhaps the smallest role of any part of the actual mechanism of candidate nomination. Again, each party sets specific rules for how the convention proceedings are arranged, and while the production and spectacle of the conventions are impressive, the voting that takes place to formally nominate candidates lacks the drama and suspense of early conventions.

Unlike brokered conventions or conventions with multiple ballots, modern party convention votes have been mere formality, with no recent convention taking more than one vote before nominating a candidate. Even in 1976, when neither Republican candidate had secured a majority of the delegates before the convention, it only took one ballot to nominate incumbent president Gerald Ford.

Modern party rules specify a voice vote of the state delegations, with the chair of the convention calling out each state in alphabetical order. Each state then announces its votes. To illustrate the ceremonial nature of these votes, it is not uncommon to see arrangements take place to ensure that a particular state is able to cast the decisive vote for a nominee. At the 2008 Democratic Convention, when it came time for Illinois (the home state of Barack Obama) to cast its votes, the state passed and allowed the vote to continue. When the vote reached New Mexico, the state's delegation yielded the floor back to Illinois, which in turn yielded the floor to New York (the adopted home state of Hillary Clinton). Hillary Clinton then took the floor, asked for the rules of the convention to be suspended, and called for Obama to be nominated by acclamation, effectively providing a unanimous nomination and ending the count of the votes.[28]

While conventions may be necessary if primaries are unable to yield a majority winner, they now are simply the culmination of a long and arduous primary season, introducing the parties' nominees to the public with much pomp and circumstance.

E. THESE RULES MATTER

Nominating contest rules matter a great deal to our electoral system because of how they narrow our choices for the general election. Consider the fact that in a general election, we merely select one candidate out of a small group of perhaps two candidates. Nominating contests winnow the field from all potential nominees down to just one candidate. Today, more than ever before in our country's history, citizens are able to play a role in this process. This has dramatically changed the nature of our democracy by wresting power away from parties who traditionally had complete control over the candidates that were offered for election. Our general election choices are totally dominated by our nominating procedures, and now that citizens have a much larger role in the process, these rules matter even more. Political science has tried to unpack just how these rules matter to the kinds of candidates we end up with.

Primary elections are often looked at as a source of some of the more negative aspects of our political system. While commonly discussed as a progressive reform, designed to pull power away from party bosses,[29] the primary system seems to have introduced a new set of problems for our political system. In particular, primaries are often seen as a primary source of political polarization.[30] This argument is made because of the ideological extremity of the voters who participate in the primary process.[31] This finding has not been universally confirmed,[32] but a number of studies have found links between primary procedures and polarization.[33]

Part of the reason for confusion in these studies might be because of the various forms that primaries take across the country, although two recent studies were unable to replicate earlier studies positive findings linking the openness of primaries to legislative extremism.[34]

Thinking more normatively, we might consider the importance of democratic participation in nomination as it relates to why these rules matter. As previously mentioned, this consideration revolves around the tension between parties as private organizations and the freedom of individuals to associate (or disassociate) with either party, at will. Should individuals be able to vote in any primary of their choosing? Should they be required to affiliate with a party before doing so? Those who would seek to protect the associational rights of the party would say yes. Taking a different look at democratic participation, we might examine the role that superdelegates play in the Democratic nomination process. Are these unpledged delegates a reasonable protection of party associational rights or a dilution of the voting power of Democratic voters? Whichever may be the case, there is much still to be examined regarding our nomination procedures and practices.

F. CHAPTER 5 DISCUSSION QUESTIONS

1.   Proponents of closed party primaries argue that primaries need to be closed to prevent voters from other parties from 'raiding' their primaries. On the other hand, open primaries offer voters a wider range of choices without the need to formally associate with a party. This debate touches a number of topics including the power of parties, candidate extremism, associational rights of parties and voters, and voter choice. Think about which considerations favor which style of primary. Do different considerations lead you to feel differently about having closed primaries versus open primaries?

2.   One criticism of primaries is their relatively low voter turnout. This means that a relatively small (and often unrepresentative) group of voters are selecting the candidates for our general elections. Before the adoption of the primary, party leaders and conventions often chose candidates for office. Do you think primary electorates or party leadership is best suited to candidate nomination? What differences do you expect to emerge between the candidates of each style of nomination? Are there alternatives that you think would yield a 'better' nominee?

3.   Superdelegates have been an especially contentious topic in recent elections. As the chapter explained, they were designed to allow the parties to retain some control in presidential nominating procedures. Recent critics have accused superdelegates of being an undemocratic feature of the Democratic nominating process. Put yourself in the position of being a Democratic Party leader and defend why the party should retain partial control of the primaries in this way.

4.   Many of the debates surrounding nominating procedures boil down to the legal status of parties in American politics. On one hand, parties have historically been seen as private organizations that can operate under any rules that they see fit to establish. On the other hand, modern parties are so entrenched in our politics that they seem to have become a political institution. In many cases, the major parties are treated preferentially. Consider this tension between the party as a private association, and parties as a government institution. Where do you think we stand today, do you think there are facets of this tension that are in conflict, and what do you think is the proper place of parties in the framework of election regulation?

---

[1]   Dallinger, Frederick W. 1903. *Nominations for Elective Office in the United States.* New York: Longmans, Green, and Co.

   [2]   Dallinger, Frederick W. 1903. *Nominations for Elective Office in the United States.* New York: Longmans, Green, and Co.

   [3]   Whitridge, Frederick. 1883. *Caucus system.* New York: Society for Political Education.

   [4]   Dallinger, Frederick W. 1903. *Nominations for Elective Office in the United States.* New York: Longmans, Green, and Co.

   [5]   Lawton, George. 1885. *The American Caucus System: Its Origin, Purpose, and Utility.* New York: G.P. Putnam and Sons.

   [6]   Epstein, Leon. D. 1986. *Political Parties in the American Mold.* Madison: University of Wisconsin Press.

   [7]   Key, V.O. 1964. *Politics, Parties, and Pressure Groups.* Crowell: New York, p. 375.

   [8]   Dallinger, Frederick W. 1903. *Nominations for Elective Office in the United States.* New York: Longmans, Green, and Co.

   [9]   Merriam, C. Edward and Louise Overacker (1928) *Primary Elections.* Chicago, IL: University of Chicago Press. Merriam, Charles E. (1908) *Primary Elections: A Study of the History and Tendencies of Primary Election Legislation.* Chicago, IL: University of Chicago Press.

   [10]   Ware, Alan (2002) *The American Direct Primary.* New York: Cambridge University Press.

   [11]   Lawrence, Eric, Todd Donovan, and Shaun Bowler. 2011. "The adoption of direct primaries in the United States." *Party Politics* 19(1): 3–18.

   [12]   Dallinger, Frederick W. 1903. *Nominations for Elective Office in the United States.* New York: Longmans, Green, and Co.

   [13]   Epstein, Leon. D. 1986. *Political Parties in the American Mold.* Madison: University of Wisconsin Press.

   [14]   Epstein, Leon. D. 1986. *Political Parties in the American Mold.* Madison: University of Wisconsin Press.

   [15]   https://www.huffingtonpost.com/2014/05/27/state-party-registration_n_5399977.html. Some of these states record party primary voting history, but they do not record this prior to the primary.

   [16]   Wisconsin Laws Ch. 5 § 62.

   [17]   10 ILCS 5/7–44.

   [18]   530 U.S. 567 (2000).

   [19]   552 U.S. 442 (2008).

   [20]   NRS 293.128.

   [21]   Council of State Governments. 2017. *The Book of The States.* Table 6.3.

   [22]   All rules elaborated in this section come from the author's interpretation of the internal rules of the parties. Democratic Party. 2014. "Delegate Selection Rules" https://demrulz.org/wp-content/files/12.15.14_2016_Delegate_Selection_Documents_Mailing_-_Rules_Call_Regs_Model_Plan_Checklist_12.15.14.pdf Republican Party. 2016 "Rules" https://prod-cdn-static.gop.com/docs/2016-Republican-Rules-FINAL.pdf.

   [23]   Busch and Mayer 2004 is one of the seminal studies of the phenomenon. Mayer, William, and Andrew Busch. 2004. *The Front-Loading Problem in Presidential Nominations.* Washington, D.C.: Brookings Institution Press.

   [24]   Norrander, Barbara. *1992. Super Tuesday: Regional Politics and Presidential Primaries.* Lexington: University Press of Kentucky.

   [25]   Mayer, William, and Andrew Busch. 2004. *The Front-Loading Problem in Presidential Nominations.* Washington, D.C.: Brookings Institution Press.

   [26]   Sanderson, Matthew T. 2009. "Two Birds, One Stone: Reversing 'Frontloading' by Fixing the Presidential Public Funding System." *The Journal of Law & Politics* 25, 279.

   [27]   Sanderson, Matthew T. 2009. "Two Birds, One Stone: Reversing 'Frontloading' by Fixing the Presidential Public Funding System." *The Journal of Law & Politics* 25, 279.

   [28]   Balz, Dan, and Anne E. Kornblut. "Democrats Nominate Obama." *Washington Post. August 28, 2008.*

   [29]   Ranney, Austin. 1975. *Curing the Mischiefs of Faction: Party Reform in America.* Jefferson Memorial Lectures. Berkeley: University of California Press.

   [30]   Fiorina, Morris P., Samuel J. Abrams, and Jeremy C. Pope. 2005. *Culture War? The Myth of a Polarized America.* New York: Pearson Longman.

   [31]   Aldrich, John H. 1983. "A Downsian Spatial Model with Party Activism." *American Political Science Review* 77(December): 974–90. Owen, Guillerrom, and Bernard Grofman. 2006. "Two-Stage Electoral

Competition in Two-Party Contests: Persistent Divergence of Party Positions." *Social Choice and Welfare* 26: 547–69.

[32] Geer, John G. 1988. "Assessing the Representativeness of Electorates in Presidential Primaries." *American Journal of Political Science* 32(4): 929–45. Norrander, Barbara. 1989. "Ideological Representativeness of Presidential Primary Voters." *American Journal of Political Science* 33(3): 570–87.

[33] Gerber, Elizabeth R., and Rebecca B. Morton. 1998. "Primary Election Systems and Representation." *Journal of Law, Economics, and Organization* 14(2): 304–24. Kanthak, Kristin, and Rebecca Morton. 2001. "The Effects of Electoral Rules on Congressional Primaries." In *Congressional Primaries and the Politics of Representation*, ed. Peter F. Galderisi, Marni Ezra, and Michael Lyons. Lanham, MD: Rowman and Littlefield.

[34] McGhee, Eric, Seth Masket, Boris Shor, Steven Rogers, and Nolan McCarty. 2013. "A Primary Cause of Partisanship? Nomination Systems and Legislator Ideology." *American Journal of Political Science.* 58:2 337–351. Rogowski, Jon C., and Stephanie Langella. 2015. "Primary Systems and Candidate Ideology: Evidence from Federal and State Legislative Elections." *American Politics Research* 43(5): 846–871.

CHAPTER 6

The Electoral College

A. INTRODUCTION

The Electoral College, the system used for the election of the President of the United States, is one of the most visible sets of election laws in our country. While some of its basic operating principles are simple and easy to understand, some of the underlying mechanisms are cloaked in confusion. Moreover, debates on the utility of the Electoral College often draw from ambiguous sources of authority, in particular, the intent of the Founders. The workability of the Electoral College seems to be a subject of debate during each election, and especially in election years when the system produces unexpected results. This was the case in recent elections like 2000 and 2016, when the Electoral College produced results that were in conflict with the results of the popular vote of the people. Examining the rationale, the evolution of rules and procedures, and the current state of the Electoral College, we can learn more about this unique plan for electing our presidents.

At its most basic, the Electoral College process follows three, and in some cases, four steps. First, on Election Day, the voters in the states vote for president and vice president of the United States. These votes, however, do not directly elect the president and vice president. Each candidate has slates, or lists, of individuals who will be elected as electors for the state, should they receive the most votes in a state. After the election, state authorities must resolve any election disputes and certify the results of the election. Second, on a date set by federal law, the electors will meet in their respective states to cast their official votes for president and vice president. Those votes are then sent to Congress to be counted. Third, Congress convenes on January 6th to open and count the results of the votes in each state. If one candidate receives a majority, they are elected to their respective office. In the case of a tie, or if one candidate does not receive a majority of the electoral votes, the election is sent a fourth step—election by the Congress.

All of these steps are laid out in their simplest form here, however, there is a long history in the fashioning of these steps, and in their revision over the years. To dive deeper into the inner workings of the Electoral College, let's look at how the original system was put into place, and how it evolved over time.

B. DEVELOPMENT

The development of the Electoral College can be thought of as a number of interrelated procedures that have been developed, often in response to political events that disturbed the operation of the system. From its initial development at the Constitutional Convention, a patchwork of procedures has been articulated to amend the process. Almost immediately after ratifying the Constitution, the elections of 1796 and 1800 laid bare important shortcomings in the original system. Throughout the nineteenth century, the college had to adapt to changing ideals of democratic participation, as well as the potential downfalls of such participation—electoral fraud. The 1876 election would be, perhaps, the toughest test of the system, and in the wake of its failures, clearer procedures for dealing with special circumstances would be adopted.

1. Crafting the College

At the Constitutional Convention, one of the most contentious debates was that of representation in the newly created Congress. The compromise plan that was adopted called for Senate representation to be equal across the new states, and House representation to be apportioned based on population. This same compromise would find its way into the method to be devised for electing the president. Considering various alternatives, the presidential system of elections could have ended up being a more democratic affair, with a system based on direct election by the people. Numerous sources cite potential problems with such a system. In one sense, it was thought to be too susceptible to the passions of a mass electorate.[1] It was also seen as politically untenable due to the issue of slavery. If popular election were to be adopted as a method of electing the president, the south would be stripped of much of its political clout, as much of its population was denied the right to vote at this point in time.[2] On the far end of the spectrum, the other possibility was election by the federal legislature. Under this system, some voting mechanism would be created to allow Congress to select a president and vice president. This system, however, was an equally distasteful option because of the potential for the domination of the legislative over the executive, and a breakdown of separation of powers.[3]

The Electoral College, as outlined by the Constitution, is a relatively basic system of indirect election. In this system, a group of individuals, called electors, cast ballots to elect the president and vice president of the United States. Each state receives an allotment of electoral votes that is equal to the size of their Congressional delegation, and the individual electors are appointed by each state in accordance with their laws. Article II, Section 1 of the Constitution allocates electors to the states in a number equal to the number of Senators and Representatives elected by each state. Each state then receives two electoral votes by virtue of their Senate representation, plus a number equal to the number of representatives. Each state, then, has a minimum of three electoral votes. When reapportionment takes place, as discussed in an earlier chapter, the number of electoral votes for a state likewise changes. This section of the Constitution also gives complete control to the state legislatures to determine the manner in which these electors are appointed. With the exception of a rule prohibiting electors from holding any other political office and a grant of authority to Congress to set the date for the election, there is little guidance on how the states should designate their electors.

Originally, the Constitution set a procedure for meetings of the electors in their respective states. These electors would cast ballots for two individuals, with the winner being elected president and the second-place finisher becoming vice president. In the case that multiple individuals received a majority of votes, or no individual received a majority, the House of Representatives would choose a president through a contingent election. In this contingency, the House would have two options. They could choose between those candidates who received a majority, or they could choose among the top five candidates if there was no individual with a majority. If this procedure was necessary, the House would allot one vote per state delegation, rather than one vote per Representative. After the selection of the president through this procedure, the remaining runner-up would become vice president. If there remained a tie for second place, the Senate would select the vice president.

The Electoral College was thought to provide a number of important benefits over direct election and legislative selection. This system would still allow for democratic participation, but the system of allocating electors would solve the political problems of southern influence. It was also assumed that this system would maintain an important role for the legislative branch. The Electoral College's majority-vote requirement left open the possibility for multiple candidates to split the vote without producing a majority winner. Without party nominations, it is plausible to think that a large field of candidates might commonly split the vote in such a way. In an election with fewer candidates, given the procedure that each elector cast two votes, there was also the possibility for more than one candidate to receive a majority. As mentioned earlier, these scenarios would throw the election to Congress. Some accounts suggest that the founders believed this to be a likely scenario. If this were to be the case, the Electoral College would essentially be acting as a nominating body, winnowing the field rather than selecting a president. The House (and Senate, if necessary) would then have the final say in electing a president, giving considerable power to the legislature.[4]

What the founders did not envision, would be how the development of the nation would render moot a number of their concerns, and how the system they constructed would fail to perform in the way they intended. In a number of ways, the development of the Electoral College is less about changes to the rules of the institution itself, but more about changes to the nation as a whole. Political parties, faster communication, retail politics, and a host of other factors ended concerns of an uninformed electorate or unknown candidates. The need for electors as intermediaries is not as clear today as it might have been during the founding. In addition, almost immediately, two-party competition would cause tremendous problems for the College as originally designed. The Electoral College has had to adapt to a changing country, and while the system itself still resembles its original form, a number of changes have refined its operation.

2. Refining the System

The original plan for the Electoral College worked well with the unanimous election of George Washington in 1792 but quickly broke down in the elections of 1796 and 1800. In 1796, Federalist John Adams won a slim victory over Democratic-Republican candidate Thomas Jefferson. However, the Federalists were not united in their selection of a vice president, with Thomas Pinckney of South Carolina and six other Federalists splitting the Federalist's electoral votes (not counting George Washington, who also received two votes). This meant that Jefferson, a member of a different political party, had more votes than any of the other Federalist candidates, and would be elected vice president.

In the election of 1800, a different problem emerged when Thomas Jefferson and Aaron Burr tied in the Electoral College. Hoping to avoid a split-party administration, Democratic-Republican electors essentially voted for a party slate, not splitting their second vote as the Federalists did in 1796. While this solved one problem, it created another. Even though it was commonly understood that Jefferson was intended to be president and Burr his running mate, the election was thrown to the House of Representatives, as the two candidates had tied (a contingent election, as mentioned earlier). The House that would make the selection was the previously sitting House, rather than the newly elected one (at this point, the inauguration of the new president and the new Congress was in March, leaving these Electoral College duties to the outgoing Congress), and a majority of its members were Federalists—political opponents of Jefferson. It would take 36 ballots and untold political efforts before Jefferson would finally be elected, providing the outcome that was intended by Republicans, but exposing another weakness of the system as originally written in the Constitution.[5]

The Twelfth Amendment, ratified in 1804, and put into effect for the elections of that year, changed the nature of the Electoral College and fixed the problems that arose in 1796 and 1800. First, the Amendment specified that electors cast one ballot for president, and one for vice president, rather than two ballots for president. This solved the issues present in both previous elections by allowing electors to vote for party slates without needing to fragment their second vote to select a vice president (as Federalists did in 1796) and without the complications of a tie vote (as the Democratic-Republicans faced in 1800). In Addition to creating separate ballots for president and vice president, the Twelfth Amendment altered the process for deciding an election that ended in a tie, or without a majority winner. Under the new system, the House would select from the top three candidates (rather than five) but the same 'one-state, one-vote' style. The Senate would similarly break ties and decide races without majority winners by selecting from the top two candidates, with each Senator receiving one vote.

The elections of 1796 and 1800 would not be the last time that the Electoral College saw difficulties in its operation. A contingent election would again take place in 1824, when a crowded field of four candidates split the electoral vote, precluding any one candidate from attaining a majority. As per the previously discussed rules, the election was thrown to a contingent election in the Congress. By 1824, the Twelfth Amendment was in force, requiring Congress to choose from the top three candidates. Of the four (John Quincy Adams, Henry Clay, William H. Crawford, and Andrew Jackson, all nominally of the Democratic—Republican Party), Henry Clay received the fewest votes and was eliminated from consideration. When the House cast their votes, state by state, John Quincy Adams emerged as the winner of the contest.

3. Creating Election Day

At this point in time, there was still little guidance in the procedures that surrounded the election of electors, their voting procedures, and the certification of that vote. While the authority existed for Congress to set more specific procedures, they would not immediately do so. For example. Congress has the Constitutional authority to set the date of the election of electors (Election Day) as well as the date when electors will cast their ballot for president.[6] In 1792, when initially setting up the procedures for the Electoral College, the Congress decided to act upon the second of those powers and set the first Wednesday in December as the date on which electors would meet in their respective state capitals to cast their votes for president.[7] At the same time, rather than set an explicit date for the election of electors (Election Day), the Congress created a 34-day window within which states could set their own election date.[8] Once electors had voted in their respective states, they were required to transmit their votes to the Congress, who would count and certify the votes of the individual states. This process was also codified early on. In each state, the electors would sign and certify a copy of their names and votes and send out three copies—one by an appointed person to the President of the Senate (the Vice President), one by mail, also to the President of the Senate, and a third to the district judge in their jurisdiction.[9] The Senate would need to receive one of these copies by the first Wednesday in January. If they had not received it, then there was a process to send a messenger to the district judge to receive what could essentially be considered a backup copy of the votes. On the second Wednesday in February, the Congress would open all of these votes and count them. The winning candidate would then begin their term as President of the United States on March 4th of that same year.[10]

Up to this point, states could set the date of election of their electors at any point within the 34-day window set by Congress. This led to the states conducting their elections on different days and opening the process up to the potential for fraud. One particular fraud made possible by the varying election days was the ability to vote in the elections of multiple states. One Senator noted the fraud, stating "It was well known that. . .frauds had been practiced in elections—that men had been transferred from one part of the Union to another, in order to vote; and that system which now had received the technical name of pipe-laying had been carried into pretty general, and in some instances, into pretty extensive operation"[11] In order to prevent these frauds, Congress could mandate a single day for the election of electors. After much debate about the administrative difficulty of holding an election in a single day, Congress decided to act.

In 1845, Congress set Election Day as the first Tuesday after the first Monday in November.[12] While there are many anecdotes about why Congress felt the need to prevent Election Day from occurring on November 1st (designating the first Tuesday *after* the first Monday precludes Election Day from every falling on the

1st of November), the record of congressional debates offers a simpler story that is directly related to one of our earlier mentioned dates. If federal law had already set a 34-day window for elections, and if electors were to meet on the first Wednesday in December, it would be possible for an Election Day of November 1 to break this 34-day rule. When November 1 falls on a Tuesday, the first Wednesday in December is 37 days later. By designating the first Tuesday after the first Monday in November, Election Day is always 29 days before the meeting of the electors. This simple provision prevented Congress from having to make changes to multiple laws.[13]

4. The General Ticket

In the earliest days of the Electoral College, the states had a wide array of methods for selecting Electors. As the Constitution lacked any guidance for these state-chosen methods, a diverse array of schemes arose.

One of the most commonly used methods of selecting electors before 1824 was selection by the state legislature. In these states, the legislatures could select electors in any proportion they saw fit, as there were no rules, state or federal, that mandated a rule to select electors as a unit. In some states, electors were chosen by the people, but in districts. In some cases, like Virginia, these districts were drawn specifically for the purpose of the Electoral College, rather than using Congressional districts. States could also opt for a combination of methods, allowing voters in districts to choose a certain number of electors, and allowing the state legislature to choose the remainder.

From 1792 to 1836, the trajectory of laws would yield two predominant rules for the selection of electors—popular vote, and winner-take-all elections. The rise of the use of the popular vote is generally attributed to increasing democratic sentiment, however, the rise of winner-take-all rules is a more complex story.[14] As has been the theme with other topics, the rules surrounding the Electoral College have, at times, been subject to political machinations in order to generate certain preferred outcomes. Indeed, that has been a key point in this book—election rules influence outcomes. As an earlier political scholar noted, "the distribution of electoral votes among the several candidates for President was determined almost as much by the mode of election as by the sense of the people."[15] In the election of 1796, for instance, Thomas Jefferson lost to John Adams by three electoral votes (71 to 68). Examining state results, a keen observer would note that Jefferson lost one vote in North Carolina, Pennsylvania, and Virginia, while winning the remainder. This was possible because these states lacked a 'unit rule' (also called a winner-take-all rule, or the general ticket system) that would have required the states to cast all of their electoral votes for Jefferson. These three votes provided the necessary margin of victory for Adams, but had they voted as a unit, Jefferson may have been our second president.

As a result of the election of 1796, Virginia would adopt a winner-take-all rule in 1800 to prevent a split vote from happening again.[16] This strategy was not lost on political observers of the time. Senator Thomas Hart Benton of Missouri said "the general ticket system [referring to winner-take-all systems], now existing in ten States, was the offspring of policy, and not of any disposition to give fair play to the will of the people. It was adopted by the leading men of those States, to enable them to consolidate the vote of the State."[17] What resulted from Virginia's move, was a wave of changes across the states to adopt similar provisions in their state laws. Majority parties would successively work to guarantee that the entire delegation of Electoral Votes within a state be cast for their party. Thinking beyond how this type of system would benefit a majority party in a state, some observers noted how it might advantage large states over small states if the small states were proportionately allocating their delegates. Again, Benton notes this trend, stating "For, when the large States consolidate their votes to overwhelm the small ones, those, in their turn, must concentrate their own strength to resist them."[18] By 1832, only Maryland and South Carolina lacked a 'general ticket' system of awarding all of the state's electoral votes to the winner of the popular vote. By 1836, only South Carolina maintained selection by the state legislature. Florida would also choose by state legislature in 1868, as would Colorado in 1876, but with the exception of these few unique cases, the people would choose electors in every state.[19]

5. 1876—Dealing with Controversy

The next changes to the Electoral College would come in the wake of the Election of 1876. In this campaign, Rutherford B. Hayes, a Republican, faced Samuel Tilden, a Democrat. The election results were close, and hinged on the results of just a few states. Florida, Louisiana, Oregon, and South Carolina had all sent the Congress multiple sets of election returns. Without a procedure to settle these disputes,[20] the Congress enacted the Electoral Commission Act, which created a 15-member Commission to adjudicate instances where multiple returns were received from a state.[21] Each house of Congress would select five members from their chamber, who would be joined by five members of the Supreme Court.[22] This commission heard arguments and delivered judgments as to which of the contested returns would be accepted. If both houses of Congress would disagree, they could overturn the decision of the Commission. Due to the partisan composition of the commission, nearly every decision they made was on an 8–7 split in favor of Hayes, who was eventually named the winner of the election.

In order to avoid a recurrence of the Electoral Commission's adjudication of Electoral College results, Congress passed the Electoral Count Act of 1887[23] which laid out new and important processes. The Act provided a new responsibility for state governors, a new safe harbor deadline for states to resolve disputes, and procedures and practices for counting and potentially objecting to state returns.

First, rather than only requiring a list of votes from the electors of a state, this law requires the governor of a state to create a certificate of ascertainment that denotes which electors were rightfully chosen in the election. These certificates are combined with the actual votes cast by those electors and sent to Congress. This important addition helps Congress to determine who the rightful electors were in case they receive two sets of votes from a state.

Second, the Act set a new deadline, known as a safe harbor date. If a state makes a final determination as to the appointment of their electors by this date (six days before the meeting of the electors in the states), Congress is mandated to afford special consideration to this determination. That is to say, Congress must abide by a state's determination of any election disputes if those disputes are reconciled by this date (this does not preclude the Congress from rejecting the return on other grounds). If a state does not resolve any disputed election results by this date, then Congress has much more latitude in determining how a state's electors should be awarded. This provision protects the prerogative of a state to resolve contests with their own rules.

Third, the Act sets a new procedure for accepting or rejecting returns, and for adjudicating between multiple sets of returns. On the second Wednesday in February (this date remained unchanged) the Congress was to meet in a joint session to open and count the election returns of the states. After each one was read, objections could be brought, so long as they were laid out in writing and supported by at least one member of both chambers. Because of the aforementioned safe harbor procedure, if a state transmitted a single set of returns and met the safe harbor deadline, Congress was very limited in the grounds upon which they could reject a return. A return would need to either be not 'regularly given' or an elector not 'lawfully certified.'[24] While the specific meaning of these terms was not set out in the act, it greatly limited the ability of Congress to object to the election returns of a state if they met the deadline and submitted a single return. If a state did not meet this deadline, then Congress had wider latitude in terms of permissible objections to state returns. If such an objection were raised, both chambers of the Congress would split up and debate the matter, with both having to approve the objection (contrary to the earlier rule, which would allow either to object).[25] In practice, if a state had still only submitted a single return, it would be unlikely for the Congress to object to the results.

In cases where two sets of returns arrive from a single state, Congress must act to determine which returns to accept. If Congress received votes from two different groups of electors, Congress need only reference the aforementioned certificate of ascertainment to determine which group of electors was rightfully elected. In cases such as this, Congress must accept the returns sent from the proper electors. In the case that there is confusion about certification of votes from multiple state authorities, and there is no clarity on which group of electors is the properly elected group, the two chambers of Congress will split and vote to determine which return to accept. If the chambers are in agreement, those returns are accepted. If the chambers disagree, the Act specifies that the Congress should give precedence to the return that comes from the governor of the state.

This procedure for determining the outcome of controversies is still in place and has been put into use twice. In 1969, a faithless elector in North Carolina cast his vote for George Wallace rather than Richard Nixon, who had won the state. In 2005, objections were raised over voting irregularities in Ohio. In both cases, the objections were in proper order and the chambers split up to consider the objections. In both cases, Congress rejected the challenges.[26] In addition to these examples, a number of objections were raised during the counting of electoral votes for the 2016 election, however, none had followed the proper procedure of having the signature of both a member of the House and the Senate. They were all rejected by Vice President Biden, acting as President of the Senate.[27] The same scenario played out in 2001.[28]

The Electoral College would not see another change in procedure until 1933, when the Twentieth Amendment to the Constitution changed the starting day of terms of both the president and Congress. The president would now be inaugurated on January 20th and the Congress on January 3rd. This significantly shortened the lame duck period for both offices, and also had the effect of changing which Congress would be in charge of counting Electoral Votes. As the date of counting votes (the second Wednesday in February) was after the new inauguration day, the law had to be rewritten and set January 6th as the new day for the Congress to count electoral votes. Since this also created problems for the date that electors meet, that date was changed to the first Monday after the second Wednesday in December (by virtue of its wording, the safe harbor deadline, fixed at six days before the meeting of the electors changed as well, although the law did not need to be rewritten.)[29]

C. TODAY'S PROCESS

Today's Electoral College bears a resemblance to the procedures originally laid out in the Constitution, but the many changes that have taken place in the intervening years have given our presidential elections a unique character. This section will briefly recapitulate the changes discussed in the last chapter by examining how the Electoral College functions today and looking at each step in the process.

1. The Allocation of Electoral Votes

As noted previously, electoral votes are allocated to the states in a sum equal to the size of the state's Congressional representation—one vote per Representative, and one per Senator, with a minimum of three electoral votes per state. D.C., which does not have voting members of Congress, still receives three electoral votes. As of the 2010 reapportionment of Congress, 535 electoral votes are allocated to the states as follows:[30]

TABLE 6.1   ELECTORAL VOTES PER STATE

State	Electoral Votes	State	Electoral Votes
Alabama	9	Montana	3
Alaska	3	Nebraska	5
Arizona	11	Nevada	6
Arkansas	6	New Hampshire	4
California	55	New Jersey	14
Colorado	9	New Mexico	5
Connecticut	7	New York	29
Delaware	3	North Carolina	15
D.C.	3	North Dakota	3
Florida	29	Ohio	18
Georgia	16	Oklahoma	7
Hawaii	4	Oregon	7

Idaho	4	Pennsylvania	20
Illinois	20	Rhode Island	4
Indiana	11	South Carolina	9
Iowa	6	South Dakota	3
Kansas	6	Tennessee	11
Kentucky	8	Texas	38
Louisiana	8	Utah	6
Maine	4	Vermont	3
Maryland	10	Virginia	13
Massachusetts	11	Washington	12
Michigan	16	West Virginia	5
Minnesota	10	Wisconsin	10
Mississippi	6	Wyoming	3
Missouri	10		

As mentioned in the previous section, all states today select electors by a vote of the people, however, two systems are used to take that vote and award electoral votes to presidential candidates. In Maine and Nebraska, popular vote totals are calculated within each congressional district, as well as statewide. Two electors are awarded to the winner of the statewide vote, and one elector is awarded to the winner in each of the congressional districts. This system is most often referred to as the district system. In practice, Maine, which has utilized this system since 1972, only first split its vote in 2016 (three for Clinton, one for Trump). This 3–1 split is the only mathematical possibility for a split so long as Maine has four electoral votes. Any candidate who would receive a majority in both districts would necessarily have a majority across the state, precluding the possibility of a 2–2 split. Nebraska, which has utilized the district system since 1992, only split its vote in 2008, awarding four votes to McCain, and one to Obama. While it is unlikely at this point, if Maine were to lose a congressional seat during reapportionment (and lose a corresponding electoral vote), it would no longer be able to split its vote, as the winner of the statewide vote and the winner of the one at-large district would always be the same.

This district system is contrasted with a winner-take-all system (or the general ticket system, or unit rule, as previously discussed), which is used in the remaining 48 states, and the District of Columbia. In these states, all of a state's electoral votes are awarded to the candidate who receives the most votes. Note that within each state, only a plurality of the vote is necessary to win the electoral votes of a state. While a majority of the electoral vote is necessary to win the Electoral College, no state requires a majority to win its individual electoral votes.

Once the ballots are tallied, the individual electors are considered elected. In order to confirm the election of these specific electors, the governor in each state prepares a document called a certificate of ascertainment. This certificate lists the names of the state's electors but does not yet confirm their vote.

2. The Electors

One might ask, at this point in the discussion, who are these electors? Unfortunately, we again have little guidance from the Constitution, with the exception of the aforementioned prohibition on electors holding an "Office of Trust or Profit under the United States."[31] In nearly every state, the parties, by various methods, select their slate of electors for the presidential election. In some cases, the electors are appointed by party leadership, and in others, they are elected at state party conventions. A few states have more interesting methods, like California, for instance, where the responsibility falls to the Democratic nominees for Congress, and Republican nominees for statewide and other offices.[32] In Pennsylvania, the presidential candidates themselves nominate a slate of electors once they have been nominated by their parties.[33]

The electors themselves come from all walks of life, and some, you might even recognize. Prominent political officials such as former president Bill Clinton and New York Governor Andrew Cuomo were both electors from New York for Hillary Clinton in 2016. Bill Clinton also fits into another category of electors—family and friends. On the Republican side, Donald Trump's son, Donald Trump Jr. was an elector from New York, although he did not cast a vote for his father because Trump did not win the state. A larger group of electors are generally chosen for their work on campaigns, or with the party. While is it impossible to know all of the wide-ranging considerations that go into the selection of electors, we can safely assume that one criterion, loyalty, is likely near the top of any list of criteria.

The apocryphal notion that electors are supposed to make independent choices, weighing the character of the various candidates, no longer holds weight. In fact, 30 states and the District of Columbia have passed laws binding electors to the results of the statewide popular vote.[34] Some of these states even prescribe penalties for faithless electors. While the Supreme Court took up the matter of the constitutionality of pledges, their decision left some ambiguity. In a case arising out of Alabama in 1952, the Court determined that states were within their authority to require pledges from their electors. However, they left open the possibility that these pledges might not be enforceable. That is to say, states may require electors to pledge themselves but might not have the authority to actually enforce that pledge.[35] While a number of these states have no penalty and accept votes as they are cast by the electors, some state levy fines or other penalties, and replace the elector with an alternate if they break their pledge. For example, the state of Washington levied $1,000 fines on four faithless electors in the 2016 election.[36] The courts have not examined the constitutionality of such penalties.

3.   The Electors Vote

Once electors have been elected, they must then perform their ceremonial duty by casting their votes for president. As mentioned earlier, these votes are generally formality now, as electors are chosen, in part, for their loyalty to the party, and the candidate. On the first Monday after the second Wednesday in December, electors gather at their respective state capitals and, in an often-overlooked ceremony, cast their ballots by completing a form called a certificate of vote. The certificate of vote is different from the governor's certificate of ascertainment, which merely lists which electors have been selected. The certificate of vote is signed by each one of the electors and states which candidates for president and vice president are receiving their respective votes.

Rather than allow faithless electors to cast their ballots, some states, including Indiana,[37] Michigan,[38] Minnesota,[39] Montana,[40] Nebraska,[41] Nevada,[42] North Carolina,[43] Oklahoma,[44] and Utah,[45] have statutes that not only require electors to cast their ballots for the top vote-getter in the state but also require the immediate replacement of any elector who attempts to cast a ballot for a different candidate. In 2016, this law came into play in Minnesota, where an elector was replaced after trying to cast his ballot for Bernie Sanders. Similar scenarios played out in Maine and Colorado, with the Maine elector changing his vote to conform, and with a Colorado elector being replaced. The status of Colorado's law was less clear than the states listed here, and the elector who was replaced has brought legal action against the state.

4.   Certification

Once the states have completed their part in the process by completing the necessary certificates of ascertainment and certificates of vote, these must be transmitted to the Congress in order for the results of the election to be officially certified. As mentioned earlier, this job is now the responsibility of the newly elected Congress, which must meet in a joint session of Congress on January 6th following the election (although the date may be changed if it falls on a Sunday.[46]

The joint session for counting votes is presided over by the President of the Senate, who is the outgoing vice president. While the composition of the Congress itself consists of newly elected members, the term of the president and vice president does not expire until inauguration day—thus the outgoing vice president still serves as President of the Senate.

Proceeding in alphabetical order, the President of the Senate, as well as two members of each chamber (called tellers) read and confirm the votes of each of the states. Once the votes are read, a tabulation is made, and the results are announced. Assuming a candidate has received a majority of the electoral votes, this ends the process of the election, and the winner is officially certified. If any issues arise with the returns of a state, or if a candidate does not receive a majority, the joint session proceeds as described in the previous section on rule development, handling objections by separately retiring to their chambers, considering the objection, and voting on its merits before reconvening.

D. ELECTORAL MATH

The math behind the Electoral College distorts and introduces biases to election results in a number of ways. This is not to say that these distortions or biases are necessarily bad, indeed some of them are part of the Electoral College by design. Broadly considered, we can think of three ways in which the college transforms or distorts the popular vote. First, because of the state-by-state winner-take-all system, the electoral vote can exaggerate the magnitude of popular vote margins, or completely invert it. Second, the Electoral College can introduce systematic biases that might make the vote of an individual in one state mean more than the vote of someone in another state.

The Electoral College, and in particular the aforementioned unit rule, has the effect of distorting the relationship between popular votes and electoral votes. This is due in large part to the varying margins of victory across states, as well as the way electoral votes are distributed to the states. Consider, for instance, three states, state X, Y, and Z. State X has 500 voters and 7 electoral votes, state Y has 600 voters and 8 electoral votes, and state Z has 1200 voters and 14 electoral votes. These states received two electoral votes, plus one electoral vote per 100 voters. This mirrors the way electoral votes are distributed to the states. In order to see how varying margins of victory, as well as the addition of the two extra electoral votes, can lead to exaggerated and inverted relationships between popular and electoral votes, let's look at two election scenarios. It is worth noting that these examples do not take into account other confounding factors like variable turnout across the states.

In one election, our two candidates, candidates A and B, split the states thusly: state X votes 300–200 in favor of A; state Y votes 350–250 in favor of B; and state Z votes 625–575 in favor of A. Totaled up, candidate A received 1175 votes and 21 electoral votes, while candidate B received 1125 votes and 8 electoral votes. In this first example, the electoral votes and the popular votes both find for the same candidate, but we can see how a winner-take-all system exaggerates the margin of victory in the Electoral College. Here we can see that candidate A only received 51 percent of the popular vote, but took home 72 percent of the electoral votes.

Let's consider another election. Here, candidate A wins state A 275–225, and state B 350–250. Candidate B takes state Z 1000–200. Here, the totals look very different. Candidate A captured 825 votes and 15 electoral votes, whereas candidate B captured 1475 votes and 14 electoral votes. Candidate A wins without capturing a majority of the popular votes. The reason for this inversion is because of the relative margins of victory in the states. In states X and Y, candidate A wins by slim margins, so they are unable to gain a large advantage in the popular vote count. However, because of the winner-take-all system, candidate A wins these states' electoral votes by a margin of 100 percent, again exaggerating their electoral margin.

These examples also reveal a second way in which electoral vote totals are not reflective of popular vote totals. Notice that each hypothetical state received one electoral vote per 100 people, but then also received two bonus electoral votes. These bonus votes correspond to the two votes given to each state by virtue of their Senate representation. Because of these bonus electoral votes, the smaller states, X and Y, have collectively more power than state Z, which has a larger combined population. Under this scenario, a candidate can win the smaller states X and Y, which have a smaller total population, and win the electoral count against a candidate who carries the larger state Z. This happened in the second of our two examples. Were the states only allotted one vote per 100 voters, candidate B would have won that election 12 votes to 11, and there would not have been an inversion of the popular vote. The Senatorial component of Electoral College votes not only creates distortions in the ratio of popular votes to electoral votes, but also may have an effect on the relative power of an individual's vote.

Another line of inquiry into the biases of the Electoral College looks at how individuals in different states are differentially impacted by this system. This is to say, does the Electoral College favor the vote of citizens in one state over another? One scholar attempted to determine if any advantage existed by examining the relative power of a single voter in one of these states. For example, if one were to be fortunate enough to cast a decisive vote in a state, that vote would carry with it the small prize of three electoral votes in a small state like Wyoming. In a larger state like California, casting the decisive vote within the state would swing 55 electoral votes. Does this mean that a voter in California has more power than a voter in Wyoming? This line of research (including more recent updates to these figures) attempted to quantify the power of an individual in a given state to affect the outcome of their own state. By also incorporating a state's power to be decisive in the outcome of the national election, these researchers created a mathematical model of how powerful a vote was in a given state. This quantification is commonly called voting power. The results of these studies routinely showed that individuals in large states like California had more voting power than those in smaller states like Montana or Wyoming. Later research on voting power questioned some of the fundamental assumptions of these studies.[47] Voters in larger states were assumed to have more voting power because of a number of mathematical assumptions based on the size of a state and the relative likelihood of casting a decisive vote. On top of this, their power was magnified by the large number of electoral votes they might wield. These more recent studies determined that there was not a significant relationship between the size of a state and an individual's likelihood of casting a decisive vote.[48] Further, these studies questioned how a state like New York or California could be so important if their electoral outcomes were so predictable. Considering this, these studies identified a more important criterion than size when calculating vote power, closeness. These studies argued that the voters which have the most voting power are the states that have the closest races—battleground states.[49] Looking at how much time candidates spend in these states[50] may lend some credence to these arguments.

E. POSSIBILITIES FOR REFORM

There are a number of modern criticisms of the Electoral College that have called for reform or replacement of the system.

1. Proportional Allocation

One proposal for reforming the Electoral College would be to implement proportional allocation systems throughout the states. As mentioned earlier, Nebraska and Maine already utilize a proportional allocation method, awarding the statewide winner two electoral votes, and awarding one electoral vote for the winner in each congressional district. This method, however, is not the only possibility for a proportional electoral college. One alternative to the district system could be a completely proportional system wherein electoral votes are allocated to presidential candidates based on the proportion of the popular vote that they receive in each state. Alternatively, some combination of proportionality and winner-take-all could be utilized, wherein the statewide winner captures two at-large electors, and the remaining electors are allocated in proportion to the statewide popular vote.

While one might be inclined to think that these proportional allocation methods are a panacea to the problems of Electoral College, particularly the problem where an individual might win the popular vote, but lose the electoral vote, they do not necessarily prevent this situation from occurring. Because electoral votes would still be allocated on a state-by-state basis, there are still biases toward the individual that wins the most states, rather than the individual who wins the most votes. For instance, in 2016, Trump won 30 states and Clinton won 20 and the District of Columbia. Even if we allocated all electoral votes proportionately using the popular Droop quota (see the chapter on apportionment for more details on this), and with no bonuses for state winners, Clinton would have received 268 electoral votes to Trump's 266 (Gary Johnson would receive two, and Stein and McMullin would receive one each). Under another proportional allocation method (using the Hare quota) Trump and Clinton would tie, each with 261 electoral votes. This method greatly helps third-party candidates, as Gary Johnson would have received 14 electoral votes, and Jill Stein and Evan McMullin would have each received one.[51] Presumably, with the election thrown to the House of Representatives in each case, Trump still would have won the presidential election, as Republicans control a majority of the state Congressional delegations. A system which would award two base delegates to the statewide winner, and the rest based on the proportional outcome of the statewide vote, would have produced an outright win for Trump, 272–261 (Johnson-3, Stein-1, McMullen-1).

Proportional allocation systems based on Congressional districts similarly suffer from biases which do not necessarily favor the winner of the popular vote.

Additionally, Congressional district systems introduce new biases based on the peculiarities of districting and gerrymandering.

2. Bonus National Delegates

An alternative plan that retains a winner-take-all Electoral College while preventing popular-vote losers from winning the Electoral College, is the National Bonus Plan. First proposed by Arthur M. Schlesinger in a 1977 Wall Street Journal article,[52] and later refined by a report of the Twentieth Century Fund[53] (later Twentieth Century Foundation), the National Bonus Plan preserves the Electoral College but adds an additional 102 electoral votes—a federal bonus. These federal bonus votes are calculated as two votes per state, with an additional two votes for the District of Columbia. They are awarded in a winner-take-all fashion to the winner of the national popular vote. This plan ensures that the popular vote winner would win the Electoral College, without dismantling the entire system. The National Bonus Plan also called for the abolition of individual electors, thereby eliminating the problem of faithless electors. Individual electoral votes would still be cast by the states, but this plan would take the actual elector, and their agency in casting an electoral vote, out of the process.

3. The National Popular Vote Interstate Compact

One proposal for altering the Electoral College is already in the process of being adopted in the states. Rather than altering the formula for allocating electors in the states, or abolishing the Electoral College totally, the National Popular Vote Interstate Compact is a plan to make the nationwide popular vote the deciding factor in elections while still retaining the Electoral College. The NPVIA is an interstate compact that binds states to award their Electoral College votes to the winner of the nationwide popular vote. Thus, the popular vote becomes the deciding factor for presidential elections, but the Electoral College is not abolished. If a number of states which control a total of 270 (or more) electoral votes would agree to cast their electoral votes as a block, the winner of the nationwide popular vote would always be the winner of the electoral college, preventing the inversion of results in 1824, 1876, 1888, 2000 and 2016. While the compact does not enter into force until enough states enact the law to total a block of 270 electoral votes, some states have already taken legislative action. As of this writing, twelve states,[54] totaling 172 electoral votes (or 64% of the needed 270) had enacted legislation to join the compact, and a number of other states have seen enacting legislation in one of their state legislative houses.

One potential problem with the compact is that it requires enforceable pledges on the part of the electors in each state to ensure that partisans would comply with the outcome of the national vote, even if that candidate did not win their particular state. As mentioned earlier, it is not clear if these pledges can be legally enforced.

4.   Abolishing the Electoral College

In addition to these ideas for reform, a number of proposals have been put forth to entirely abolish or replace the Electoral College. Presumably, if the Electoral College were abolished, we would elect the president based on the outcome of the nationwide popular vote. While this method offers the benefit of always electing the candidate who receives the most popular votes, it does have some potential downsides, although their importance is debatable.

First, eliminating the Electoral College would completely eliminate the role of the states in the presidential election, although the importance of federalism in our elections is subjective. The focus on states, and in particular, the relative advantage that small states have compared to large states, typifies the federalism built into the Electoral College. By eliminating the role of the states, we would diminish this facet of the federal-state relationship.

Second, it might create new difficulties with regard to election recounts. If a national election were to be extremely close, a national recount in each of the states might be an untenable prospect. As logistically, or as administratively difficult as a national recount might be, each state already has recount procedures in place (the final chapter will discuss the capabilities of states to recount elections). Additionally, sometimes our current system warrants recounts that would not be necessary if we took a national count of votes. In 2000, the closeness of Florida precipitated a recount, however, Gore had a national margin over .5 percent. This margin of victory would only trigger a recount in three states under their current laws (again, see the final chapter on recounts for more details).

Third, there is no guarantee that a candidate might reach a majority threshold in the national popular vote. Only 13 of the last 20 presidential elections have ended with a candidate receiving 50 percent or more of the popular vote. One method of resolving this dilemma would be to introduce a ranked-choice voting method, which would allow for the calculation of a runoff winner instantly (see the upcoming chapter on counting votes for a more detailed explanation of this voting method). Alternatively, we could arrange a system that allowed for a plurality winner.

While numerous proposals to abolish the Electoral College have been introduced in Congress, none have ever been proposed to the states. One attempt, sponsored by Emanuel Celler (D-NY) in the House and Birch Bayh (D-IN) (commonly called the Bayh-Celler amendment), came very close. In the wake of the 1968 election, in which Nixon captured a mere 0.6% of the popular vote more than Hubert Humphrey, the House voted to approve a proposed amendment which would have abolished the electoral vote and replaced it with a plurality system based on the national popular vote (with a 40% runoff threshold). When the proposal went before the Senate, it passed safely through the Judiciary Committee, but never received a vote of the full Senate, falling short of the threshold required to invoke cloture. No proposal to alter the Electoral College has received an affirmative vote in either chamber of the Congress since this attempt.

F. THESE RULES MATTER

The presidency is, perhaps, the most visible office in the country, and the framework of the Electoral College imparts a number of biases to the selection of the president. The Electoral College, as originally formulated by the framers, bears little resemblance to the system as it now operates. The Electoral College matters in a two-fold way. First, its very existence preconditions our presidential elections, and second, the specific formulation of the system can alter outcomes.

In order to see that the very existence of the Electoral College matters, we need only to look at recent elections where the college has produced winners that are at odds with the outcome of the popular vote across the country. This offers us clear and convincing evidence that the use of this electoral system can alter outcomes. Under a popular vote system, one result would occur, while under the Electoral College system, a different winner emerges. This is an overly simplistic look at why the College matters, but it is too important of a consequence to omit.

The Electoral College also conditions the actions of voters and candidates. One way in which this may occur is that the College may have an impact on voter turnout. One series of studies have examined whether or not turnout is depressed in non-battleground states. The theory behind these studies is that, because of the winner-take-all nature of the Electoral College, voters in states that are perceived to be 'safe,' are disincentivized to vote compared to voters in battleground states, or what would otherwise be the case in a popular election system. These studies found strong evidence for their hypothesis that turnout was reduced in uncompetitive states under the Electoral College system.[55] In addition to affecting voters, the Electoral College has been shown to affect candidate strategies, particularly in the way candidates target specific state, in ways that would not necessarily be the case if presidents were elected by popular vote.[56]

The specific rules of the Electoral College also matter, as shown in the previous section on potential reforms. The structure of the Electoral College as it is today is not the only way to arrange a system of indirect election. In particular, as shown in the section on proportional allocation, we would experience very different election outcomes if Electoral Votes were allocated to candidates on a proportional basis rather than in a winner-take-all fashion. As mentioned in the previous paragraph, a proportional allocation system might also have an impact on voter turnout and candidate strategies which were preconditioned by the winner-take-all nature of the College.

G. CHAPTER 6 DISCUSSION QUESTIONS

1.   The framers of the Constitution settled on an indirect system of electing the president. Given what you know about their early concerns, do you think that we still need an indirect system of elections? What has changed (or conversely, what has not changed) about the nature of the electorate to make you feel this way?

2.   Two alternative plans to the Electoral College were legislative election and direct election. Consider these two options by placing yourself back during the time of the founding, and again today. Do you think different plans would have been better in different times? Consider what would have happened throughout history had we adopted a different system of election. If we had adopted a system of legislative election, do you think we would be advocating for reform today? Why or why not?

3.   The Electoral College math seems to present a contradiction of sorts in the sense that while smaller states have an advantage in absolute voting power (population per vote), they also seem to have less power in terms of the race to 270 votes. Do you think small states are unfairly advantaged or disadvantaged by the Electoral College? Alternatively, are small states *fairly* advantaged? If the system were to be abolished, do you think this would harm or benefit smaller states?

4.   Consider the alternative plans to reform the Electoral College (excepting its complete abolition). What do you see as the relative pros and cons of these plans? How do each of them address the current deficiencies in our system? Can you foresee them introducing any new problems? If you had to advocate for one plan, which would it be?

1 Dougherty, J. Hampden. 1906. *The Electoral System of the United States.* New York: Putnam.

2 O'Neil, Charles A. 1889. *The American Electoral System.* New York: Putnam.

3 Dougherty, J. Hampden. 1906. *The Electoral System of the United States.* New York: Putnam.

4 Longley, Lawrence D. And Neal R. Peirce. 1999. *The Electoral College Primer 2000.* New Haven: Yale University Press.

5 Ferling, John (2004). *Adams vs. Jefferson: The Tumultuous Election of 1800.* New York: Oxford University Press.

6 U.S. Constitution Article II, Section 1, Clause 4.

7 Statutes at Large, 2nd Congress, 1st Session, p. 239.

8 Statutes at Large, 2nd Congress, 1st Session, p. 239.

9 Statutes at Large, 2nd Congress, 1st Session, p. 240.

10 Statutes at Large, 2nd Congress, 1st Session, p. 241.

11 Congressional Globe 28th Congress 1st Session p. 728.

12 Statutes at Large, 28th Congress, 2nd Session, p. 721.

13 Congressional Globe 28th Congress 2nd Session pg.14 "His object in making this change was to avoid the necessity of changing the laws in relation to the day on which the electoral colleges now meet; for the first Tuesday of November might, in some cases, be more than thirty days from the first Wednesday in December."

14 Peirce, Neal R. 1968. *The People's President: the Electoral College in American History and the Direct-Vote Alternative.* New York: Simon and Schuster.

15 Wilmerding, Lucius. 1958. *The Electoral College.* New Brunswick: Rutgers University Press. p. 48.

16 Wilmerding, Lucius. 1958. *The Electoral College.* New Brunswick: Rutgers University Press. p. 61.

17 Annals of Congress 1824. p. 169.

18 Register of Debates in Congress, Appendix 127 Gales and Seaton.

19 Paullin, Charles A. 1932. *Atlas of the Historical Geography of the United States* Washington D.C.: Carnegie Institution of Washington. Peirce, Neal R. 1968. *The People's President: the Electoral College in American History and the Direct-Vote Alternative.* New York: Simon and Schuster.

20 The Congress had previously adopted a rule called the Twenty-second Joint Rule, which allowed either of the two chambers to object to the acceptance of a state's election returns. This rule was no longer in force by 1876.

21 19 Stat. 227.

22 Haworth, Paul L. 1906. The Hayes-Tilden disputed presidential election of 1876. New York: Russell & Russell. p. 202.

23 24 Stat. 373 90.

24 24 Stat. 373.

25 See 22nd Joint Rule.

26 Maskell Jack and Elizabeth Rybicki. 2016. "Counting Electoral Vote: An Overview of Procedures at the Joint Session, Including Objections by Members of Congress." Congressional Research Service.

27 Williams, Brenna. 2017. "11 Times VP Biden was interrupted during Trump's electoral vote certification." *CNN* January 6, 2017. Accessed at https://www.cnn.com/2017/01/06/politics/electoral-college-vote-count-objections/index.html.

28 Walsh, Edward and Juliet Elipherin. 2001. "Gore Presides As Congress Tallies Votes Electing Bush." *Washington Post.* January 7, 2001. Accessed at https://www.washingtonpost.com/archive/politics/2001/01/07/gore-presides-as-congress-tallies-votes-electing-bush/0461e40f-3317-4a7e-a1ad-2232aae304db/?utm_term=.778aa1e4c818.

29 48 Stat. 390.

30 U.S. Census. 2010. Apportionment Population and Number of Representative, By State: 2010 Census.

31 U.S. Constitution Article II Section 1, Clause 2.

32 California Elections Code § 7100 (Democrats) § 7300 (Republicans).

[33] Pennsylvania Statutes § 2878.

[34] National Conference of State Legislators, and Fair Vote: The Presidential Elections Reform Program.

[35] *Ray v. Blair*, 343 U.S. 214 (1952).

[36] Brunner, Jim. 2016. "Four Washington 'faithless electors' to be fined $1,000 each for not casting Clinton votes" *Seattle Times*. December 29, 2016.

[37] Indiana Code 3–10–4–9.

[38] Michigan Compiled Laws 168.47.

[39] Minnesota Statutes 208.46.

[40] Montana Code 13–25–307.

[41] Nebraska Revised Statutes 32–714.

[42] Nevada Revised Statute 298.075.

[43] North Carolina General Statute 163–212.

[44] Oklahoma Statutes 26–10–108.

[45] Utah Code 20A–13–304.

[46] 3 U.S.C. 15.

[47] Gelman, Andrew, Jonathan Katz, and Joseph Bafumi. 2004. "Standard Voting Power Indexes Do Not Work: An Empirical Analysis". *British Journal of Political Science*. 34:4 657–674.

[48] Gelman, Andrew, Jonathan Katz, and Joseph Bafumi. 2004. "Standard Voting Power Indexes Do Not Work: An Empirical Analysis". *British Journal of Political Science*. 34:4 657–674.

[49] Gelman, Andrew, Gary King and W. John Boscardin. 1998. "Estimating the probability of events that have never occurred: when is your vote decisive?" *Journal of the American Statistical Association*. 93:441 1–9.

[50] FairVote maintained a campaign event tracker and noted that 94% of campaign events took place in just 12 states, of which, 11 were commonly described by political watchers as being battleground states.

[51] This calculation is based on the FEC election results, and a calculation using the Hare quota (see the chapter on apportionment for a detailed explanation of this method).

[52] Arthur Schlesinger, Jr., 1977. "The Electoral College Conundrum," *The Wall Street Journal*. April 4, 1977.

[53] Winner Take All: Report of the Twentieth Century Fund Task Force on Reform of the Presidential Election Process New York, 1978.

[54] Maryland, New Jersey, Illinois, Hawaii, Washington, Massachusetts, D.C., Vermont, California, Rhode Island, New York, and Connecticut had enacted laws to join the National Popular Vote Compact as of May 24, 2018.

[55] See Cebula, R. J., & Murphy, D. 1980. "The Electoral College and voter participation rates: an explanatory note." *Public Choice*. 35(2): 185–190. As well as later updates to this work.

[56] Shaw, Daron R. 1999. "The Methods behind the Madness: Presidential Electoral College Strategies, 1988–1996." *The Journal of Politics*. 61(4): 893–913.

CHAPTER 7

Campaign Finance

A. GENERAL TERMS

Money is, perhaps, the most important resource to a political campaign. According to the Center for Responsive Politics, $6,444,253,265[1] was spent on all federal elections during the 2016 election cycle, making it the most expensive election cycle in American history. With this huge influx of money in our electoral process, there has recently been a renewed interest into the rules surrounding campaign finance. Boiling campaign finance down to its most basic parts, federal rules govern donations, expenditures, and disclosure. These rules vary for different types of organizations and groups, and different parts of the federal government are involved in enforcing regulations.

The Federal Election Commission promulgates regulations under the authority of the Federal Election Campaign Act of 1974. The FEC regulates campaign finance for groups that engage in advocacy for and against candidates in federal elections. The Internal Revenue Service, or IRS, is also an important player in regulating campaign finance. While they do not enforce specific campaign finance regulations, they do enforce the laws that allow for the incorporation of nonprofit entities and other tax-exempt organizations like political committees. In this sense, these organizations share responsibility in regulating campaign finance.

Three important parts of federal law that are relevant to a discussion of campaign finance are 26 U.S. Code § 501, 26 U.S. Code § 527, and Part 11 of the Code of Federal Regulations. Title 26 is the section of the U.S. Code which deals with IRS regulations, and sections 501 and 527 of that title of the U.S. Code deal with regulating certain tax-exempt organizations. Part 11 of the Code of Federal Regulations contains the rules that the Federal Election Commission uses to regulate political committees. One of the largest sources of confusion about campaign finance comes from the wide array of political organizations and committees that operate under different campaign finance rules. While these will all be discussed in more depth later in the chapter, it is worthwhile to discuss a basic framework in this introduction.

1.   501(c) Groups

Section 501 of the U.S. Code, particularly subsection (c) deals with the classification of tax-exempt, nonprofit organizations. Perhaps the most common of these types of organizations is the 501(c) 3 group, so named because it is the third of 29 different nonprofit groups listed in this part of the code. 501(c) 3 groups are nonprofit organizations that are operated for "religious, charitable, scientific, testing for public safety, literary, or educational purposes, or to foster national or international amateur sports competition. . . or for the prevention of cruelty to children or animals."[2] The remaining subsections deal with a wide array of other groups including unions,[3] chambers of commerce,[4] credit unions,[5] and recreational clubs.[6] While many of these are not relevant to campaign finance, 501(c) 3 charitable organizations and 501(c) 4 social welfare organizations will be important in our upcoming discussions.[7] Generally, these two organizations are distinct from other types of groups because they are limited in their ability to participate in political activity.

Nonprofit 501(c) organizations are not designed to facilitate participation in political activity. Donors to 501(c) 3 organizations, for example, are allowed to claim tax deductions for their donations. Moreover, these donations are not required to be disclosed to any agency (beyond the disclosure necessary for an individual to claim a tax deduction). 501(c) 4 organizations are designed to allow some political participation, but not direct advocacy for or against political candidates. As their involvement in the political process is generally limited to lobbying and issue advocacy, they are not regulated by the FEC in the same way that other political organizations are.

Once an organization decides that they want to enter the political realm more completely, and begin to advocate for or against political candidates, they must move out of the 501 framework and operate as a 527 organization.

2.   527s and PACs

Section 527 of the U.S. Code deals with a very different type of organization—political organizations. While these groups also enjoy tax-advantaged status, they are distinct from 501(c) groups in they are specifically organized as political organizations. Official candidate campaign committees, political parties, political action committees (PACs), political organizations affiliated with interest groups and associations, and even the newer category of super PACs, are all 527 political organizations, in that they are governed by this section of the law. There are, however, very important distinctions between these groups.

Official candidate committees, PACs, political parties, and other groups which engage in advocacy for or against political candidates fall under an additional set of regulations promulgated not by the IRS, but by the FEC. As mentioned earlier, these rules are contained in the Code of Federal Regulations. All 'other' 527 organizations are not subject to FEC rules, because they are supposed to engage in advocacy on issues and not for or against particular candidates. Because of this distinction, they are only regulated by the IRS, not the FEC. In common parlance, these 'other' 527 groups are the only ones that are generally referred to by the name 527. Groups that are regulated by the FEC are generally referred to as PACs (although there are many distinctions within this category of groups as well). To think about this in another way, all PACs are 527 organizations, but not all 527 organizations qualify as PACs.

B. CREATING A REGULATORY FRAMEWORK

Campaign finance is regulated in the United States through a framework that has seen many changes over the last century. This section will discuss early laws designed to regulate the country's campaign finance system, and introduce the Federal Election Campaign Act, which is the primary source of campaign finance regulations today.

1. Early Attempts at Regulation

Campaign finance has been regulated by the federal government in some form or fashion since the Tillman Act of 1907.[8] These laws have taken a number of different forms and have attempted to regulate different features of campaign finance. Two important concepts in this regulation are limits and disclosure. By limits, we mean restrictions on the types and amounts of certain financial transactions, and by disclosure, we mean the requirement to document and report transactions of different kinds.

Limitations on campaign finance have generally come in two distinct types— contribution limits and spending limits. Contribution limits place specific dollar amount limitations on the contributions that can be made to different political actors. Contribution limits may also limit who may contribute to campaigns.

Alternately, spending limits focused on how much a candidate may spend on their campaign. A wholly different area of regulation has come in the form of disclosure laws, which require certain entities to disclose their transactions like donations, receipts, or expenditures.

The Tillman Act, the first major attempt at regulating campaign finance, operated by prohibiting campaign contributions from corporations. Thus, the act was a limitation on contributions. This early prohibition was notable for its omission of regulation on labor unions, which would not see similar treatment until the Smith-Connally Act of 1943.[9] In addition to these early restrictions on contributions to campaigns, the Taft-Hartley Act of 1947[10] would add spending rules to the campaign finance landscape by further restricting both corporations and labor unions from making independent expenditures in federal elections. Thus, corporations and labor unions were restricted from contributing to campaigns, and from making expenditures to try and influence the outcome of the election.

Disclosure rules would be added to the regulatory framework by another law, passed in 1910, which regulated entities participating in Congressional elections by requiring them to disclose donors and expenses for general elections.[11] This did not necessarily place limitations on spending or contributions, but required entities to report contributions. An amendment to that law passed the following year extended the disclosure law to include primary elections, and incorporated limits on expenditures.[12] These laws (excepting the aforementioned Smith-Connally Act and Taft-Hartley Act, which came later) were codified in a law known as the Federal Corrupt Practices Act of 1925.[13] Unfortunately, this law fell short in a number of ways, not least of which was the reality that these laws applied only to political committees that operated in more than one state, or committees that were affiliated with a national organization like a political party. This meant that individual campaigns were generally exempted from much of this early regulation.

2.   FECA and Buckley v. Valeo

The next large push for campaign finance regulation would not come until 1971,[14] with the passage of the Federal Election Campaign Act. This new law created a stronger framework for campaign finance disclosure and enacted new limits on contributions and spending. These rules would be bolstered by amendments to the law which came in 1974, creating the Federal Election Commission, an independent agency, which would carry out the enforcement and regulation of campaign finance. With the enactment of the 1974 amendments, the newly created FEC was set to begin to regulate campaign contributions and spending in federal elections for the 1976 federal elections. However, before the FEC could begin enforcing these new rules, a challenge arose from a number of plaintiffs, including elected officials and political parties. The case would come before the Supreme Court as *Buckley v. Valeo*,[15] and their decision would change the nature of federal regulatory power over campaign finance.

In their *per curiam* opinion, eight justices[16] grappled with the appropriate way to view the legitimate governmental interests to regulate campaign finance, and struck a middle ground, overturning parts of the law and allowing others to stay. Before looking at the decision itself, it is worthwhile to look at how the justices viewed this governmental interest. When considering campaign finance, there is often a competing pull between two opposing forces—equality and free speech. On one hand, political equality is a central component to a fair and democratic electoral process. Looking back at the previous chapter on gerrymandering, we see how the courts evoke the principle of 'one person, one vote' in cases like *Baker v. Carr*,[17] *Reynolds v. Sims*,[18] and others. Does the naturally unequal distribution of wealth necessarily create inequalities in political participation or the expression of political speech? Does the desire to equalize voices in our democracy provide a legitimate governmental interest for regulating campaign finance? Conversely, does the regulation of campaign finance create an unconstitutional abridgment of free speech?

Perhaps surprisingly, the court did not frame their ruling in *Buckley* as a matter of free speech or political equality. The opinion specifically rejected the "ancillary interest in equalizing the relative financial resources of candidates competing for elective office,"[19] stating "the concept that government may restrict the speech of some elements of our society in order to enhance the relative voice of others is wholly foreign to the First Amendment."[20] Instead, the only legitimate governmental interest that the courts found was the "prevention of corruption and the appearance of corruption."[21]

In rendering their decision, the court upheld the FECA's limitations on contributions as such a safeguard against corruption. However, the court viewed expenditure limits, including limitations on the use of a candidate's personal money, as an abridgment of First Amendment freedom of speech. Moreover, the ruling created a framework for the regulation of independent expenditures, that is, expenditures by groups without the involvement of a candidate's committee or party. While the FECA limited these independent expenditures, *Buckley* created a new framework, delineating between issue advocacy—advertising about broad political issues, and express advocacy—advertising which clearly supports or opposes a candidate. The decision left open a loophole which, while prohibiting groups from engaging in unregulated express advocacy, allowed these groups to spend unregulated amounts of money on issue advocacy. In doing so, the court opined that a number of terms might indicate that an ad is engaged in express advocacy. These 'magic words' include 'vote for,' 'elect,' 'support,' 'cast your ballot for,' 'Smith for Congress,' 'vote against,' 'defeat,' and 'reject.'[22]

Congress would amend the FECA once more in 1976 in order to bring the law into compliance with this new ruling.[23] With the exception of minor amendments in the coming years, this version of the FECA would govern campaign finance until the next push for reform in the early 2000s.

a.   *Public Financing*

One aspect of the Federal Election Campaign Act that was not discussed in the previous section is public financing of political campaigns. Arising from multiple pieces of legislation in the early 1970s, the public financing system for presidential elections provides public funds for primary elections, conventions (although this part of the law was recently repealed), and general elections. This money is diverted from the general treasury by individual marking the '$3 tax checkoff' on their federal income tax form (the amount was previously $1). Checking this box does not increase an individual's tax liability, it only designates $3 of their taxes to the presidential election campaign fund. Qualifying candidates and parties were able to, under the original law, receive matching grants for money raised during the primary season, receive grants to hold the major party conventions, and receive grants for the general election. All three of these offers came with their own qualifications and restrictions.

The basic qualification for public financing is viability. In the case of public funding for primary elections, candidates must show that they can raise money across a large geographic area, before qualifying for matching grants. Candidates must be able to raise $5000 in 20 different states and may only apply a maximum of $250 of each individual donation towards this total. Once candidates reach this threshold, they are able to receive matching grants for the first $250 of each individual donation that they receive, up to a specific maximum in each state, and nationally. The FEC calculates an aggregate spending maximum across all states based off of a cost of living adjustment of the original amount provided in law ($10 million). In 2016, this maximum was $48.07 million. Each state is also assigned a maximum spending limit based on the greater of either $200,000 or 16 cents per person, using the voting age population of a state (both of these numbers are similarly adjusted for cost of living). The sum of all the individual state limits exceeds the aggregate limit, meaning a candidate may not spend the maximum in every state. Additionally, while the amount a candidate receives is based on their individual ability to fundraise, matching grants are limited to half of the spending ceiling.[24]

For the general election, the major party candidates do not need to 'qualify' as they are automatically eligible to receive assistance by virtue of their nomination by the parties. Minor party candidates can qualify for partial funding if their party's candidate received more than 5 percent of the popular vote in the previous election. Parties qualify as major parties once they receive over 25 percent of the popular vote in the previous presidential election. The amount that major party candidates are entitled to is based on a cost of living adjusted figure set in statute. In 2016, the national party candidates were eligible for $96.14 million in assistance. Similar to the conditions set out in primary election grants, general election grants come with limitations. General election grants, however, completely limit candidate spending to the amount of the grant, and do not allow any other outside funding. The only exception to this is that candidates may use some of their own personal money. This trade-off means that candidates are entitled to this sum of money but are limited to spending only that amount.

The third facet of public financing deals with the party conventions. The FECA originally provided financial assistance to the parties in order to fund their quadrennial national conventions. In addition, Congress has more recently supplemented this money with grants to state and local governments to assist in providing security for the conventions. In 2014, however, Congress repealed the part of the law which provided assistance to the parties, but left in place support for convention security. In 2016 these security grants totaled $100 million for both conventions.

Today, the public financing system is a shell of its former self. With the immense sums of money that candidates are able to fundraise on their own, public funding is now rarely used by major party candidates for either the primary or general elections. Barack Obama was the first major candidate to decline public funding in 2008, and in that same year, John McCain became the last major party candidate to accept public funding. In both 2012 and 2016, neither major party candidate accepted public funding for the general election, and all of the major candidates raised sums that dwarfed what they would have received under the public financing system. Participation in the primary matching system has also waned, with 2008 being the last year when a significant number of major party candidates participated in the system. No major party candidates participated in 2012, and only Martin O'Malley, a Democratic candidate, participated in 2016.

3.   BCRA and Deregulation

One of the largest changes to the FECA came in 2002 with the Bipartisan Campaign Reform Act (BCRA), also called the McCain-Feingold Act after its two primary sponsors, John McCain (R-AZ) and Russ Feingold (D-WI). The Act was designed to counter the proliferation of previously discussed issue ads, as well as 'soft money.'

Since *Buckley,* issue ads had become a pervasive issue in American political campaigns, with large amounts of money being spent by groups on ads which closely resembled express advocacy but did not include the court's 'magic words.' In an attempt to stem the growing tide of these ads, the BCRA crafted a new term to regulate advertising that brought together express advocacy and issue ads. The new term used by the Act was 'electioneering communications.' This term encompassed express advocacy and the types of issue ads which were clearly advocating for a candidate but escaping regulation by avoiding certain terms. Electioneering communications would now encompass any ad that had clearly referred to a candidate within 60 days of a general election or 30 days of a primary election.[25] These electioneering communications would now face FEC regulation.

A second issue that the BCRA was designed to combat was the ride of 'soft money.' Under the FECA, individuals could contribute without limit to political parties. Parties could then use this money to engage in activities like get-out-the-vote drives, state election support, party advertising, and other 'party building' activities. Parties were able to raise hundreds of millions of dollars in 'soft money' as a result.[26] The BCRA banned the receipt of these funds, cutting off a significant source of income for the parties.

In order to compensate for restrictions on soft money, the BCRA also increased limits on donations to candidates and committees, and it provided for increases to these limits with inflation. Additionally, these limits could be increased further under a 'millionaire's provision,' which allowed for increased contribution limits if a candidate's opponent used more than $350,000 of their own personal money.

As with the original adoption of the FECA, the BCRA faced legal challenges almost immediately after it was enacted. A number of groups, including Senator Mitch McConnell of Kentucky joined to file suit against the FEC in *McConnell vs. FEC*[27] in 2003. Unlike in *Buckley*, the court upheld many of the most important features of the BCRA. Over the next decade, however, a number of other cases would gradually erode most of the key provisions of the Act.

One of the first largely successful challenges to the BCRA was in *FEC v. Wisconsin Right to Life*.[28] The opinion in this case relaxed the standard set on electioneering communications and brought campaign finance law back closer to the court's earlier distinction between express advocacy and issue advocacy. *Citizens United v. FEC*[29] would take this decision even further, completely overruling BRCA limitations on corporate electioneering communications and independent expenditures, allowing corporations to enter the electoral fold and directly advocate for or against candidates, so long as their expenditures were independent.

In addition to overruling independent expenditure and electioneering communication prohibitions on corporations (and presumably any group, even though non-corporate entities were not specifically mentioned in the decision), other provisions of the FECA and BRCA have been similarly ruled unconstitutional. The BCRA's aforementioned 'millionaire's provision' was struck down in 2008 in *Davis v. Federal Election Commission*,[30] and the FECA's aggregate limits on donations discussed in the previous section were ruled unconstitutional in *McCutcheon v. Federal Election Commission*.[31]

While a number of key provisions of both the FECA and BCRA still remain in effect, the landscape of campaign finance has changed dramatically with the introduction of unlimited independent expenditures. To look at what regulations remain in place, and how they govern campaign finance today, let's look at each of the major players and dive deeper into the specific rules that govern their actions in the electoral sphere.

C. CONTRIBUTORS AND CONTRIBUTIONS

Within the basic framework of the FECA and BCRA exist a number of different legal entities. These players, including political committees, corporations, unions, candidate committees, parties, and super PACs, all play an important role in the electoral process. Importantly, they are not all treated the same in terms of what they are and are not allowed to. Different organizations must play by different rules. To unpack campaign finance more completely. Let's look at how these groups differ in their organization, in their participation political process, and in how they are regulated.

1. Political Committees

Political committees are, generally, any group that raises and spends funds, and that meets a number of criteria listed in federal regulations.[32] As political committees, these groups are subject to FEC regulations on contributions and expenditures. Political committees can include a candidate's official authorized campaign committee, a committee set up by an elected official for the benefit of other candidates, a political party, a committee set up by a corporation or labor union, or a committee that is unconnected to any business or sponsoring organization. Generally speaking, the term PAC, or political action committee, is used to refer to a smaller subset of these committees. Committees that are sponsored by organizations or businesses, nonconnected (meaning not connected to a candidate) political committees, and committees sponsored by public officials for the benefit of other candidates are all generally referred to as PACs. However, authorized candidate committees and party committees, while technically political committees, are not generally referred to as PACs. Similarly, while political parties meet the definition of political committees, they are also not commonly referred to as PACs.

One of the largest categories of PACs are those set up by corporations and labor unions. These corporations and labor unions, while barred from using general treasury funds to donate to candidates, can set up a PAC using funds that are separate from their general treasury funds. These separate funds are commonly called separate segregated funds, or SSFs. Sponsoring organizations are allowed to pay some of the costs of organization and administration of the PAC with corporate funds, however, all other funds must remain separated from general treasury money in these SSFs. Once established, the PAC can solicit contributions, subject to FEC rules and limits, and disperse those contributions to candidates or other PACs.

SSF PACs are limited in that they may only solicit contributions from a limited group of individuals associated with the organization.[33] These restrictions are in place to prevent SSF PACs from compelling their employees to donate through force or coercion. SSFs are allowed to solicit contributions from only a small group of individuals (called a restricted class) including stockholders and executive personnel for corporations, and executives and members for unions, at any time.[34] Twice a year, corporations and their SSFs may ask for contributions from their other employees, but again, not from the general public.[35]

In some cases, PACs do not have sponsoring organizations. These PACs are generally referred to as nonconnected PACs. A key distinction between these groups and SSFs is that nonconnected PACs can solicit donations from anyone, so long as they adhere to standard FEC contribution limits and rules. One type of nonconnected PAC is the leadership PAC, which is a PAC that is organized by an elected official for the benefit of *other* candidates for office. These PACs operate entirely separate from any authorized candidate committee, although transfers can be made between authorized committees and leadership PACs, subject to FEC limits. Leadership PACs are often formed by prominent public officials in order to leverage their fundraising ability for other candidates. If any of these PACs support at least five candidates and has reached a minimum threshold of contributions, it attains multicandidate status, which allows it to give larger contributions to candidates.

PACs, and political committees in general, are all held together by common abilities and regulations. These groups are allowed to expressly advocate for the election or defeat of candidates, are allowed to coordinate with each other (excepting super PACs, a special category of PACs that will be discussed later), and are subject to contribution limits, and disclosure rules. Contribution limits for PACs are different from those for candidate committees because they are limited by year, rather than by election. The table below lists these limits.

TABLE 7.1   DONATION LIMITS FOR POLITICAL COMMITTEES

Donor	Donation Limit (per year)
Individuals	$5,000
Candidate Committees (Other Candidates' Committees)	$5,000
Multicandidate PACs	$5,000
Non-multicandidate PACs	$5,000
State, District & Local Party Committee	$5,000
National Party Committee	$5,000

In addition to facing limits on receipts, PACs must also follow disclosure rules, forcing them to keep records of contributions to the PAC itself as well as disbursements from the PAC to candidates, parties, or other PACs. In addition to monetary contributions, PACs can engage in coordinated communications (advertisements) or provide other services to campaigns, however, these communications and services are considered 'in-kind' contributions (which will be discussed more in the next section) and their fair value counts towards donations limits.

2. Candidate Committees and Hard Money

Perhaps the most important type of committee is the candidate campaign committee. Campaign finance, at its simplest, involves contributions of money or services to the campaign committees of candidates. The framework of the FECA calls for candidate committees to register as 'authorized committees', to submit reports on contributions and expenditures to the FEC, and to be subject to limitations on contributions (recall that *Buckley v. Valeo* struck down limitations on expenditures, but preserved contribution limits and disclosure rules).

The most basic rules that apply to campaign committees are contribution limits. Contributions consist of anything of value, including money, goods, or services. Donations of goods and services are called 'in-kind contributions.' These in-kind contributions must be valued at fair market prices and reported in the same way as a monetary donation.[36] For example, if an individual purchases and provides food for a campaign event, the campaign must report the value of the purchased food as a donation, and the value of the food would count towards the individual's donation limit. For standard campaign committees, contribution limits vary across six distinct donor groups.

TABLE 7.2   DONATION LIMITS TO CANDIDATE COMMITTEES

Donor	Donation Limit (per election) 2017–2018
Individuals	$2,700
Candidate Committees (Other Candidates' Committees)	$2,000
Multicandidate PACs	$5,000
Nonmulticandidate PACs	$2,700
State, District & Local Party Committee	$5,000
National Party Committee	$5,000

These donation limits apply for each election, however, primary elections, runoff elections, and general elections are all treated as separate elections. Additionally, individual limits are indexed for inflation in odd-numbered years.[37] This rule allows these limits to rise with inflation without having to rewrite the regulation. As noted earlier, while the FECA originally enforced aggregate caps on donations (a maximum donation across multiple candidates), the Supreme

Court ruled these caps unconstitutional in *McCutcheon v. FEC.* Today an individual faces no limits to the amount they may donate, so long as they adhere to these per-candidate limits.

Candidates must maintain records and submit disclosure forms to the FEC to ensure that individuals and other groups do not exceed their contribution limits for any given election cycle. Candidates are only allowed to gather donations for elections in which they contest the election, and donations generally need to be made before the election. This is to say, a candidate committee is not allowed to collect donations under a general election limit if they are defeated in the primary or if they drop out of the election.[38] Moreover, candidates are limited in their ability to accept donations for an election after Election Day (they may only take donations after Election Day to offset remaining campaign debts).[39]

Rules are very specific regarding the records that must be kept for contributions. For contributions over 50 dollars, the campaign must make a record of the name and address of the person giving the contribution, as well as a digital image or record of the check or credit card authorization.[40] When contributions exceed 200 dollars, the campaign must also record the occupation, and employer of the donor. As mentioned earlier, in-kind donations must be assigned a fair value and reported in the same way as a monetary donation. Because of these reporting rules, campaigns are not allowed to accept anonymous donations in excess of 50 dollars or cash donation in excess of 100 dollars.[41]

In addition to these sources of money, candidates are allowed to use their own personal money. Donations of personal funds to a candidate's own campaign are not limited, but still must be disclosed like other contributions.[42] Within certain limits, candidates may consider their own personal funds as loans to their committee and may be eligible for repayment from committee funds. Additionally, campaigns are allowed to secure traditional bank loans without regard to donation limits, but still subject to some restrictions on the terms of the loan.[43] However, any other individuals who may wish to loan money to a campaign are still subject to individual level donation limits.[44]

Candidate committees are also subject to some prohibitions on *who* may contribute. Banks, corporations, and labor unions are all prohibited from making any donations from their general treasuries to the campaign committees of candidates.[45] Monetary donations are not the only form that impermissible contributions might take. Consider in-kind donations that we discussed above. If a local sign-maker were to print and donate lawn signs to a campaign, this would constitute an in-kind donation to the campaign in the amount of the fair market value of the signs. Since this in-kind donation is coming from the signmaker's business, it would constitute an illegal corporate contribution (assuming the signmaker did not personally purchase the signs from his own business first, and then donate them as an individual in-kind donation). This is not to say that corporations do not play a role in campaign finance. Corporations are allowed to form PACs with so-called separate segregated funds (money that is separate from their corporate treasuries). Additionally, under recent court decisions, these organizations may now spend money independently from candidate campaigns (via super PACs). These exceptions to restrictions on corporate and labor union donations will be discussed in an upcoming section of this chapter.

Another important restriction on candidate committees is that these committees cannot receive donations from any foreign national.[46] This restriction includes foreign citizens, governments, parties, and corporations. However, this restriction does not include non-citizens who are permanent residents or U.S. nationals.[47]

On the other side of the financial ledger, candidate committees are also required to make disclosures for campaign expenditures. Again, *Buckley* found that limits on expenditures were unconstitutional, but left in place some regulations on expenditures, including disclosure, and some impermissible uses of campaign funds. While campaigns are granted wide latitude in how they choose to spend money, there are some limitations, particularly with respect to personal use. Campaign committees are not allowed to use funds for personal expenses for the candidate.[48] These limitations include things like household items, food, clothing, mortgage payments, tuition, club fees, or vacation expenses.[49] The general rule for these restrictions is that campaign funds cannot be used for expenses that the candidate would make 'irrespective' of their campaign.[50] In addition to these minor restrictions on spending, campaigns must keep records of all expenditures (commonly called disbursements), and file reports including details like the date, amount, payee, and purpose of an expenditure.[51]

3. Parties, Soft Money, and BCRA

Parties are another type of special political committee which are subject to a number of important campaign finance rules. As previously mentioned, before the adoption of the BCRA, national parties were allowed to raise and spend unlimited quantities of money, called soft money, so long as those funds were used for a limited set of so-called 'party building activities.' Today, parties face a number of new restrictions on their ability to raise and spend money.

Rules regarding the formation of party committees differ from the rules that govern party status for ballot access as described in Chapter 5. While political party committees can only be formed by organizations that qualify as political parties according to state, or federal law. A local, state, or national party committee must meet additional qualifications set by the FEC, which may differ from the qualifications set by the individual states. These qualifications are generally related to the party's ability to contest elections regularly and promulgate a coherent platform of issues. Since parties may engage in advocacy on behalf of federal and non-federal candidates, they often segregate funds (either through keeping records or maintaining separate accounts) for federal and non-federal races.

As with other political committees, parties are subject to FEC contribution limits in terms of who may contribute to parties and the value of those contributions. The table below lists the various donation limits to national, state, and local committees. Each party's House and Senate campaign committees are treated as additional national party committees, subject to their own individual limits. State and local parties (of the same party) are considered affiliated parties, and thus their donation limits are aggregated for each state. This means that these limits apply as an aggregate cap on all donations to a single party's state and local organizations within a single state.

TABLE 7.3   DONATION LIMITS TO NATIONAL AND STATE/LOCAL PARTIES

Donor	National Party Committee	State/Local Party
Individual	$33,900 per year	$10,000 per year (total)
Candidate committee	Unlimited	Unlimited
Multicandidate PAC	$15,000 per year	$5,000 per year (total)
Nonmulticandidate PAC	$33,900 per year	$10,000 per year (total)
State/Local Party	Unlimited	Unlimited
National Party	Unlimited	Unlimited

4. The Super PAC

Perhaps the most important recent development in campaign finance has been the emergence of independent expenditure political committees, commonly known as Super PACs. The term Super PAC is a nod to the extraordinary ability of these groups to accept donations without restrictions and spend money to influence elections under the condition that they do not coordinate with political campaigns. Due to the Supreme Court's decision in *Citizen's United v. FEC,* corporations (and by extension, unions and other groups) are now allowed to make independent expenditures in federal campaigns. The courts reasoned that if the only legitimate state interest in regulating campaign finance is the prevention of corruption, and if independent expenditures necessarily lack the required coordination for corruption or *quid pro quo* arrangements, then independent expenditures cannot be limited.[52] This has spurred the creation of this new class of unregulated political committees. Because these organizations do not make direct contributions to candidate committees, party committees, or traditional PACs, they face no limitations on the value of contributions they can accept from individuals or groups like corporations or unions.[53] While SuperPACs can raise and spend unlimited amounts of money, a federal court decision[54] did uphold registration and disclosure requirements on these organizations, requiring them to report their donors and expenditures just as a normal PAC would.

D. DARK MONEY

Dark money is a term used to describe funds that are spent for political purposes, where a donor cannot be identified. Unlike the vast majority of political spending that we have discussed in this chapter, dark money enjoys an uncommon amount of anonymity. Given all of the regulations discussed in this chapter, how can this money be spent anonymously? Dark money has existed in some form since *Buckley v. Valeo.* While *Citizens United* is often cited as the case that allowed the development of dark money, recall that Citizens United merely allowed corporations to make unlimited independent campaign expenditures. While individuals may be able to claim some degree of anonymity behind a corporate shield, other cases that came before *Citizens United* had a larger impact on the dark money framework as we now know it. Cases like *FEC v. Massachusetts Citizens for Life*[55] and *FEC v. Wisconsin Right to Life,*[56] set the stage for *Citizens United* by relaxing restrictions on nonprofits engaging in independent expenditures (MCFL) even in cases where the nonprofit organization receives some of its funding from corporate sources (WRTL). The decision in *Citizens United* took these decisions to their next logical step by deregulating the political activity of corporations. Taken together, these cases dramatically loosened restrictions on nonprofit organizations and corporations alike, allowing them to participate in the political sphere to a much greater degree. While 501 organizations still must abide by certain restrictions to maintain their 501 status, the advocacy that they are able to engage in has now become less restricted. One of the ways that corporations and 501 organizations have seen increased use are as a channel for anonymous political spending or dark money.

Generally speaking, there are two avenues through which anonymous political spending can flow. Both require some form of 501(c) nonprofit group. As mentioned earlier in this chapter, nonprofit 501(c) are groups that are regulated by the IRS rather than the FEC since they are not designed for the primary purpose of political activity. 501 organizations may raise unlimited amounts of money, and because they are regulated by the IRS, rather than the FEC, they are not required to report their donors. This lack of transparency, coupled with their newfound ability to engage in political advocacy, means that any money spent on election communications by 501 organizations would be untraceable to donors. This spending is what is commonly referred to as dark money. Again, the only limitation on 501(c) nonprofit group spending is the requirement that this sort of political activity is not their 'primary activity.' It is not entirely clear what constitutes primary activity, but even in a very restrictive sense, these groups now function as an effective vehicle for anonymous participation in the political process.

One way to get around this limitation on 'primary activity' is to couple a 501(c) group, or shell corporations with an independent expenditure PAC, or SuperPAC. With this second avenue for dark money, a SuperPAC does not have to maintain any exterior appearance of being a social welfare nonprofit, like a 501(c) 4 would. Rather, the super PAC can dedicate all of their activities to political advocacy. The one weakness of super PACs within the dark money framework is that while they are allowed to receive contributions and make political expenditures without limits, they are required to disclose their donors. By coupling a 501(c) 4, which does not disclose donors, or a shell corporation that could shield the identity of individuals, with a super PAC, those disclosure rules become meaningless. If a SuperPAC were to receive a donation from a 501(c) 4, they would merely list that 501 group as the donor. They would not have to trace the source of the money back past the 501 group. Since the 501 group does not disclose donors, the connection between the super PAC spending and the individual donors would be broken. Similarly, if a corporation were to make a donation to a SuperPAC, the corporation, and not any individual in control of the corporation, would be listed as the donor. These machinations allow for unlimited and anonymous independent expenditures.

E. STATE LAW

All of the laws discussed in this chapter have applied to federal elections. This does not mean that states do not similarly regulate campaign finance for statewide, state legislative, judicial, or even local elections. Indeed, in nearly every state, there are contribution limits similar to those imposed by the FEC on federal candidates. A handful of states do not regulate campaign finance, including Alabama, Indiana, Iowa, Mississippi, Nebraska, North Dakota, Oregon, Pennsylvania, Texas, Utah, and Virginia.[57] In states that provide for judicial election, similar laws apply. In many cases, these state campaign finance systems involve disclosure laws as well. A few states have experimented with limiting the amount of money that a candidate can receive from non-residents or out-of-state PACs. These prohibitions take a number of different forms, for example, in Hawaii, a candidate cannot take more the 30 percent of their total contributions from non-residents.[58] Alaska, Oregon, and Vermont have also experimented with non-resident contribution limits, but have faced legal challenges. In Oregon and Vermont, the restrictions have been overturned, but they remain in effect for Alaska and Hawaii.[59] While the details of all of these campaign finance systems vary, in general, they mirror the federal campaign finance system to some degree. In some cases, state laws have provisions for local or municipal elections, but some localities choose to regulate campaign finance on their own.

F. THESE RULES MATTER

Money is one of the most valuable resources to a candidate, and the regulation of campaign finance is of critical importance to our democracy. Money often finds itself listed as one of the necessary evils of politics, and while the point of this book is not to determine the relative place of money on a spectrum of good and evil, it is surely necessary to politics. Campaign finance rules matter and are perhaps most studied in the sense that campaign spending matters. At the presidential level, studies have shown that the candidate who spends more, wins more votes.[60] However, incumbency effects in Congressional races have complicated the study of money and legislative election. Much research has shown that the more a challenger spends, the better they fare. Interestingly, this finding has not held for incumbents, where evidence has shown that the more they spend, the worse they fare. This conclusion may seem paradoxical but consider what these two candidates might look like. If a challenger is able to spend a large amount of money, that spending probably suggests a strong candidate who has been able to a raise good deal of money. On the other hand, if an incumbent is spending a good deal of money, it might be the case that they are facing a greater challenge and need to spend more to protect their seat. Thus, challengers spend when they are doing well, and incumbents must spend when they are doing poorly. Beyond these endogenous effects, research has been able to identify the actual effects of spending in elections, suggesting that increased spending by challengers can help to equalize the advantage of incumbents.[61] This increased spending can even signal to voters that a candidate is a viable one.[62]

Other lines of research have focused directly on the relationship between the regulation of campaign finance and electoral outcomes. One line of inquiry has focused on how lessening campaign finance restrictions might lead to more moderate legislators. The theory behind this is that corporations and parties will focus on more appealing to swing voters, who favor moderate candidates.[63] At this point, this line of inquiry is far from settled, and it is unclear how the dramatic increase in outside spending has affected our elections. Part of this problem stems from the recency of the court cases opening up outside spending, and another part of the problem is that it can be difficult to track some outside spending (particularly dark money). Most of the extant literature on independent expenditures has merely tried to explain the phenomenon and get a handle on who is spending, how they are spending, and how much they are spending.[64]

G. CHAPTER 7 DISCUSSION QUESTIONS

1. In recent years, the courts have come to the conclusion that political donations and independent expenditures are akin to speech. Under this view, the courts have been very reluctant to limit money in politics. Do you agree with this view that money constitutes speech?

2. A key aspect of campaign finance has been the idea of disclosure—that candidates should have to report the sources of their donations. Arguments in favor of disclosure laws contend that this helps to prevent the possibility of quid-pro-quo arrangements between donors and candidates. There are other arguments that suggest that individuals should be able to make donations to candidates without having to reveal their identity. This might protect them if they did not want their political views to be made public. Should donors be able to remain secret, or does the possibility of corruption outweigh privacy concerns?

3. How much money is too much money to be spent in our political campaigns? While some political observers lament the increasing influence of money in our elections, some have pointed out that it is a relatively small amount per voter. Are we spending too much? Or not enough?

4.   The Supreme Court has wrestled with the wording of ads and advocacy in political advertisements in a number of cases. Ads can be classified as issue ads, or express advocacy ads. Do you think this is a reasonable distinction in regulating advertisements? Why or why not?

---

[1]   Open Secrets—The Center for responsive politics.

[2]   26 U.S. Code § 501 (c) 3.

[3]   26 U.S. Code § 501 (c) 5.

[4]   26 U.S. Code § 501 (c) 6.

[5]   26 U.S. Code § 501 (c) 14.

[6]   26 U.S. Code § 501 (c) 7.

[7]   According to the Center for Responsive Politics, 501 (c) 4 social welfare groups spent nearly five times the amount that unions (501 (c) 5) or trade associations (501 (c) 6) spent.

[8]   34 Stat. 864.

[9]   57 Stat. 163.

[10]   61 Stat. 136.

[11]   36 Stat. 822.

[12]   37 Stat. 25.

[13]   43 Stat. 1053.

[14]   86 Stat. 3.

[15]   424 U.S. 1 (1976).

[16]   The case was heard on November 10, 1975, and John Paul Stevens did not take his seat on the court until December 19.

[17]   369 U.S. 186 (1962).

[18]   377 U.S. 533.

[19]   *Buckley v. Valeo,* 424 U.S. 54 (1976).

[20]   *Buckley v. Valeo,* 424 U.S. 48–49 (1976).

[21]   *Buckley v. Valeo,* 424 U.S. 25 (1976).

[22]   *Buckley v. Valeo,* 424 U.S. 54 (1976) at Footnote 52.

[23]   90 Stat. 47.

[24]   11 CFR 9031–9039; 11 CFR 110.8.

[25]   Pub. L 107–155.

[26]   Ansolabehere, Stephen and James M. Snyder, Jr. 2000. "Soft Money, Hard Money, Strong Parties." *Columbia Law Review* 100(3): 598–619. p. 605.

[27]   *McConnell v. Federal Election Commission,* 540 U.S. 93 (2003).

[28]   *Federal Election Commission v. Wisconsin Right to Life, Inc.,* 551 U.S. 449 (2007).

[29]   *Citizens United v. Federal Election Commission,* 558 U.S. 310 (2010).

[30]   *Davis v. Federal Election Commission,* 554 U.S. 724 (2008).

[31]   *McCutcheon v. Federal Election Commission,* 572 U.S. 185 (2014).

[32]   11 CFR 100.5.

[33]   11 CFR 114.5.

[34]   11 CFR 114.1(i).

[35]   11 CFR 114.6.

[36]   11 CFR 100.52.

[37]   11 CFR 110.1.

[38]   11 CFR 110.1.

[39] 11 CFR 110.1(b)(3).

[40] 11 CFR 102.9(a)(1).

[41] 11 CFR 110.4.

[42] 11 CFR 110.10.

[43] 11 CFR 100.82.

[44] 11 CFR 100.52.

[45] 11 CFR 114.2.

[46] 11 CFR 110.20.

[47] 11 CFR 110.20(a)(3).

[48] 11 CFR 113.1(g).

[49] 11 CFR 113.1(g)(1) A–J.

[50] 11 CFR 113.1(g).

[51] 11 CFR 102.9(b)(1).

[52] *Citizens United v. Federal Election Commission*, 558 U.S. 310 (2010).

[53] See *Speechnow.org v. FEC*, 599 F.3d 686 (D.C. Cir. 2010).

[54] *Speechnow.org v. FEC*, 599 F.3d 686 (D.C. Cir. 2010).

[55] 479 U.S. 238 (1986).

[56] 551 U.S. 449 (2007).

[57] According to the National Council of State Legislatures.

[58] Hawaii Revised Statutes 2: 11–362.

[59] Wallace, Ben. 2018. "A Vote against State Nonresident Contribution Limits." *Louisiana Law Review* 78(2): 598–630.

[60] Bartels Larry. 2008. *Unequal Democracy: The Political Economy of the New Golden Age.* New York: Russell Sage.

[61] Jacobson Gary. 2013. *The Politics of Congressional Elections.* New York: Pearson. 8th Ed.

[62] Kahn Kim F. and Patrick Kenney. 1999. *The Spectacle of U.S. Senate Campaigns.* Princeton, NJ: Princeton Univ. Press.

[63] La Raja, Raymond J. and Brian F. Schaffner. 2015. *Campaign Finance and Political Polarization: When Purists Prevail.* Ann Arbor: University of Michigan Press.

[64] Boatright, Robert, Michael J. Malbin, and Brendan Glavin. 2016. "Independent expenditures in congressional primaries after Citizens United: Implications for interest groups, incumbents and political parties." *Interest Groups & Advocacy.* 5(2)119–14.

CHAPTER 8

Casting, Counting, and Recounting

A. ELECTION DAY

Election Day has arrived, and with it, a host of important election rules come to the forefront. While we previously discussed the right to vote, there are a number of rules which determine how and when individuals cast their ballot. States across the country currently use a wide array of balloting methods, some still hand-counting paper ballots, and others using new electronic voting technology. While many voters will cast their ballots at the polls on Election Day, a growing number will vote early. Early voting and vote-by-mail elections are becoming more common, adding to older and more common methods of absentee voting. Once ballots are cast, winners must be determined. As simple a task as this might seem, states and localities utilize different voting systems, electing candidates who win through electoral pluralities, or electoral majorities. Runoff elections may occur in some jurisdictions, sometimes weeks after Election Day, and sometimes instantly through new ranked choice voting systems. Election authorities will tally the votes in their respective jurisdictions in different ways, and candidates and voters who are displeased with the results have varying rights to election recounts and audits. This chapter will explore the diverse array of casting, counting, and recounting votes to see how rules matter in this final act of the election year.

B. VOTING SYSTEMS

One of the most basic characteristics of an election is the type of voting system that is used. While we might just think that the candidate with the most votes wins, this perception oversimplifies the range of possibilities for declaring a winner. While it is true that winning candidates often receive more votes than the other candidates, this mere fact is not always enough to win an election. In some cases, an objective standard, such as a majority, must be reached in order to be declared the winner. This may require multiple rounds of voting. Sometimes, multiple rounds, or ranked choice voting, may mean that the candidate who received the most votes in the initial round of voting ends up losing the election. We may also, rather than declare a single winner, want to declare multiple winners. This section will look at some of the various voting systems in use throughout the country.

1. Plurality Voting

Plurality voting, or first-past-the-past voting, is perhaps the simplest of all voting methods. Under this method, the candidate with the most votes is declared the winner, regardless of the specific percentage of the vote garnered by the candidate. While there are some disadvantages to plurality voting, such as the fact that more candidates might vote *against* a winning candidate than for them, its simplicity makes it a common choice for voting systems. Another common criticism of the plurality system is the probability that a third candidate might play a spoiler role. Since no candidate is required to win a majority, and since there is no runoff election in a plurality system, a third candidate that can draw enough support from one of the two top candidates could swing the election. This is commonly called the spoiler effect.

Plurality voting is used in Congressional elections in the United States, as well as in a number of state races. Interestingly, while the Electoral College requires a majority of electoral votes, individual states generally allot their electoral votes on a plurality basis.

2. Majority Voting and Two Round Systems

Up to now, we have only discussed voting systems that generate a winner from a single round of voting. There are, however, voting systems that allow for multiple rounds of voting. Why would multiple rounds of voting be required? Perhaps instead of wanting to declare a plurality winner, we want to set the bar at an absolute majority. If we have a race with only two candidates, we will be guaranteed to see a majority winner, however, if there are more candidates in the race, a single election is not guaranteed to produce a majority result. Thus, in order to guarantee a majority winner in an election, two-round systems eliminate all but the top two candidates and then proceed to have a second election at a later date between the top two candidates.

Two-round systems in the American context are often called runoff elections. While not found everywhere, runoff elections are an interesting regional feature of southern politics in the United States. Because of the one-party nature of the south, there was a desire to avoid plurality election in primaries, as this was the only meaningful election in these states.[1] In Arkansas, the runoff system was ostensibly created to avoid the nomination of a Ku Klux Klan-supported candidate. Often these candidates could gather a small plurality of the vote, but runoff systems allowed for a second round of voting, wherein an anti-Klan majority could emerge.[2]

Today, a number of states continue to use runoff primary elections, including Alabama, Arkansas, Georgia, Mississippi, North Carolina, Oklahoma, South Carolina, and Texas. With the exception of North Carolina, which has a 40 percent threshold, all of these states require a candidate to gain 50 percent or more in order to avoid a runoff election. South Dakota also has a runoff law, but only requires a candidate to receive 35 percent of the vote to be elected, thus, runoffs are rare. Perhaps even rarer are Vermont runoffs, which only occur if the primary results in a tie.[3]

Louisiana operates a majority system wherein the November general election operates as an open primary. A runoff election is then contested in December in order to determine a winner. The Electoral College is also a majoritarian system, however, a runoff does not occur in the case of a tie, as explained in Chapter 6.

One of the problems with majority voting, and in particular, two-round voting systems, is the cost and difficulty of administering two separate elections. However, there are voting systems that can allow for a majority winner to emerge in just a single round of voting.

3.   Ranked Choice

Ranked choice voting is a term that encompasses a number of different voting systems that rely on a ranking of candidates in order to determine a winner. Utilizing this voting system can ensure that the election winner will receive a majority of the votes, even when there are more than two candidates. When one individual is being elected (as opposed to multi-member districts, discussed in the next section), ranked choice voting is commonly called instant runoff voting or the alternative vote. Instant-runoff voting (IRV) ballots contain all of the candidates for a particular office. Voters rank order their choices rather than selecting one candidate. Under some rule systems, voters are required to rank all candidates, whereas in others, they are allowed to stop when they no longer prefer any of the candidates.

Ranked choice ballots are counted in an instant-runoff system by first tallying the first preferences of all voters. It may be the case that one candidate is able to amass a majority of the votes in this initial round of counting. If so, the candidate with the majority is declared the winner and counting ends. If no candidate is able to gather a majority of the votes, we then begin the instant-runoff process by eliminating the candidate who is in last place, and then redistribute those votes to voters' second choices. Since voters rank-ordered all of the candidates on one ballot, this second round of counting can take place without a second round of voting, hence the name, instant runoff. If, after this redistribution of votes, a candidate has the requisite majority of votes, that candidate is declared the winner and the election ends. Again, if no candidate gains a majority of the votes, the candidate with the next fewest votes is eliminated, and their votes redistributed. The table below shows how an instant-runoff voting system might proceed through four rounds to declare a winner. In this case, there are four candidates from two parties and one independent candidate. We will assume that partisans from the Teal and Bronze parties both prefer the candidates of their party first, the independent candidate third, and opt not to rank the opposing party candidates. We will also assume that independent voters prefer the Teal candidates evenly, that is to say, half of the independent voters prefer Candidate A as a second choice, and the other half prefer Candidate B. While any number of other preferences may arise in a real-world scenario, the underlying process does not change.

TABLE 8.1   SIMPLE INSTANT-RUNOFF VOTING EXAMPLE

Cand.	Party	Round 1	Transfer	Round 2	Transfer	Round 3	Transfer	Round 4	Result
A	Teal	320	0	320	80	400	250	650	Elected
B	Teal	170	0	170	80	250	−250	Eliminated	Eliminated
C	Independent	160	0	160	−160	Eliminated	---	---	Eliminated
D	Bronze	250	100	350	0	350	0	350	Lost
E	Bronze	100	−100	Eliminated	---	---	---	---	Eliminated

As we can see from this example, no candidate has a majority of the 1000 votes needed for election (501 votes). Candidate E has the fewest votes in the initial round of voting and is eliminated. Candidate E's votes are then redistributed to those voters' second choice, the remaining Bronze party candidate (Candidate D). In the second round, we still do not have a majority winner, so the independent candidate (who now has the fewest number of votes) is eliminated. The independent voters' votes are now distributed to those voters' second choices—half for Candidate A, and half for B. In the third round, we still cannot declare a winner, so candidate B is eliminated, and those votes are transferred to B-voters' second choice, Candidate A, who finally crosses the majority threshold with 650 votes, and is declared the winner.

As we can see from this example, the final winner was the same candidate who garnered a plurality of the vote in the first round, however, it is entirely plausible that instant runoff voting will produce winners that differ from the candidates who lead after the first round of voting. Let's now imagine that the independent voters in our example, who previously supported teal candidates, now support Bronze party candidates. While the first rounds remain the same, independent voters put their support behind candidate D in the third round, which gives the Bronze party candidate enough votes for a majority. Here, ranked-choice voting has given us a winner that is different from the one that would emerge under simple plurality voting.

TABLE 8.2 ALTERNATIVE SIMPLE INSTANT-RUNOFF VOTING EXAMPLE

Candidate	Party	Round 1	Transfer	Round 2	Transfer	Round 3	Result
A	Teal	320	0	320	0	320	Lost
B	Teal	170	0	170	0	170	Lost
C	Independent	160	0	160	−160	160	Eliminated
D	Bronze	250	100	350	160	510	Elected
E	Bronze	100	−100	Eliminated	Eliminated	Eliminated	Eliminated

In what way are these two scenarios important for elections? To think about a concrete example, let's consider a race with only two candidates, in which a third-party candidate enters the race. A notable example of this, in presidential elections, is the 1912 election between Roosevelt, Taft, and Wilson. Roosevelt, who sought and lost the Republican presidential nomination to Taft, entered the race as a third-party candidate for the Progressive party. This had the effect of splitting (or, more commonly, 'spoiling') the Republican Party vote, and allowing Wilson to win the presidency. While presidential elections have an added layer of complexity with the Electoral College, let's assume for now that we will declare our winner based on the outcome of the popular vote. In 1912, none of the three candidates received a majority of the popular vote in the first round.[4]

TABLE 8.3 1912 POPULAR VOTE RESULTS
UNDER TRANSFERRABLE VOTE

	Round 1	Transfer	Round 2	Result
Taft	4,119,207	3,483,922	7,603,129	Winner
Roosevelt	3,483,922	−3,483,922	Eliminated	Eliminated
Wilson	6,293,152	0	6,293,152	Loser
Total	13,896,281			
Majority	6,948,142			

Under plurality rules, Wilson would be declared the winner in this race. However, under instant-runoff rules, Roosevelt would be eliminated, and his votes would be transferred to (presumably) Taft. Now, Taft is able to garner a majority of the popular vote and be elected. One of the most compelling features of ranked choice voting and instant runoff voting systems is their ability to prevent spoiler candidates, as this example shows.

In addition to proceeding through multiple rounds of calculation, there are two methods that can be used to conduct a compressed version of ranked voting. One method is by using batch elimination. Batch elimination calls for the simultaneous elimination of candidates once their election becomes mathematically impossible. Mathematical impossibility is usually calculated by determining whether or not it is possible for a candidate to overtake the next highest candidate if they were to win the transferred votes of all candidates behind them. This method of elimination saves time but yields the same result as performing sequential rounds of elimination. An alternative to this is to eliminate all but the top-two candidates. This system has various names including top two IRV, the contingent vote and the double-choice primary, and can lead to an outcome that would be different under sequential elimination. Top-two IRV is rarely used, and was only used for a short time in the United States in a handful of states including Alabama, Florida, and Louisiana.[5] Alabama experimented with the system after a 1915 law was passed to eliminate their traditional runoff primary and conduct an instant runoff between the top two candidates.[6] After disappointing results (one account noted 130,814 votes for a first choice, but only 34,668 votes for a second choice[7]) the system was eliminated.

Today, instant runoff voting is used in a number of jurisdictions, including some in the United States. Most often, it is used in local elections, as it is in

Oakland, San Francisco, St. Paul, Minnesota, and others.[8] In 2018, Maine became the first state to use instant runoff voting statewide, although in its first year of use, it only applied to primary elections and general elections for U.S. House and Senate. This was due to a conflict with the state constitution, which mandated that state officials were to be elected by a plurality vote.[9]

4. Multiple Winners

Voting systems can also be created to yield multiple winners. For instance, consider an imaginary city council with members elected at-large. Let's assume that in this election, three members must be elected to the council, which has elections on a rotating cycle. Rather than a ward or district system where one winner would emerge from each individual district, these city council members are elected at-large, so the election must yield three winners. How, then, would the city organize its elections to ensure that three winners emerge?

Perhaps the simplest system one could imagine is one where each voter casts one ballot, and the three candidates with the most votes would win. This is commonly called single voting, or single non-transferable voting. Consider a two-party election with five candidates vying for three spots. There are 1,000 voters in our imaginary city, and we know the underlying partisan breakdown to be 600 Teal party voters, and 400 Bronze party voters. Our imaginary election outcomes might look like the following:

TABLE 8.4 SIMPLE MULTIPLE-WINNER CITY COUNCIL ELECTION

Candidate	Party	Votes	Elected
A	Teal	300	X
B	Teal	200	X
C	Teal	100	
D	Bronze	250	X
E	Bronze	150	

Here, we see two Teal candidates elected, and two Bronze candidates elected. This proportion of representation represents the 60/40 split in our city as fairly as possible. However, let's consider an example where the Teal party has a more crowded field of candidates. In this election, there are seven candidates for three spots, and the Teal party fields five candidates. They split the vote and end up with an unrepresentative result.

TABLE 8.5   MULTIPLE-WINNER CITY COUNCIL ELECTION (CROWDED)

Candidate	Party	Votes	Elected
A	Teal	150	
B	Teal	250	X
C	Teal	75	
D	Teal	100	
E	Teal	25	
F	Bronze	175	X
G	Bronze	225	X

In this example, the Teal party has fragmented their vote to the point where the Bronze party, with only two candidates, was able to capture two seats to Teal's one seat. Since we know that the Teal party is a majority, this result seems unfair.

We may try to counteract this problem by allowing our voters to each vote for three candidates (commonly called block voting or multiple non-transferable vote). However, this can cause other problems that lead to disproportionate results. If the Teal party can be sure to limit its field of candidates to three, as in the first example, they are likely to each receive 600 votes. Bronze candidates would only receive 400 votes each and the three Teal candidates will sweep the election (even if Bronze had only one candidate, that candidate cannot receive more than one vote per voter, so long as they have a number of candidates at or below the number of seats, we can assume they will only receive 400 votes). Moreover, this does not solve the problem of a party fragmenting the vote with too many candidates.

Our solution to this problem comes in the form of the transferable vote. Single transferable vote or STV voting is a form of ranked choice voting where voters can rank order their choices of candidates. Returning to our original example, if we assume that individual will create a rank ordering that prefers candidates of their own party, we would likely see the same result. Here, candidate C is eliminated because they have the lowest vote total. Supporters of candidate C ranked other Teal candidates second, so those votes are added to their totals (mathematically it would not matter which candidate, A or B, received the support of the 100 candidate C supporters, because A and B would still have a vote total larger than E, the next candidate to be eliminated). Next, candidate E is eliminated, and presumably, those votes are transferred to candidate D, the other

Bronze candidate. Having only three remaining candidates, the election concludes, and candidates A, B, and D are elected.

TABLE 8.6   SINGLE TRANSFERRABLE VOTE— SIMPLE CITY COUNCIL ELECTION

Candidate	Party	Round 1	Transfer	Round 2	Transfer	Round 3	Elected
A	Teal	300	+50	350	0	350	X
B	Teal	200	+50	250	0	250	X
C	Teal	100	−0	0	0	0	
D	Bronze	250	0	250	+150	400	X
E	Bronze	150	0	150	−150	0	

Let us see what happens in our second example where the Teal party fractured their vote:

TABLE 8.7   SINGLE TRANSFERRABLE VOTE— CITY COUNCIL ELECTION, CROWDED FIELD

Cand.	Party	Round 1	Transfer	Round 2	Transfer	Round 3	Transfer	Round 4	Transfer	Round 5	Elected
A	Teal	150	+25	175	+50	225	+75	300	0	300	X
B	Teal	250	0	250	0	250	+75	325	0	325	X
C	Teal	75	0	75	−75	0	0	0	0	0	
D	Teal	100	0	100	+50	150	−150	0	0	0	
E	Teal	25	−25	0	0	0	0	0	0	0	
F	Bronze	175	0	175	0	175	0	175	−175	0	
G	Bronze	225	0	225	0	225	0	225	+175	400	X

In this example, it took four transfers to resolve the election, but we end up with a result that is in proportion to the underlying partisanship of our city. The simple transfers here allowed candidates that voted for more unpopular Teal candidates to switch their votes to the more popular Teal candidates. Take note that the transfers here are arbitrary and assume that voters will switch to another candidate of their party. In this example, the transfers could be split in a number of other ways that would yield the same result. This is not to say that single-transferable vote with a simple transfer method like this solves all problems that arise when voting for multiple candidates. Let's imagine one more scenario where Teal, rather than having a few candidates that are roughly equal in popularity (and that roughly split transferred votes as above), has one extremely popular candidate and others which are much less popular.

TABLE 8.8   SINGLE TRANSFERRABLE VOTE—CITY COUNCIL ELECTION, ONE POPULAR CANDIDATE (PART 1)

Candidate	Party	Round 1	Transfer	Round 2	Transfer	Round 3
A	Teal	150	0	150	0	150
B	Teal	250	+25	275	+75	350
C	Teal	75	0	75	−75	0
D	Teal	100	0	100	0	100
E	Teal	25	−25	0	0	0
F	Bronze	175	0	175	0	175
G	Bronze	225	0	225	0	225

As we can see, after only two transfers, if Candidate B is much more popular than the other Teal candidates, they might sweep the transfer vote and begin to amass an unnecessarily high number of votes. As the election resolves, Teal only elects one council member, and Bronze elects 2, another disproportionate result.

TABLE 8.9   SINGLE TRANSFERRABLE VOTE—CITY COUNCIL ELECTION, ONE POPULAR CANDIDATE (PART 2)

Candidate	Party	Round 3	Transfer	Round 4	Transfer	Round 5	Elected
A	Teal	150	0	0	−150	0	
B	Teal	350	+100	450	+150	600	X
C	Teal	0	0	0	0	0	
D	Teal	100	−100	0	0	0	
E	Teal	0	0	0	0	0	
F	Bronze	175	0	175	175	175	X
G	Bronze	225	0	225	225	225	X

This election has yielded a number of wasted votes for the Teal party, and has allowed the Bronze party to take a majority of the council seats. One way to counteract this would be with a more sophisticated transfer mechanism. If the goal of transferring votes is to avoid wasted votes, why not continue to transfer votes once a candidate is guaranteed election? To do this, we only need to calculate some minimum number of votes that would guarantee a win. We might instinctively say that if we are electing three seats, then we would just need to divide the total votes by the number of seats to know how many votes would be enough to guarantee election. This is referred to as the Hare quota, (named for Thomas Hare, a British proponent of single transferable vote) and while it is true that 333 (rounding down) votes would guarantee election in this example, it is not the *minimum* number of seats that would guarantee election for three candidates. Rather, taking the total number of votes, and dividing by the number of seats, plus one, and adding one vote to that result, we would get the minimum number of votes that three candidates could equally receive, while ensuring a fourth candidate could not reach the quota. In this example, the minimum quota would be 251 votes—this is often referred to as the Droop quota (after mathematician H.R. Droop). Three candidates could each receive 251 votes, for a total of 753 votes. The remainder, 247 votes, would not be enough for a fourth candidate to reach the quota (to see how the Hare method would be different, imagine three candidates with 333 votes, this would mean that a fourth candidate would have one vote—in this sense it is the maximum number, rather than minimum, that three candidates would have to win an election). A simple scenario shows us why this quota can be an important factor in transferring votes. Rather than looking at aggregate vote totals, let's look at groups of vote preferences first.

TABLE 8.10 PREFERENCE ORDERING

Teal Party				Bronze Party		
A Voters	**B Voters**	**C Voters**	**D Voters**	**E Voters**	**F Voters**	**G Voters**
400 Votes	290 Votes	40 Votes	30 Votes	180 Votes	40 Votes	20 Votes
A	B	C	D	E	F	G
B	A	A	C	F	E	E
C	C	B	A	G	G	F
D	D	D	B	X	X	X

In this example, there are 1000 total votes. The Teal party has a majority of voter support with 760 of the total votes possible. Teal runs four candidates, and each of their supporters has a different preference ranking. The Bronze party has 240 votes total and has fielded three candidates. Looking at the simpler Hare quota (333) we can immediately elect A. Candidate A's excess votes are then transferred to candidate B who is also immediately elected, with their excess votes being transferred to candidate C. At this point, no candidate has the required quota so the lowest candidate (G) is eliminated. This elimination does not yield an election, so D, and in the next round, F, are subsequently eliminated. In the next round, C is eliminated, and with no active candidate to transfer those votes to, the only remaining candidate, E is elected. Thus, A, B, and E are elected, with Teal winning two seats, and Bronze winning one.

TABLE 8.11 HARE QUOTA EXAMPLE

Cand.	Round 1	Transfer	Round 2	Transfer	Round 3	Transfer	Round 4	Transfer	Round 5	Transfer	Round 6	Transfer	Result
A	400	−67	Elected	Elected	Elected	Elected	Elected	Elected	Elected	Elected	Elected	Elected	Elected
B	290	+67	357	−24	Elected	Elected	Elected	Elected	Elected	Elected	Elected	Elected	Elected
C	40	0	40	+24	64	0	64	+30	94	0	94	−94	Eliminated
D	30	0	30	0	30	0	30	−30	Eliminated	---	---	---	Eliminated
E	180	0	180	0	180	+20	200	0	200	+40	240	Elected	Elected
F	40	0	40	0	40	0	40	0	40	−40	---	---	Eliminated
G	20	0	20	0	20	−20	Eliminated	---	---	---	---	---	Eliminated

Changing our quota to the Droop method, we can again immediately elect A and after transferring excess votes, B. At this point we must begin to eliminate candidates as no candidate meets the quota. First, we eliminate G, and with no candidate meeting the quota, proceed to eliminate D. With the transfer of D's votes to C, they are elected, giving Teal all three seats—a decisive victory through no change in the actual votes.

TABLE 8.12 DROOP QUOTA EXAMPLE

	Round 1	Transfer	Round 2	Transfer	Round 3	Transfer	Round 4	Transfer	Result
A	400	−149	Elected	Elected	Elected	Elected	Elected	Elected	Elected
B	290	+149	439	−188	Elected	Elected	Elected	Elected	Elected
C	40	0	40	+188	228	0	228	+30	Elected (258)
D	30	0	30	0	30	0	30	−30	Eliminated
E	180	0	180	0	180	+20	200	0	Eliminated (200)
F	40	0	40	0	40	0	40	0	Eliminated (40)
G	20	0	20	0	20	−20	Eliminated	Eliminated	Eliminated

While the Hare quota was common in early days of STV, most jurisdictions that use single transferable vote now use the Droop method of calculating vote quotas. While the Droop method minimizes wasted votes, in the sense that winning candidates only need to cross a minimum threshold, it also advantages the majority party as shown in this example.

The determination of quotas is not the only factor that can alter outcomes in transferable-vote systems. There are a number of other considerations that come into play, including how votes are transferred to other candidates, and how votes are transferred to winning candidates once they have crossed the threshold. For example, after all ballots are counted, and a candidate meets a quota, *which* ballots are transferred to other candidates? In real-world scenarios, preference orderings are not as simple as those presented here, and supporters of a candidate could have different second or third preferences. How, then, do we determine which ballots will be counted for the first-choice candidate and be counted in their total, and which ballots will be transferred to other candidates. Some methods suggest a random drawing of ballots, however, more modern ballot tabulating technology can allow us to calculate the total of all voters' second and third choices and allocate votes proportionately (this often leads to fractions of votes being transferred). In addition to this, decisions must be made with regard to whether or not votes are transferred to candidates who have already won election, and then subsequently re-transferred, or merely transferred to a voter's next choice, skipping any candidates who have already won. All of these decisions are made when forming a voting system and have an incredibly important impact on the outcome of elections.

C. BALLOTING METHODS

As odd as it may seem, Federal law is relatively silent on the matter of balloting in U.S. elections. As we have seen in other areas, this has led to a patchwork of methods for casting ballots across the country. Even within states, there is little uniformity in ballot technology, with some states utilizing both hand-counted paper ballots, as well as electronic voting systems with no physical record. The earliest elections in America were conducted by a public voice vote, with citizens loudly announcing their candidate of choice in front of an election judge. While some states continued to use voice voting until the middle part of the nineteenth century, paper balloting had been on the ascendancy since the American Revolution.[10]

Early forms of paper balloting included written and pre-printed ballots. Sometimes these ballots were printed by the candidates themselves, in order to ensure that voters would correctly cast their ballot, and not have their vote disqualified for illegibility or because of their own illiteracy.[11] With the increased organization of parties, full party tickets would become the norm throughout the country. The party ticket was, simply, a preprinted ballot with the names of all of a party's candidates on it. Voters could cast a straight-ticket vote by placing the party ticket in the ballot box. Split-ticket voting was a more difficult process, entailing the cutting and pasting of party ballots into a new fusion ballot that the voter could then cast.[12]

Party tickets themselves were usually easily identifiable, printed on unique colored papers, or on papers of easily distinguishable size. These features continued to render voting a highly public process, subject to fraud or intimidation. Indeed, some unscrupulous individuals would print the names of candidates of one party on paper that resembled the ballots of another party in order to confuse illiterate voters.[13] While some states began to intervene by regulating the appearance of party tickets, these rules were often ineffectual and did little to remedy the defects of party tickets. In many states, white was prescribed as the color for all ballots, however, parties would print on paper of slightly different shades of white (cream, or bright white, for example).[14] Another example of the early regulation of balloting was the advent of clear glass ballot boxes. While these innovations may have made it harder to stuff the ballot box, they did little to counter corruption in the counting of ballots.[15]

The sea change in balloting would take place with the eventual adoption of the Australian ballot, or the secret ballot. Taking its name from its place of origin, the Australian ballot was a system wherein the state would print ballots with the names of all candidates. Voters would then mark or indicate their choice of candidate when they cast their vote. These ballots were generally printed in one of two forms, the office block ballot, or the party column ballot. With the office block ballot, a voter must read each candidate's name or party affiliation and select their choice for that office. The party column ballot easily arranged these choices, allowing for easy straight-ticket voting. While these methods saw parity in the early years of the Australian ballot, many more states later opted to use party column ballots, easing the burden of voting for illiterate voters.[16]

FIGURE 8.1 OFFICE BLOCK AND PARTY COLUMN BALLOTS

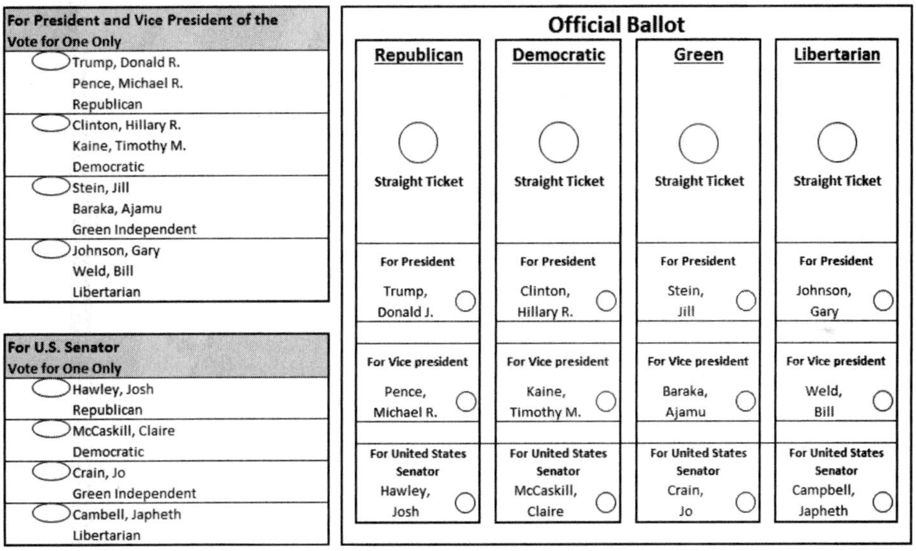

What would come over the next century, would be a number of innovations in voting technologies, from mechanical voting machines to machine-read punch card ballots. Today, the country is a laboratory for testing different ballot systems. The vast majority of states use one of two systems, optical scan ballots, or direct-recording electronic (or DRE) devices. Optical scan ballots are paper ballots where voters use one of a number of methods to designate their vote. These paper ballots are then read by an optical scanner. DRE devices are the modern version of older mechanical voting machines, substituting a computer and touchscreen for gears and levers. Each system comes with its own benefits and shortfalls.

1. Hand Counted Paper Balloting

The simplest method for casting and counting ballots is the hand-counted paper ballot. While few jurisdictions continue to perform hand counts, recounts, audits, and counts of absentee ballots are still sometimes conducted by hand.[17] Proponents of hand counts note that there are far fewer opportunities for fraud or corruption (assuming that the count is conducted publicly) than with newer electronic voting methods. One recent study, however, showed significant limitations in the accuracy hand counts, and cited the potential for an error of up to two percent depending on the counting method.[18]

Two methods are commonly used to count paper ballots, read-and-mark, and sort-and-stack.[19] In the read-and-mark system, one team of counters looks at the paper ballot and calls out each vote aloud. A second team makes a hash mark or similar tally for each vote, and those marks are then added up to determine the total number of votes for each candidate and race. In the sort-and-stack method, ballots are sorted into stacks depending on the vote for a particular office that is being counted (meaning only one race is counted at a time). Ballots can be stacked crosswise in a particular multiple for ease of counting, or a tally sheet can be used. These methods are illustrative of the types of systems used to hand count, but the specific procedures are often more complicated and involve multiple readers and counters, and multiple checks to verify accurate counting.[20]

To be sure, hand counting paper ballots is one of the simplest ways to tally election results, but in large jurisdictions, the labor involved can be prohibitive. Further, hand counting requires strict controls over the physical ballots themselves, and cautious oversight of those who count ballots. It is precisely these weaknesses that caused the initial departure from hand-counted ballots and the emergence of the mechanical voting machine.

2. Direct Recording

Direct recording electronic (DRE) devices are a second category of balloting methods. These devices include older mechanical devices, as well as newer electronic voting machines. With these devices, the key distinction is that voters cast their ballot through the machine, and the count is tallied internally, rather than having a multi-step system of casting a ballot and separately counting that ballot.

The earliest direct recording devices were mechanical voting machines. These machines appeared around the turn of the twentieth century, and while New York is frequently associated with these machines, they were widely used across the country. These machines were a collection of switches, gears, and levers which directly tallied votes. Voters would turn a large lever to one side in order to initialize the machine, and then designate their choices by flipping the switches next to their desired candidates. These switches would engage odometer-like counters in the mechanism of the machine and would advance the count once the voter turned the large lever back, casting their ballot. The voting machine had the capability to take write-in votes and included protections for overvoting (casting a ballot for more than the allowed number of candidates). In order for a count of the votes to take place, election officials, and often police officers, would unlock the back of the voting machine, revealing rotating counters for each office. It was often the procedure to take a photograph of the counters before reading, counting, and double-checking the votes.

Today's DRE machines are usually touchscreen computer devices that operate in a way very similar to older mechanical voting machines. Voters are presented with the image of a ballot and may indicate their choices on the touchscreen. Internal software then maintains a running count of the votes cast just as the mechanical counters of older machines would. DRE voting machines are often distinguished between their ability to maintain a vote verification system. In election administration parlance, the term VVPAT is used to refer to voter-verifiable paper audit trails. This means that the DRE system creates some sort of paper record of each vote cast on the machine. This allows election officials to have a separate record of the votes cast in the case of an error or the need to conduct an audit or recount. Not all DRE systems are equipped with VVPAT systems.

3. Punch Cards

Another balloting method is the punch card system. A descendant of early systems used for computer programming, the punch card was a heavy paper card where data would be stored by creating (punching out) holes in the card. The cards generally contained small perforated squares that were easily detached from the card using a small metal stylus. These cards could then be read by a tabulating device which would use electrical or light conductance to detect the location of holes in the cards in order to read the data that was punched on the card. The earliest form of this device, the IBM Votomatic, was a device that allowed voters to insert their punch card and punch holes in the appropriate location to indicate their votes.

The election of 2000 brought widespread attention to many problems associated with punch card technology. Specifically, the election highlighted the incidence of incorrectly punched cards. These ballots could be incorrectly marked in a number of ways. Voters might punch a hole that corresponded to the wrong candidate (See image of 2000 ballot). There were concerns that some voters may have incorrectly voted punched their ballot for Pat Buchannan rather than Al Gore because of the confusing placement of names on the ballot.[21] Although Al Gore was listed second on the left half of the ballot, because of the 'butterfly' printing, Pat Buchannan, first on the right, was assigned to the second punch hole, and Gore, the third.

FIGURE 8.2 BUTTERFLY BALLOT

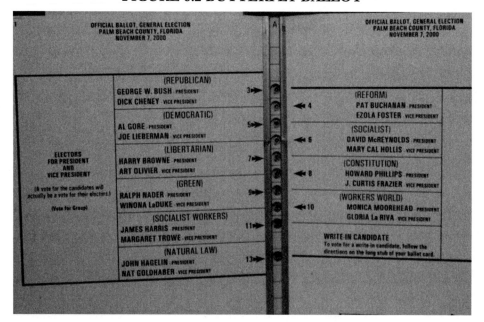

Other ballots might have been incorrectly marked because voters punched too many holes (overvoting) or by not being able to depress the punch with sufficient force to completely detach the perforated segment of the card. The waste pieces of card that were perforated and detached were called 'chad,' and would accumulate in a waste tray below the card holder. If these trays were not regularly emptied, the buildup of chad could prevent the voter from completely depressing the stylus and breaking off the perforated segment of the ballot. A number of creative names were used to describe the condition of the chad on the ballot—it may have been dimpled (still attached to the card but with an imprint of the stylus), or hanging by one, two, or even three of its corners. During the manual recount of the 2000 election results in Florida, election officials had to determine the intent of voters by examining the position of chad on punch cards.

4. Optical Scan

Optical scan ballots have now become the most frequently used paper ballot across the country. Rather than count paper ballots by hand, or have machines read specifically punched cards, optical scan ballots combine the familiarity of a hand-marked ballot with the efficiency of a machine-read punch card. Optical Scan ballots generally take one of two forms, an oval style, or an arrow style. With oval style ballots, voters must completely darken the oval next to their preferred candidate to cast their ballot. With arrow style ballots, voters are required to connect the stub of the arrow to the point of the arrow, filling in the missing part of the shape.

FIGURE 8.3 OVAL AND ARROW BALLOT INDICATORS

Candidate A ⬭   Candidate A ◀ ■

Candidate B ⬭   Candidate B ◀▬

Candidate C ⬭   Candidate C ◀ ■

Once the ballot is marked by the voter, it can either be placed into a ballot box to be counted later at a central counting location or in some instances, the ballot is placed into an optical scan reader and counted at the voting precinct. If the ballots are scanned at the precinct, the paper ballot is still collected in a ballot box to be saved as a record of the vote. Ballot scanning devices are able to detect marks on the ballot and can automatically tally all votes for a given candidate.

In addition to being able to mark these ballots by hand, some locations that use optical scan ballots are equipped with automated ballot marking devices. In the wake of the Help America Vote Act of 2002, efforts were made to make optical scan balloting more accessible for individuals who were unable to mark their ballot by themselves. Ballot marking devices allow individuals to use a number of different adaptive devices, such as a touchscreen, keyboard, or sip-puff device to input choices, or headphones to hear the ballot read aloud. Individuals who need assistance in marking their ballots can insert their paper ballot into the machine, use the necessary adaptive devices to select their choices, and the machine will make the appropriate marks on the paper ballot. The ballot is then removed from the device and the individual is able to cast their ballot through the optical scan device or into the ballot box.

In addition to the aforementioned advantages of simple design and efficient tabulation, optical scan ballots also provide an important physical paper trail which can allow for meaningful recounts of election results. Additionally, if optical scan devices fail, ballots remain intact and voting can continue uninterrupted. One caveat to these advantages is the need for important safety protocols and chain-of-custody procedures to ensure the integrity of the ballots as they are transported for tabulation, or as they are being recounted.

5.   Spoiled Ballots

While the vast majority of ballots are cast without incident, there are cases where individuals do not cast a vote. Some individuals may simply decline to cast a ballot for a specific race, however, there are times when voter error can mean a ballot is not counted. Perhaps the most common voter error is a failure to properly mark an optical scan ballot. While direct recording electronic voting machines do not suffer from this defect, optical scan ballots must be properly marked in order for the optical scanner to correctly read and count the ballot. One style of optical scan ballot that suffers from this problem more than others is the 'connect the arrow' ballot. These ballots list candidates and have broken arrows beside the candidate. In order to properly indicate their choice, a voter must darken the portion of the arrow between the point and the stump.

FIGURE 8.4 CONNECT THE ARROW BALLOT

Below are four different ways that an individual might attempt to designate their choice. In the top left example, the voter simply marked their vote with an X, in the top right they circled the entire arrow, in the bottom left, the voter mistook the 'stump' of the arrow for a checkbox, and in the bottom right, the voter correctly connected the two parts of the arrow.

FIGURE 8.5 DIFFERENT MARKINGS OF
CONNECT THE ARROW BALLOT

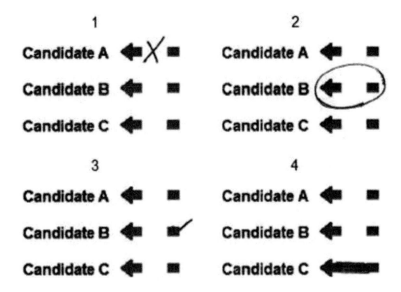

In all of these cases, an observer might note that the voter's intention is clear. There are no confusing, duplicate, or stray marks, however, an optical scan machine would likely designate ballots 1–3 as undervotes, meaning that the computer did not detect a valid vote, and only count ballot number four as valid. One study directly linked an increased incidence of undervotes to use of the connect-the-arrow ballot.[22]

This is not to say that 'connect the arrow' ballots are the only ones to suffer from potential voter errors. Any optical scan ballot, even the common 'fill in the bubble' ballots, may be improperly marked by something as simple as a stray mark. If an individual fills in a bubble indicating one choice, and accidentally makes a stray mark in another bubble, the optical scanner may mark that ballot as an invalid overvote, meaning the computer detected too many votes.

One method to counteract improperly marked optical scan ballots is to institute optical scanning at the precinct. If these scanners are properly configured, they can notify voters and election officials immediately that an error is present on the ballot. This notification can allow individuals to request a new ballot and make the appropriate corrections. Unfortunately, when ballots are counted at a central location, this type of error checking and correction is impossible. With few exceptions, such as a manual recount of the election, there is no remedy for spoiled, or rejected ballots, even when the intent of the voter is clear.

D. EARLY, ABSENTEE, AND PROVISIONAL BALLOTS

While most voters will cast a regular ballot on Election Day, a significant number of voters will end up casting early ballots, absentee ballots, or provisional ballots.

Early voting the term used to describe voting performed prior to Election Day. While absentee voting is typically performed before Election Day, early voting is commonly used to describe a process where voters are able to visit voting sites and cast a ballot before the election, rather than needing to apply for either an excuse, or no-excuse absentee ballot which is mailed back in (See Chapter 2 for a larger discussion of absentee voting methods).

Provisional ballots act as a backup or failsafe for voters who encounter difficulty at their polling place on Election Day. In all states, pursuant to the 2002 Help America Vote Act, states must provide provisional ballots to allow voters in certain situations, including when a voter does not appear on the registration list, when they are challenged by an election official, when they do not have appropriate voter identification, or when a polling place is ordered to stay open later than the usual closing time. If states offer Election Day registration, they may not have some of these issues, like a voter's absence from the voting rolls. However, these states may still need to offer provisional ballots in case of other problems, like a voter not having appropriate identification.

There are a number of reasons why a voter may have a problem voting. As mentioned at various points throughout this book, voters must arrive at their appropriate precinct on Election Day having registered to vote, and in some cases, prepared to show some sort of identification. When poll workers attempt to validate the registration and identity of a voter, problems can arise. For various reasons, including administrative or technical errors, a voter's name might not appear on the list of registered voters, even though the voter is correctly registered. Voters, likewise, may have made a mistake by going to the wrong polling place or forgetting the appropriate identification documents. Voters may also be mistaken in their belief that they are registered. If one of these problems arise, rather than deny the voter a ballot, they are given specially marked provisional ballots, which are held separately from regular ballots. After the election, provisional ballots are examined to determine if the issue facing the voter can be reconciled. In some cases, this requires voters to return to an elections office to show the identification they forgot to bring to the polling place. In other cases, states may be able to simply match signatures on the provisional ballot to signatures on voter registration forms to confirm a voter's identity. Once these issues are resolved, the provisional ballot is either cast and added to the vote totals or discarded without being counted. Often, jurisdictions do not start processing provisional ballots until a window of time has elapsed (presumably to allow individuals time to bring any necessary documentation to election officials). Once this window closes, processing these provisional ballots still takes a good deal of time, which can delay the final certification of election results.

E. COUNTING, AUDITING, CERTIFYING

Once the polls close and votes have been cast, it is time for election authorities to count votes. However, the process is not as simple as the vote tallies that we watch on television. What we see on television on election night are vote totals being collected by a number of freelance journalists, commonly called 'stringers' and reported back to reporting agencies like the Associated Press. In addition to these totals, some jurisdictions post unofficial vote totals on state or county websites. This is commonly referred to as election night reporting, and state laws differ as to the nature of what must be reported.

The official count of ballots is usually referred to as a canvass. While each state specifies a different procedure for their canvass of votes, there are a number of procedures which are fairly universal. The process of canvassing votes usually begins at the polling place. Voting machines and balloting equipment must immediately be properly secured when the polling place closes to prevent any further voting. Next, depending on the balloting method used, states might conduct an initial review of ballots in different ways.

In states which use direct recording electronic voting machines, poll workers can reconcile ballots by checking the number of votes cast on the machines against the written record (usually a sign-in sheet or poll book) of how many voters voted. Each individual voting machine will have a record of the votes cast, which can be transferred off of the individual voting machine through the use of specifically designed devices, or via some type of memory card. Depending on state rules, these memory devices can be transported to a central location for tabulation, or tabulated at the precinct, with those tabulated results then being transmitted to central election authorities.

States that utilize paper ballots will perform some similar reconciliation procedure, ensuring that the number of ballots voted, spoiled, and unused, appropriately reflects the number of ballots originally delivered to the polling place. At this point, an initial count of the votes may take place at the precinct, or, in cases where a central count in performed, the optical scan ballots must be secured and transported to these counting sites.

The next procedures typically occur at the county level. Judges, canvassing boards, election boards, or other government bodies will count votes if a central count in performed, or a tabulation of results already prepared by the precincts will begin to take place. Reconciliation procedures or more formal auditing procedures (discussed in an upcoming section) may be used to ensure that all ballots are accounted for. Depending on which elections are being contested (particularly in the case of local elections), some elections will end here, at the county level. When elections involve multiple counties or statewide offices, county governments will then transmit the results of their counts and audits to the appropriate state authority, such as a board of elections, so that the state can tabulate votes and certify the winners of the election. Sometimes these county or state-level canvasses do not take place until a number of days after the election. This can provide time to ensure that all ballots are accounted for, as well as time to process any provisional or absentee ballots.

One the ballots are all counted, we may think that the electoral process has come to an end. However, there are two processes that may still need to take place after Election Day, specifically audits and recounts.

Audits often take place between the end of voting and the certification of the election returns. Audits are procedures that check to ensure that the tabulation of votes was completed accurately and that all voting equipment performed without malfunction on Election Day. Many states have post-election audit procedures in place to verify the results of elections.

A typical audit involves the verification of the vote in a certain number of randomly selected voting precincts. The specific auditing procedures that are available depend on the type of voting technology used. In states with optical scan balloting, post-election audits can include a hand count of ballots in a selected number of precincts. This hand count can then be compared to the optical scan reader count to verify that the scanner performed accurately. In states with VVPAT capable DRE systems, a hand-count of the audit trail can be compared to machine-generated results in order to verify the accurate tabulation of votes. A meaningful audit, however, is not always possible. For example, direct recording electronic voting machines that do not have a paper audit trail leave limited avenues for a meaningful audit of votes. In other words, without some physical record of each individual vote, it is impossible to discern whether or not the voting machine correctly tabulated all of the votes. This is not to say that audits in states with DRE equipment are entirely useless. In South Carolina, for instance, audit procedures involve checking to see that all voting machines were correctly closed and that each individual machine's votes were properly downloaded for tabulation. Audits can also detect errors that may have occurred, alerting election officials to potential problems.[23] Unfortunately, this limited audit capability does not eliminate the possibility that a voting system has failed due to an undetectable software error (or a change in the software under more nefarious circumstances). The ability for an audit to detect these types of changes or errors is entirely reliant on this concept of 'software-independence.'[24]

Best practices for auditing have now begun to focus on the implementation of risk-limiting audits. These audits are so-named because they utilize a statistical method and as well as a determined 'risk limit' to calculate the number of ballots to examine as opposed to an audit method that specifies a flat percentage of ballots. The risk limit in this calculation is simply a pre-determined tolerance or chance that the audit would complete and not detect an incorrect election outcome. Thus, a risk limit can be set at 10%, meaning that there remains a 10% chance that the audit would complete and not detect an incorrect outcome. This is not to say there is always a 10% chance of an incorrect result, but that *if* the original election outcome is wrong, there is a 90% chance that the audit will detect the error and a 10% chance that it will not. The procedure can be adjusted for any level of risk tolerance.

Risk-limiting audits work by either recounting a random sample of ballots until we can be confident in the results of the election (a ballot-polling audit) or by comparing a hand interpretation of a random sample of ballots to their respective machine interpretations until we are confident in the performance of the voting system's interpretation of ballots (a comparison audit). In both cases, the audit examines ballots until one of two outcomes occur—either we reach a level of statistical certainty that the reported outcome is correct, or the audit continues until every vote has been hand counted. The number of ballots that need to be audited to reach any level of statistical certainty is determined by a mathematical formula that is dependent on the number of ballots cast, and the reported margin of victory. Thus, in close races, more ballots will need to be audited to reach our confidence thresholds. Additionally, the ballots that are examined need to be randomly selected to comply with some of the underlying assumptions of probability and sampling.

The actual conduct of a risk-limiting audit involves a repeating sequence of checking ballots, comparing to official results, and calculating our confidence in those results. Risk-limiting audits are adaptable in the sense that we gain statistical confidence in official election results by only counting a small sample of ballots. As ballots are audited and begin to match official counts, statistical formulas suggest to the auditors that we can be confident in the election outcome. Statistically, we will approach a confidence threshold as the audit continues, and, assuming the official results are correct, the audit will end long before a full recount. This adaptability saves valuable election administration resources. Conversely, if audited ballots do not match the official results, the audit procedure will not terminate, and will instead require that more ballots be examined. In such a case, it is possible that we will still reach a level of statistical confidence in the official results once we have examined a larger sample of ballots (perhaps there were some small errors, but not enough to change the outcome of the election). In the case of an incorrect election result, the audit procedure will continue to require the examination of more ballots until a complete hand count of the election has taken place. Thus, an election result is never corrected unless a complete recount takes place.[25]

F. RECOUNTS

Once votes are counted, audited in some cases, and certified, the need for an election recount may arise. These recounts are important in ensuring candidates and voters that the results of an election are accurate. Recounts are governed by state laws, and special requirements must be met in order for a recount to take place. Generally speaking, recounts can be initiated automatically, or a losing candidate may make a formal petition for a recount. Automatic recounts are triggered by the margin of an election. If the results of a race are particularly close, an automatic recount is performed. In most states that allow automatic recounts, the margin between the candidates must be below a fixed percentage, usually .5 percent or smaller in some cases. Alaska, for example, only allows automatic recounts in the case of exact ties.[26]

In addition to automatic recounts, many states allow candidates, voters, or even parties, to petition for a recount if the margin of the race is outside the bounds necessary for an automatic recount. In these cases, the individuals requesting the recount are expected to pay the costs of conducting the recount, however, many states allow for reimbursement if the recount ends up changing the result of the election.

Not all states allow automatic or petition recounts. Hawaii, for example only allows complaints to be filed with the State Supreme Court,[27] which would require evidence that the election result should be challenged.

Recounts usually consist of one of two types of action. Recounts can be done as a retabulation of the votes by machine, or as a manual hand count of ballots. For optical scan balloting methods, a machine recount consists of rescanning all ballots. In the case of a manual recount, this requires election officials to examine each individual ballot. While this is time-consuming, it can address spoiled ballots that machine counting may have been unable to read. One problem with recounts revolves around the voting technology that a state utilizes. As previously mentioned, some states use DRE machines that have no voter-verifiable paper audit trail. This means there is no secondary source or independent record that can be verified in the case of a recount. Machine recounts can still take place by performing a retabulation of the individual machine results, but with these systems a manual recount is impossible.

Once recounts are finished, there are few legal avenues that a losing candidate can pursue. Those that are available are unlikely to be successful unless there is evidence of serious violations of the law.

G. THESE RULES MATTER

The rules which govern the casting, counting, and recounting of votes matter greatly to the operation of our electoral system. Voting methods can have an impact on the determination of specific winners. As mentioned throughout this chapter, counting votes in different ways can yield different winners. Voting methods can also have an impact on the larger political landscape as well. Plurality voting, for example, is often linked to the presence of a two-party system (Duverger's law).[28] It is suggested that this is often the case because supporters of third parties will often strategically vote for a second or third-choice candidate that has a better chance of winning. Thus, by simply choosing to adopt one voting method over another, we can set favorable conditions for the emergence of a specific type of party system.

Ballot design may seem like an aesthetic choice, but as shown here, circles, arrows, and checkmarks can lead to confusion and invalid votes. A good deal of research has examined how ballots can be more efficiently designed in order to minimize the impact of design on election outcomes. One recent study looked at various ballot features and rates of unrecorded votes in order to determine if there were certain features that were more or less likely to cause voters to cast an incomplete ballot. For example, the authors of the study found that 'connect-the-arrow' ballots result in a 15 percent increase in unrecorded votes. Looking at overvotes and undervotes specifically, there was a 413 percent increase in overvotes when using the arrow ballot method.[29] Candidate order on the ballot can also impact elections. One study found that ballot position can have an impact on election results.[30] By merely altering the position of a candidate or an item on a ballot, we can affect the outcome of an election.

Thinking beyond ballot design to balloting methods, there has been a great deal of debate on the relative benefits of specific voting systems. Recently, optical scan devices have seen an increasing number of proponents due to the ability to maintain an auditable, recountable, paper trail. In addition to this, one study on balloting systems found a significant decrease in uncounted ballots when precinct-count optical scan devices were used.[31]

How we choose to cast, count, and recount our ballots should not be a process shrouded in mystery. These rules matter a great deal in ensuring the fairness and legitimacy of our electoral system. Even when ballot systems or voting methods fail us, it is important to have robust procedures in place to audit and potentially recount votes. These procedures can help us to ensure that we can continue to have confidence in our democratic processes.

H. CHAPTER 8 DISCUSSION QUESTIONS

1.   Consider our discussion of plurality versus majority voting systems. Is the majority produced by a two-round system an actual majority, distinct from the plurality that would have emerged otherwise? Consider what happens to voters who supported candidates that are eliminated from the second round of voting. If they choose not to participate, and only supporters of the top two candidates vote, does the two-round process yield a meaningfully different result?

2.   Ranked choice is a relatively new voting system in the American context. Many jurisdictions have been hesitant to experiment with a new voting system due to its complexity and the fact that some voters might be confused by the system. If you were an election administrator, do you think the advantages of ranked choice voting would outweigh the potential downfalls of a new and complicated voting system?

3.   Consider a situation where election official must look at a ballot that was not properly scanned by an optical scan machine. While an improperly filled bubble may suggest the intent of the voter to cast a vote for that candidate, one could imagine a number of different scenarios taking place. Perhaps the bubble only contains an accidental stray mark, or perhaps the voter made a mark and attempted to scratch out the mark, making it look like a filled bubble. Consider the tension between wanting to respect the intent of voters and count all votes,

versus the potential for misinterpreting a voter's intent. Is it worse to throw out a real vote or count an accidental vote? Why do you feel this way?

4.   Some political observers have called for the replacement of DRE voting machines without paper trails. They contend that these machines lack the capability for meaningful audits and recounts. On the other hand, one could argue that jurisdictions do not have the capability to secure and properly count physical paper ballots, and that the invitation for fraud or inaccuracy grows as time elapses after Election Day. Do you think the accuracy and integrity of elections would be better served by moving toward devices that produce auditable and recountable paper records, or towards technology that only stores vote counts digitally (or mechanically, as was in the case of older voting machines)?

---

1   See Key, V.O. 1949. *Southern Politics in State and Nation.* New York: Knopf.

2   Bullock, Chuck and Loch Johnson. 1992. *Runoff Elections in the United States.* Chapel Hill: UNC Press.

3   http://www.ncsl.org/research/elections-and-campaigns/primary-runoffs.aspx http://archive.fairvote.org/?page=2293.

4   Congressional Quarterly, Inc. 1997. *Presidential elections, 1789–1996.* Washington, D.C.: Congressional Quarterly.

5   Tarr, Dave and Bob Benenson. 2012. *Elections A to Z.* Washington: CQ Press.

6   J. Mills Thornton III. 2014. "Alabama Politics, J. Thomas Heflin, and the Expulsion Movement of 1929," *Alabama Review* 67:1. p. 16.

7   Tarr, Dave and Bob Benenson. 2012. *Elections A to Z.* CQ Press; Washington.

8   Ranked Choice Voting Resource Center https://www.rankedchoicevoting.org/where_used.

9   Maine Secretary of State. 2018. Timeline of Ranked-Choice Voting in Maine. https://www.maine.gov/sos/cec/elec/upcoming/pdf/rcvtimeline.pdf.

10   Evans, Eldon Cobb. 1917. *A history of the Australian ballot system in the United States.* Chicago: University of Chicago Press.

11   Jones, Douglas and Barbara Simons. 2012. *Broken Ballots: Will your vote count in the electronic age?* Stanford: CSLI Publications.

12   Brewin, Mark. 2010. "Bonfires, Fistfights, and Roaring Cannons. Election Day and the Creation of Social Capital in the City of Philadelphia." in Social Capital in the City: Community and Civic Life in Philadelphia. ed. Dilworth Richardson. Philadelphia: Temple University Press.

13   Evans, Eldon Cobb. 1917. *A history of the Australian ballot system in the United States.* Chicago: University of Chicago Press.

14   Evans, Eldon Cobb. 1917. *A history of the Australian ballot system in the United States.* Chicago: University of Chicago Press.

15   Jones, Douglas and Barbara Simons. 2012. *Broken Ballots: Will your vote count in the electronic age?* Stanford: CSLI Publications.

16   Jones, Douglas and Barbara Simons. 2012. *Broken Ballots: Will your vote count in the electronic age?* Stanford: CSLI Publications. Also See Ludington, Arthur. 1909. "Present status of ballot laws in the United States." *American Political Science Review* 3: 252–61 for a discussion of early ballot laws.

17   Jones, Douglas and Barbara Simons. 2012. *Broken Ballots: Will your vote count in the electronic age?* Stanford: CSLI Publications.

18   Jones, Douglas and Barbara Simons. 2012. *Broken Ballots: Will your vote count in the electronic age?* Stanford: CSLI Publications.

[19]   Goggin, Stephen N., Michael D.Byrne, and Juan E. Gilbert. 2012. "Post-Election Auditing: Effects of Procedure and Ballot Type on Manual Counting Accuracy, Efficiency, and Auditor Satisfaction and Confidence". *Election Law Journal.* 11(1) 36–51.

[20]   Goggin, Stephen N., Michael D.Byrne, and Juan E. Gilbert. 2012. "Post-Election Auditing: Effects of Procedure and Ballot Type on Manual Counting Accuracy, Efficiency, and Auditor Satisfaction and Confidence". *Election Law Journal.* 11(1) 36–51.

[21]   Wand, Jonathan N., Kenneth W. Shotts, Jasjeet S. Sekhon, Walter R. Mebane, Jr., Michael C. Herron and Henry E. Brady. 2001. "The Butterfly Did It: The Aberrant Vote for Buchanan in Palm Beach County, Florida" *The American Political Science Review* 95(4): 793–810.

[22]   Bullock, Charles S. and M.V. Hood. 2002. One Person—No Vote; One Vote; Two Votes: Voting Methods, Ballot Types, and Undervote Frequency in the 2000 Presidential Election. Social science Quarterly 83: 981–993.

[23]   Buell, D. A., E. Hare, F. Heindel, C. Moore, and B. Zia. 2011. "Auditing a DRE-based election in South Carolina." *Proceedings of the 2011 conference on Electronic voting technology/workshop on trustworthy elections.* August 08–09, 2011, San Francisco, CA.

[24]   Rivest, Ronald R. 2008. "On the notion of 'software independence' in voting systems." *Philosophical Transactions of the Royal Society A.* 366 (1881): 3759–3767.

[25]   See Lindeman Mark and Philip B. Stark. B. 2012. "A gentle introduction to risk-limiting audits." *IEEE Security & Privacy* (5): 42–49. For a more comprehensive discussion of risk-limiting audits.

[26]   Alaska Statutes § 15.20.430.

[27]   Hawaii Revised Statutes 11–172.

[28]   Duverger M. 1963. *Political Parties: Their Organization and Activity in the Modern State.* New York: Wiley. Also see Duverger, Maurice. 1972. *Party Politics and Pressure Groups.* New York: Thomas Y. Crowell.

[29]   Kimball, David C., and Martha Kropf. 2005. "Ballot Design and Unrecorded Votes on Paper-Based Ballots." *Public Opinion Quarterly.* 69(4): 508–29.

[30]   Koppell, Jonathan GS & Steen, Jennifer A. 2004. "The Effects of Ballot Position on Election Outcomes." *The Journal of Politics.* 66(1): 267–81.

[31]   Kimball, David C., and Martha Kropf. 2005. "Ballot Design and Unrecorded Votes on Paper-Based Ballots." *Public Opinion Quarterly.* 69(4): 508–29.

CHAPTER 9

Conclusion

A. REFLECTING

If this book has impressed any point upon its readers, hopefully, they have come away with the knowledge that the rules which govern our electoral institutions have important implications on the outcomes of those systems. Election law, procedures, and rules are not merely arbitrary structures. Many of our most basic rules have their roots in Constitutional debates. Legislatures and courts have refined, interpreted, and refined again these practices and procedures. We have greatly expanded the franchise, approaching a system of almost universal suffrage. We have opened public office to a wider portion of the population than ever before. We have worked to equalize the relative power of voters in districts and ensure that everyone's political voice is heard. We have made great strides in democratizing the nomination of our political candidates and have worked to limit the potentially corrupting influence of money in our elections.

In Chapter 2 we examined citizens and the right to vote. Tracking the expansion of the franchise, we saw how the history of voting in America is a history of fits and starts. We also discussed the current status of voting rights in the country, paying particular attention to the Voting Rights Act. While the act's preclearance procedures are no longer in effect, its basic principles still protect our voting rights. Whether or not Congress sees fit to amend and restart preclearance still remains to be seen. We also discussed the modern framework for voting, examining rules in states that govern registration, voting, voter identification, and other eligibility rules. These rules mattered because they set the limits of participation, determining the most important players in elections—the voters. Looking forward, it is unclear what path these rules are on. Some states are seeking to adopt more restrictive measures in the name of election security, while others are radically reinventing their election procedures to incorporate new technologies and innovative ways of voting.

We then turned our attention to the candidates in elections, discussing the basic Constitutional qualifications for office as well as a number of rules that govern the eligibility of candidates in the states. Once these candidates are deemed eligible, we looked to see how they gained access to the ballot. By examining the barriers to access for independent and third-party candidates, we saw how the rules advantage and protect our two-party system. These rules are important because they set the limits of our choices. If candidates are ineligible or cannot get their names on the ballot, they are eliminated from consideration. Thus, the universe of our choices is not only set by the candidates who proffer themselves for election, but by the rules that qualify and disqualify those candidates.

Having looked at the major players in elections we began to look at electoral processes by first examining the processes of apportionment, districting, and gerrymandering. In addition to the actors in the game, the playing field is equally important. Setting the bounds of the playing field for legislative elections can have a tremendous impact on electoral outcomes. Whether because of malapportionment, or racial or political gerrymandering, we saw how the districting process can affect the makeup of a districts electorate, and by extension, the outcome of an election, or even the composition of a legislature.

In Chapter 5 we turned our attention to nominating procedures, looking at how we developed our system of direct primaries for sub-presidential offices, as well as examining our complex system of presidential nomination. The procedures we use for selecting candidates for office are just as important as our previously explored qualifications for office.

The Electoral College is another integral part of the American election landscape, and perhaps one of the most unique of our institutions. We explored its history and took an in-depth look at some of the processes that are often less explored. We then engaged in the debate over whether or not the Electoral College should still be used, or whether or not we should reform our system of presidential election. Exploring four different reform proposals, we saw how considerations like federalism and indirect election can introduce factors that confound what could otherwise be a simple popular vote.

Money was another important part of our inquiry into election rules. As the lifeblood of the modern political campaign, the regulation of campaign finance is of critical importance to our electoral environment. With recent elections breaking fundraising records, the importance of money in elections has never been higher. By discussing the history of campaign finance regulations, we saw how the federal government slowly assembled a regulatory framework, before seeing it begin to unravel with recent court decisions.

Finally, we examined how we cast, count, audit, and recount ballots. While many of our elections are simply decided by a plurality vote, we explored new and innovative voting systems, such as the new ranked-choice system being used in Maine. We also looked at how we cast our votes, entering into a particularly topical debate on voting technology, the use of electronic voting machines, and the future of how we cast our ballots. Finally, we discussed how election official canvass, audit, and recount ballots to determine who has won our elections. These rules are critical to the legitimacy of our electoral system. Citizens need to have confidence that their ballot is secure and that their choice will be accurately counted. Likewise, candidates must have confidence in the results of an election and have appropriate recourse in the event that problems occur on Election Day.

The rules of the game do not exist in a vacuum, and they can be tailored in ways to be more or less likely to produce certain outcomes. As shown throughout this book, determining what outcomes are desirable may not be a simple task. One of the most critical parts of any attempt to change or reform electoral rules is to consider the normative outcomes that are most desirable. To illustrate the point again, let us look at voter turnout. To many, increased voter turnout is seen as normatively positive for democracy. Higher voter turnout can be seen as a proxy for the legitimacy of an elected government. However, the right to choose to abstain from voting seems every bit as democratic as voting itself, much more so than coerced voting, for example. Indeed, we might see extremely high turnout in an election in a despotic regime, but that turnout might speak little to legitimacy.

Other concepts yield similarly frustrating contradictions. Our discussion of representation and the creation of majority-minority districts highlights one such tension. Our desire to ensure descriptive and substantive representation of minorities and the requirement that we not let race become a controlling factor in redistricting seem like completely contradictory goals.

Our ability to affect change through electoral laws can also lead to perversions of our democratic principles. Consider our discussion of voting rights in the first chapter of this book. While national trends were expanding the franchise for new groups of voters, concerted efforts to minimize the voting rights of black citizens were extremely successful. Given a desired outcome, restricting black participation, southern states were able to successfully craft an electoral system which effectively disenfranchised black voters for generations.

As time has marched on, it is important to take note that while some of our rules have changed, some have remained the same. In this sense, we cannot always count on our rules to reflect the values of today's political environment. Are we as concerned today that our chief executive is a natural born citizen? Do we still feel the need to have an indirect system of electing our president? These rules were designed in an eighteenth-century world. Do they still apply to the twenty-first century?

Elections are one of the cornerstones of our democracy, and it is important to remember that our elections are only as democratic as the rules which govern them. These rules set the bounds of participation, the geographic extent of representation, the process of nomination, the limitations of the campaign, and the standards for election. Democracies hold elections, but not all elections are held in democracies. Electoral rules can be bent or even broken to the point that elections themselves cease to protect the democratic nature of a government. To ensure that our elections remain a bulwark for democracy, we must be sure that we have crafted a fair and free system, and we must be sure to remain vigilant against changes that would erode the quality of our institutions. Understanding our system, its history, and its operation today is one of the best ways of ensuring that it will continue to stand for democratic governance.

List of State Rules

Alabama

Election Code Source:

Alabama Code Title 17

Rules for Voters

Voter Registration: Yes Deadline: 14 Days Before Election

Absentee Voting: Excuse Required

Early Voting: Absentee Mail Only

Felon Disenfranchisement: Disenfranchised longer than sentence/parole/probation

Voter ID: Must present photo ID

Alternative ID Option: Voters without ID can cast provisional ballot, or vote if election judges attest to voter's identity

Primary Participation: Semi-Open

Rules for Candidates

Independent Filing Deadline: Day of Primary

Sore Loser Law: Yes

Gubernatorial Term Limits: 2 Consecutive Terms

State Legislative Limits: None

Redistricting Authority

State Legislative Districts: State Legislature with Gubernatorial Veto

Congressional Districts: State Legislature with Gubernatorial Veto

Alaska

Election Code Source:

Alaska Statutes Title 15

Rules for Voters

Voter Registration: Auto Deadline: 30 Days Before Election

Absentee Voting: No Excuse Absentee

Early Voting: In Person Early Voting

Felon Disenfranchisement: Disenfranchised until after sentence/parole/probation

Voter ID: Must present ID—need not have a photo

Alternative ID Option: Voters without ID can vote if election judges attest to knowing the person

Primary Participation: Semi-Closed—R

Rules for Candidates

Independent Filing Deadline: Day of Primary

Sore Loser Law: Yes

Gubernatorial Term Limits: 2 Consecutive Terms

State Legislative Limits: None

Redistricting Authority

State Legislative Districts: Independent Commission

Congressional Districts: At Large

Arizona

Election Code Source:

Arizona Revised Statutes Title 16

Rules for Voters

Voter Registration: Yes Deadline: 29 Days Before Election

Absentee Voting: No Excuse Absentee

Early Voting: In Person Early Voting

Felon Disenfranchisement: Disenfranchised longer than sentence/parole/probation

Voter ID: Must present ID—need not have a photo

Alternative ID Option: Voters may cast provisional ballot, but must return with ID later

Primary Participation: Closed for presidential; open for others

Rules for Candidates

Independent Filing Deadline: Same as Party Deadline

Sore Loser Law: Yes

Gubernatorial Term Limits: 2 Consecutive Terms

State Legislative Limits: Lower: 8 Years; Upper: 8 Years

Redistricting Authority

State Legislative Districts: Independent Commission

Congressional Districts: Independent Commission

Arkansas

Election Code Source:

Arkansas Code Title 7

Rules for Voters

Voter Registration: Yes Deadline: 31 Days Before Election

Absentee Voting: Excuse Required

Early Voting: In Person Early Voting

Felon Disenfranchisement: Disenfranchised until after sentence/parole/probation

Voter ID: Must present photo ID

Alternative ID Option: Voters without ID may cast provisional ballot

Primary Participation: Semi-Open

Rules for Candidates

Independent Filing Deadline: After Party Deadline, Before Primary

Sore Loser Law: Yes

Gubernatorial Term Limits: 2 Terms

State Legislative Limits: 16 Years Total (Either/Both Houses)

Redistricting Authority

State Legislative Districts: Political Commission

Congressional Districts: State Legislature with Gubernatorial Veto

California

Election Code Source:

California Election Code

Rules for Voters

Voter Registration: Auto Deadline: 15 Days Before OR EDR at Specific Sites

Absentee Voting: No Excuse Absentee

Early Voting: In Person Early Voting

Felon Disenfranchisement: Disenfranchised until after sentence/parole/ probation

Voter ID: Non-Photo ID required for first time voters

Alternative ID Option: N/A—No ID Required

Primary Participation: Semi-Open—D, Closed—R for presidential; Top—Two Nonpartisan for others

Rules for Candidates

Independent Filing Deadline: Same as Party Deadline

Sore Loser Law: Yes

Gubernatorial Term Limits: 2 Terms

State Legislative Limits: 12 Years Total (Either/Both Houses)

Redistricting Authority

State Legislative Districts: Independent Commission

Congressional Districts: Independent Commission

Colorado

Election Code Source:

Colorado Revised Statutes Title 1

Rules for Voters

Voter Registration: Auto Deadline: Election Day Registration

Absentee Voting: N/A—All Mail Voting

Early Voting: N/A—All Mail Voting

Felon Disenfranchisement: Disenfranchised until after sentence/parole/probation

Voter ID: Must present ID—need not have a photo

Alternative ID Option: N/A—All Mail Elections

Primary Participation: Semi-Open

Rules for Candidates

Independent Filing Deadline: After Primary

Sore Loser Law: Yes

Gubernatorial Term Limits: 2 Consecutive Terms

State Legislative Limits: Lower: 8 Years; Upper: 8 Years

Redistricting Authority

State Legislative Districts: Political Commission

Congressional Districts: State Legislature with Gubernatorial Veto

Connecticut

Election Code Source:

Connecticut General Statutes Title 9

Rules for Voters

Voter Registration: Yes Deadline: 7 Days Before OR EDR at Specific Sites

Absentee Voting: Excuse Required

Early Voting: Absentee Mail Only

Felon Disenfranchisement: Disenfranchised until after sentence/parole/probation

Voter ID: Must present ID—need not have a photo

Alternative ID Option: Voters without ID may sign affidavit/oath

Primary Participation: Semi-Open (Affiliation required, can change on Election Day)

Rules for Candidates

Independent Filing Deadline: After Party Deadline, Before Primary

Sore Loser Law: No

Gubernatorial Term Limits: No Limits

State Legislative Limits: None

Redistricting Authority

State Legislative Districts: State Legislature—No Veto, Backup Commission

Congressional Districts: State Legislature, No Veto, Backup Commission

Delaware

Election Code Source:

Delaware Code Title 15

Rules for Voters

Voter Registration: Yes Deadline: Fourth Saturday Before Election

Absentee Voting: Excuse Required

Early Voting: Absentee Mail Only

Felon Disenfranchisement: Disenfranchised longer than sentence/parole/probation

Voter ID: No ID required

Alternative ID Option: N/A—No ID Required

Primary Participation: Closed

Rules for Candidates

Independent Filing Deadline: After Party Deadline, Before Primary

Sore Loser Law: Yes

Gubernatorial Term Limits: 2 Terms

State Legislative Limits: None

Redistricting Authority

State Legislative Districts: State Legislature with Gubernatorial Veto

Congressional Districts: At Large

District of Columbia

Election Code Source:

D.C. Code Division 1, Title 1, Ch 10

Rules for Voters

Voter Registration: Auto Deadline: Election Day Registration

Absentee Voting: No Excuse Absentee

Early Voting: In Person Early Voting

Felon Disenfranchisement: Disenfranchised until completion of sentence

Voter ID: Non-Photo ID may be required for first time voters

Alternative ID Option: N/A—No ID Required

Primary Participation: Closed

Rules for Candidates

Independent Filing Deadline: After Primary

Sore Loser Law: Yes

Gubernatorial Term Limits: No Limits (Mayor)

State Legislative Limits: None

Redistricting Authority

State Legislative Districts: N/A

Congressional Districts: N/A

Florida

Election Code Source:

Florida Statutes Title IX

Rules for Voters

Voter Registration: Yes Deadline: 29 Days Before Election

Absentee Voting: No Excuse Absentee

Early Voting: In Person Early Voting

Felon Disenfranchisement: Disenfranchised until completion of sentence

Voter ID: Must present photo ID

Alternative ID Option: Voters without ID may cast provisional ballot

Primary Participation: Closed

Rules for Candidates

Independent Filing Deadline: After Party Deadline, Before Primary

Sore Loser Law: Yes

Gubernatorial Term Limits: 2 Consecutive Terms

State Legislative Limits: Lower: 8 Years; Upper: 8 Years

Redistricting Authority

State Legislative Districts: State Legislature—No Veto

Congressional Districts: State Legislature with Gubernatorial Veto

Georgia

Election Code Source:

Georgia Code Title 21

Rules for Voters

Voter Registration: Auto Deadline: Fifth Monday Before Election

Absentee Voting: No Excuse Absentee

Early Voting: In Person Early Voting

Felon Disenfranchisement: Disenfranchised until after sentence/parole/probation

Voter ID: Must present photo ID

Alternative ID Option: Voters may cast provisional ballot, but must return with ID later

Primary Participation: Semi-Open

Rules for Candidates

Independent Filing Deadline: After Primary

Sore Loser Law: Yes

Gubernatorial Term Limits: 2 Consecutive Terms

State Legislative Limits: None

Redistricting Authority

State Legislative Districts: State Legislature with Gubernatorial Veto

Congressional Districts: State Legislature with Gubernatorial Veto

Hawaii

Election Code Source:

Hawaii Revised Statutes Title 2

Rules for Voters

Voter Registration: Yes Deadline: Election Day Registration

Absentee Voting: No Excuse Absentee

Early Voting: In Person Early Voting

Felon Disenfranchisement: Disenfranchised until completion of sentence

Voter ID: Non-Photo ID may be required for first time voters

Alternative ID Option: Voters without ID may sign affidavit/oath

Primary Participation: Pure-Open

Rules for Candidates

Independent Filing Deadline: Same as Party Deadline

Sore Loser Law: Yes

Gubernatorial Term Limits: 2 Consecutive Terms

State Legislative Limits: None

Redistricting Authority

State Legislative Districts: Political Commission

Congressional Districts: Politician Commission

Idaho

Election Code Source:

Idaho Statutes Title 34

Rules for Voters

Voter Registration: Yes Deadline: Election Day Registration

Absentee Voting: No Excuse Absentee

Early Voting: In Person Absentee

Felon Disenfranchisement: Disenfranchised until after sentence/parole/probation

Voter ID: Must present photo ID

Alternative ID Option: Voters without ID may sign affidavit/oath

Primary Participation: Open—D, Closed—R

Rules for Candidates

Independent Filing Deadline: Same as Party Deadline

Sore Loser Law: Yes

Gubernatorial Term Limits: No Limits

State Legislative Limits: None

Redistricting Authority

State Legislative Districts: Independent Commission

Congressional Districts: Independent Commission

Illinois

Election Code Source:

Illinois Revised Statutes Ch. 10, Act 5

Rules for Voters

Voter Registration: Auto Deadline: Election Day Registration

Absentee Voting: No Excuse Absentee

Early Voting: In Person Early Voting

Felon Disenfranchisement: Disenfranchised until completion of sentence

Voter ID: Non-Photo ID may be required for first time voters

Alternative ID Option: N/A—No ID Required

Primary Participation: Semi-Open

Rules for Candidates

Independent Filing Deadline: After Primary

Sore Loser Law: Yes

Gubernatorial Term Limits: No Limits

State Legislative Limits: None

Redistricting Authority

State Legislative Districts: State Legislature with Veto—Backup Commission

Congressional Districts: State Legislature with Gubernatorial Veto

Indiana

Election Code Source:

Indiana Code Title 3

Rules for Voters

Voter Registration: Yes Deadline: 29 Days Before Election

Absentee Voting: Excuse Required

Early Voting: In Person Absentee

Felon Disenfranchisement: Disenfranchised until completion of sentence

Voter ID: Must present photo ID

Alternative ID Option: Voters may cast provisional ballot, but must return with ID later

Primary Participation: Semi-Open

Rules for Candidates

Independent Filing Deadline: After Primary

Sore Loser Law: Yes

Gubernatorial Term Limits: No more than 8 years in 12

State Legislative Limits: None

Redistricting Authority

State Legislative Districts: State Legislature with Gubernatorial Veto

Congressional Districts: State Legislature with Veto—Backup Commission

Iowa

Election Code Source:

Iowa Code Title II

Rules for Voters

Voter Registration: Yes Deadline: Election Day Registration

Absentee Voting: No Excuse Absentee

Early Voting: In Person Absentee

Felon Disenfranchisement: Disenfranchised longer than sentence/parole/probation

Voter ID: Non-Photo ID may be required for first time voters; No ID

Alternative ID Option: Voters without ID may sign affidavit/oath

Primary Participation: Semi-Open (Affiliation required, can change on Election Day)

Rules for Candidates

Independent Filing Deadline: After Primary

Sore Loser Law: No

Gubernatorial Term Limits: No Limits

State Legislative Limits: None

Redistricting Authority

State Legislative Districts: State Legislature with Veto—Advisory Commission

Congressional Districts: State Legislature with Veto—Advisory Commission

Kansas

Election Code Source:

Kansas Statutes Chapter 25

Rules for Voters

Voter Registration: Yes Deadline: 21 Days Before Election

Absentee Voting: No Excuse Absentee

Early Voting: In Person Early Voting

Felon Disenfranchisement: Disenfranchised until after sentence/parole/probation

Voter ID: Must present photo ID

Alternative ID Option: Voters may cast provisional ballot, but must return with ID later

Primary Participation: Semi-Closed

Rules for Candidates

Independent Filing Deadline: After Party Deadline, Before Primary

Sore Loser Law: Yes

Gubernatorial Term Limits: 2 Consecutive Terms

State Legislative Limits: None

Redistricting Authority

State Legislative Districts: State Legislature with Gubernatorial Veto

Congressional Districts: State Legislature with Gubernatorial Veto

Kentucky

Election Code Source:

Kentucky Revised Statutes Chapter 117

Rules for Voters

Voter Registration: Yes Deadline: Fifth Monday Before Election

Absentee Voting: Excuse Required

Early Voting: Absentee Mail Only

Felon Disenfranchisement: Disenfranchised longer than sentence/parole/probation

Voter ID: Must present ID—need not have a photo

Alternative ID Option: Voters without ID may sign affidavit/oath

Primary Participation: Closed

Rules for Candidates

Independent Filing Deadline: After Primary

Sore Loser Law: Yes

Gubernatorial Term Limits: 2 Consecutive Terms

State Legislative Limits: None

Redistricting Authority

State Legislative Districts: State Legislature with Gubernatorial Veto

Congressional Districts: State Legislature with Gubernatorial Veto

Louisiana

Election Code Source:

Louisiana Revised Statutes Title 18

Rules for Voters

Voter Registration: Yes Deadline: 30 Days Before Election

Absentee Voting: Excuse Required

Early Voting: In Person Early Voting

Felon Disenfranchisement: Disenfranchised until after sentence/parole/probation

Voter ID: Must present photo ID

Alternative ID Option: Voters without ID may sign affidavit/oath

Primary Participation: Closed for presidential primary; runoff system for other races

Rules for Candidates

Independent Filing Deadline: After Party Deadline, Before Primary

Sore Loser Law: Yes

Gubernatorial Term Limits: 2 Consecutive Terms

State Legislative Limits: Lower: 12 Years; Upper: 12 Years

Redistricting Authority

State Legislative Districts: State Legislature with Gubernatorial Veto

Congressional Districts: State Legislature with Gubernatorial Veto

Maine

Election Code Source:

Maine Revised Statutes Title 21-A

Rules for Voters

Voter Registration: Yes Deadline: Election Day Registration

Absentee Voting: No Excuse Absentee

Early Voting: In Person Absentee

Felon Disenfranchisement: Not Disenfranchised

Voter ID: Non-Photo ID may be required for first time voters; No ID

Alternative ID Option: N/A—No ID Required

Primary Participation: Closed (Unaffiliated may affiliate at the polls)

Rules for Candidates

Independent Filing Deadline: After Party Deadline, Before Primary

Sore Loser Law: Yes

Gubernatorial Term Limits: 2 Consecutive Terms

State Legislative Limits: Lower: 8 Years; Upper: 8 Years

Redistricting Authority

State Legislative Districts: State Legislature with Veto—Advisory Commission

Congressional Districts: State Legislature with Veto—Advisory Commission

Maryland

Election Code Source:

Maryland Code—Election Law

Rules for Voters

Voter Registration: Auto Deadline: 22 Days Before OR During Early Voting (NO EDR)

Absentee Voting: No Excuse Absentee

Early Voting: In Person Early Voting

Felon Disenfranchisement: Disenfranchised until completion of sentence

Voter ID: Non-Photo ID may be required for first time voters; No ID

Alternative ID Option: N/A—No ID Required

Primary Participation: Closed

Rules for Candidates

Independent Filing Deadline: After Primary

Sore Loser Law: Yes

Gubernatorial Term Limits: 2 Consecutive Terms

State Legislative Limits: None

Redistricting Authority

State Legislative Districts: State Legislature—No Veto

Congressional Districts: State Legislature with Gubernatorial Veto

Massachusetts

Election Code Source:

Massachusetts General Laws Part I, Title VIII

Rules for Voters

Voter Registration: Yes Deadline: 20 Days Before Election

Absentee Voting: Excuse Required

Early Voting: In Person Early Voting

Felon Disenfranchisement: Disenfranchised until completion of sentence

Voter ID: Non-Photo ID may be required for first time voters; No ID

Alternative ID Option: N/A—No ID Required

Primary Participation: Semi-Closed

Rules for Candidates

Independent Filing Deadline: After Party Deadline, Before Primary

Sore Loser Law: Yes

Gubernatorial Term Limits: No Limits

State Legislative Limits: None

Redistricting Authority

State Legislative Districts: State Legislature with Gubernatorial Veto

Congressional Districts: State Legislature with Gubernatorial Veto

Michigan

Election Code Source:

Michigan Compiled Laws Chapter 168

Rules for Voters

Voter Registration: Yes Deadline: 30 Days Before Election

Absentee Voting: Excuse Required

Early Voting: Absentee Mail Only

Felon Disenfranchisement: Disenfranchised until completion of sentence

Voter ID: Must present photo ID

Alternative ID Option: Voters without ID may sign affidavit/oath

Primary Participation: Pure-Open

Rules for Candidates

Independent Filing Deadline: After Party Deadline, Before Primary

Sore Loser Law: Yes

Gubernatorial Term Limits: 2 Terms

State Legislative Limits: Lower: 6 Years; Upper: 8 Years

Redistricting Authority

State Legislative Districts: State Legislature with Gubernatorial Veto

Congressional Districts: State Legislature with Gubernatorial Veto

Minnesota

Election Code Source:

Minnesota Statues Ch. 200–212

Rules for Voters

Voter Registration: Yes Deadline: Election Day Registration

Absentee Voting: No Excuse Absentee

Early Voting: In Person Absentee

Felon Disenfranchisement: Disenfranchised until after sentence/parole/ probation

Voter ID: No ID required

Alternative ID Option: N/A—No ID Required

Primary Participation: Pure-Open

Rules for Candidates

Independent Filing Deadline: Same as Party Deadline

Sore Loser Law: Yes

Gubernatorial Term Limits: No Limits

State Legislative Limits: None

Redistricting Authority

State Legislative Districts: State Legislature with Gubernatorial Veto

Congressional Districts: State Legislature with Gubernatorial Veto

Mississippi

Election Code Source:

Mississippi Code Title 23

Rules for Voters

Voter Registration: Yes Deadline: 30 Days Before Election

Absentee Voting: Excuse Required

Early Voting: Absentee Mail Only

Felon Disenfranchisement: Disenfranchised longer than sentence/parole/ probation

Voter ID: Must present photo ID

Alternative ID Option: Voters may cast provisional ballot, but must return with ID later

Primary Participation: Semi-Open

Rules for Candidates

Independent Filing Deadline: Same as Party Deadline

Sore Loser Law: Yes

Gubernatorial Term Limits: 2 Terms

State Legislative Limits: None

Redistricting Authority

State Legislative Districts: State Legislature—No Veto, Backup Commission

Congressional Districts: State Legislature with Gubernatorial Veto

Missouri

Election Code Source:

Missouri Revised Statutes Title IX

Rules for Voters

Voter Registration: Yes Deadline: Fourth Wednesday Before Election

Absentee Voting: Excuse Required

Early Voting: Absentee Mail Only

Felon Disenfranchisement: Disenfranchised until after sentence/parole/probation

Voter ID: Must present photo ID

Alternative ID Option: Provisional ballot with non-photo id; If no ID, can vote if election judges attest to voter's identity

Primary Participation: Semi-Open

Rules for Candidates

Independent Filing Deadline: After Party Deadline, Before Primary

Sore Loser Law: Yes

Gubernatorial Term Limits: 2 Terms

State Legislative Limits: Lower: 8 Years; Upper: 8 Years

Redistricting Authority

State Legislative Districts: Political Commission

Congressional Districts: State Legislature with Gubernatorial Veto

Montana

Election Code Source:

Montana Code Title 13

Rules for Voters

Voter Registration: Yes Deadline: 30 Days Before OR EDR at specific sites

Absentee Voting: No Excuse Absentee

Early Voting: In Person Absentee

Felon Disenfranchisement: Disenfranchised until completion of sentence

Voter ID: Must present ID—need not have a photo

Alternative ID Option: Voters without ID may cast provisional ballot

Primary Participation: Pure-Open

Rules for Candidates

Independent Filing Deadline: After Party Deadline, Before Primary

Sore Loser Law: Yes

Gubernatorial Term Limits: No more than 8 years in 16

State Legislative Limits: Lower: 8 Years; Upper: 8 Years

Redistricting Authority

State Legislative Districts: Independent Commission

Congressional Districts: At Large

Nebraska

Election Code Source:

Nebraska Revised Statues Ch. 32

Rules for Voters

Voter Registration: Yes Deadline: Second Friday Before Election

Absentee Voting: No Excuse Absentee

Early Voting: In Person Early Voting

Felon Disenfranchisement: Disenfranchised longer than sentence/parole/probation

Voter ID: Non-Photo ID may be required for first time voters; No ID

Alternative ID Option: N/A—No ID Required

Primary Participation: Semi-Closed

Rules for Candidates

Independent Filing Deadline: After Primary

Sore Loser Law: Yes

Gubernatorial Term Limits: 2 Consecutive Terms

State Legislative Limits: Unicameral: 8 Years

Redistricting Authority

State Legislative Districts: State Legislature with Gubernatorial Veto

Congressional Districts: State Legislature with Gubernatorial Veto

Nevada

Election Code Source:

Nevada Revised Statutes Title 24,

Rules for Voters

Voter Registration: Yes Deadline: Third Tuesday Before Election

Absentee Voting: No Excuse Absentee

Early Voting: In Person Early Voting

Felon Disenfranchisement: Disenfranchised longer than sentence/parole/probation

Voter ID: No ID required

Alternative ID Option: N/A—No ID Required

Primary Participation: Closed

Rules for Candidates

Independent Filing Deadline: After Party Deadline, Before Primary

Sore Loser Law: Yes

Gubernatorial Term Limits: 2 Terms

State Legislative Limits: Lower: 12 Years; Upper: 12 Years

Redistricting Authority

State Legislative Districts: State Legislature with Gubernatorial Veto

Congressional Districts: State Legislature with Gubernatorial Veto

New Hampshire

Election Code Source:

New Hampshire Revised Statutes Title LXIII

Rules for Voters

Voter Registration: Yes Deadline: Election Day Registration

Absentee Voting: Excuse Required

Early Voting: Absentee Mail Only

Felon Disenfranchisement: Disenfranchised until completion of sentence

Voter ID: Must present photo ID

Alternative ID Option: Voters without ID may sign affidavit/oath

Primary Participation: Semi-Open (Affiliation required, can change on Election Day)

Rules for Candidates

Independent Filing Deadline: After Party Deadline, Before Primary

Sore Loser Law: Yes

Gubernatorial Term Limits: No Limits

State Legislative Limits: None

Redistricting Authority

State Legislative Districts: State Legislature with Gubernatorial Veto

Congressional Districts: State Legislature with Gubernatorial Veto

New Jersey

Election Code Source:

New Jersey Statutes Annotated Title 19; New Jersey Administrative Code Title 10 Subchapter 10

Rules for Voters

Voter Registration: Auto Deadline: 21 Days Before Election

Absentee Voting: No Excuse Absentee

Early Voting: In Person Absentee

Felon Disenfranchisement: Disenfranchised until after sentence/parole/ probation

Voter ID: Non-Photo ID may be required for first time voters; No ID

Alternative ID Option: N/A—No ID Required

Primary Participation: Semi-Closed

Rules for Candidates

Independent Filing Deadline: Day of Primary

Sore Loser Law: Yes

Gubernatorial Term Limits: 2 Consecutive Terms

State Legislative Limits: None

Redistricting Authority

State Legislative Districts: Political Commission

Congressional Districts: Politician Commission

New Mexico

Election Code Source:

New Mexico Statutes Ch. 1

Rules for Voters

Voter Registration: Yes Deadline: 28 Days Before Election

Absentee Voting: No Excuse Absentee

Early Voting: In Person Early Voting

Felon Disenfranchisement: Disenfranchised until after sentence/parole/ probation

Voter ID: Non-Photo ID may be required for first time voters; No ID

Alternative ID Option: N/A—No ID Required

Primary Participation: Closed

Rules for Candidates

Independent Filing Deadline: After Primary

Sore Loser Law: Yes

Gubernatorial Term Limits: 2 Consecutive Terms

State Legislative Limits: None

Redistricting Authority

State Legislative Districts: State Legislature with Gubernatorial Veto

Congressional Districts: State Legislature with Gubernatorial Veto

New York

Election Code Source:

New York Election Law

Rules for Voters

Voter Registration: Yes Deadline: 25 Days Before Election

Absentee Voting: Excuse Required

Early Voting: Absentee Mail Only

Felon Disenfranchisement: Disenfranchised until after sentence/parole/probation

Voter ID: Non-Photo ID may be required for first time voters; No ID

Alternative ID Option: N/A—No ID Required

Primary Participation: Closed

Rules for Candidates

Independent Filing Deadline: After Primary

Sore Loser Law: No

Gubernatorial Term Limits: No Limits

State Legislative Limits: None

Redistricting Authority

State Legislative Districts: State Legislature with Veto—Advisory Commission

Congressional Districts: State Legislature with Veto—Advisory Commission

North Carolina

Election Code Source:

North Carolina General Statutes Ch. 163A

Rules for Voters

Voter Registration: Yes Deadline: 25 Days Before OR During Early Voting (NO EDR)

Absentee Voting: No Excuse Absentee

Early Voting: In Person Early Voting

Felon Disenfranchisement: Disenfranchised until after sentence/parole/probation

Voter ID: Non-Photo ID may be required for first time voters; No ID

Alternative ID Option: N/A—No ID Required

Primary Participation: Semi-Closed

Rules for Candidates

Independent Filing Deadline: After Party Deadline, Before Primary

Sore Loser Law: Yes

Gubernatorial Term Limits: 2 Consecutive Terms

State Legislative Limits: None

Redistricting Authority

State Legislative Districts: State Legislature—No Veto

Congressional Districts: State Legislature, No Veto

North Dakota

Election Code Source:

North Dakota Century Code Title 16.1

Rules for Voters

Voter Registration: No Deadline: N/A

Absentee Voting: No Excuse Absentee

Early Voting: In Person Early Voting

Felon Disenfranchisement: Disenfranchised until completion of sentence

Voter ID: Must present ID—need not have a photo

Alternative ID Option: Voters may cast provisional ballot, but must return with ID later

Primary Participation: Pure-Open

Rules for Candidates

Independent Filing Deadline: After Primary

Sore Loser Law: Yes

Gubernatorial Term Limits: No Limits

State Legislative Limits: None

Redistricting Authority

State Legislative Districts: State Legislature with Gubernatorial Veto

Congressional Districts: At Large

Ohio

Election Code Source:

Ohio Revised Code Title XXXV

Rules for Voters

Voter Registration: Yes Deadline: 30 Days Before Election

Absentee Voting: No Excuse Absentee

Early Voting: In Person Absentee

Felon Disenfranchisement: Disenfranchised until completion of sentence

Voter ID: Must present ID—need not have a photo

Alternative ID Option: Voters may cast provisional ballot, but must return with ID later

Primary Participation: Semi-Open

Rules for Candidates

Independent Filing Deadline: After Party Deadline, Before Primary

Sore Loser Law: Yes

Gubernatorial Term Limits: 2 Consecutive Terms

State Legislative Limits: Lower: 8 Years; Upper: 8 Years

Redistricting Authority

State Legislative Districts: Political Commission

Congressional Districts: State Legislature with Veto—Backup Commission

Oklahoma

Election Code Source:

Oklahoma Statutes Title 26

Rules for Voters

Voter Registration: Yes Deadline: 25 Days Before Election

Absentee Voting: No Excuse Absentee

Early Voting: In Person Absentee

Felon Disenfranchisement: Disenfranchised until after sentence/parole/probation

Voter ID: Must present ID—need not have a photo

Alternative ID Option: Voters without ID may cast provisional ballot

Primary Participation: Semi-Closed—D

Rules for Candidates

Independent Filing Deadline: Same as Party Deadline

Sore Loser Law: Yes

Gubernatorial Term Limits: 2 Terms

State Legislative Limits: 12 Years Total (Either/Both Houses)

Redistricting Authority

State Legislative Districts: State Legislature with Veto—Backup Commission

Congressional Districts: State Legislature with Gubernatorial Veto

Oregon

Election Code Source:

Oregon Revised Statutes Ch. 254

Rules for Voters

Voter Registration: Auto Deadline: Automatic Voter Registration

Absentee Voting: N/A—All Mail Voting

Early Voting: N/A—All Mail Voting

Felon Disenfranchisement: Disenfranchised until completion of sentence

Voter ID: No ID required

Alternative ID Option: N/A—No ID Required

Primary Participation: Closed

Rules for Candidates

Independent Filing Deadline: After Primary

Sore Loser Law: Yes

Gubernatorial Term Limits: No more than 8 years in 12

State Legislative Limits: None

Redistricting Authority

State Legislative Districts: State Legislature with Gubernatorial Veto

Congressional Districts: State Legislature with Gubernatorial Veto

Pennsylvania

Election Code Source:

Pennsylvania Election Code

Rules for Voters

Voter Registration: Yes Deadline: 30 Days Before Election

Absentee Voting: Excuse Required

Early Voting: Absentee Mail Only

Felon Disenfranchisement: Disenfranchised until completion of sentence

Voter ID: Non-Photo ID may be required for first time voters; No ID

Alternative ID Option: N/A—No ID Required

Primary Participation: Closed

Rules for Candidates

Independent Filing Deadline: After Primary

Sore Loser Law: Yes

Gubernatorial Term Limits: 2 Consecutive Terms

State Legislative Limits: None

Redistricting Authority

State Legislative Districts: Political Commission

Congressional Districts: State Legislature with Gubernatorial Veto

Rhode Island

Election Code Source:

Rhode Island General Laws Title 17

Rules for Voters

Voter Registration: Auto Deadline: 30 Days Before OR EDR for Presidential Elections ONLY

Absentee Voting: Excuse Required

Early Voting: Absentee Mail Only

Felon Disenfranchisement: Disenfranchised until completion of sentence

Voter ID: Must present photo ID

Alternative ID Option: Voters without ID may cast provisional ballot

Primary Participation: Semi-Closed

Rules for Candidates

Independent Filing Deadline: After Party Deadline, Before Primary

Sore Loser Law: Yes

Gubernatorial Term Limits: 2 Consecutive Terms

State Legislative Limits: None

Redistricting Authority

State Legislative Districts: State Legislature with Veto—Advisory Commission

Congressional Districts: State Legislature with Veto—Advisory Commission

South Carolina

Election Code Source:

South Carolina Code of Laws Title 7

Rules for Voters

Voter Registration: Yes Deadline: 30 Days Before Election

Absentee Voting: Excuse Required

Early Voting: Absentee Mail Only

Felon Disenfranchisement: Disenfranchised until after sentence/parole/probation

Voter ID: Must present photo ID

Alternative ID Option: Those with an impediment can be exempted

Primary Participation: Semi-Open

Rules for Candidates

Independent Filing Deadline: After Primary

Sore Loser Law: Yes

Gubernatorial Term Limits: 2 Consecutive Terms

State Legislative Limits: None

Redistricting Authority

State Legislative Districts: State Legislature with Gubernatorial Veto

Congressional Districts: State Legislature with Gubernatorial Veto

South Dakota

Election Code Source:

South Dakota Codified Laws Title 12

Rules for Voters

Voter Registration: Yes Deadline: 15 Days Before Election

Absentee Voting: No Excuse Absentee

Early Voting: In Person Absentee

Felon Disenfranchisement: Disenfranchised until after sentence/parole/ probation

Voter ID: Must present photo ID

Alternative ID Option: Voters without ID may sign affidavit/oath

Primary Participation: Semi-Closed—D

Rules for Candidates

Independent Filing Deadline: After Party Deadline, Before Primary

Sore Loser Law: Yes

Gubernatorial Term Limits: 2 Consecutive Terms

State Legislative Limits: Lower: 8 Years; Upper: 8 Years

Redistricting Authority

State Legislative Districts: State Legislature with Gubernatorial Veto

Congressional Districts: At Large

Tennessee

Election Code Source:

Tennessee Code Title 2

Rules for Voters

Voter Registration: Yes Deadline: 30 Days Before Election

Absentee Voting: Excuse Required

Early Voting: In Person Early Voting

Felon Disenfranchisement: Disenfranchised longer than sentence/parole/probation

Voter ID: Must present photo ID

Alternative ID Option: Voters may cast provisional ballot, but must return with ID later

Primary Participation: Semi-Open

Rules for Candidates

Independent Filing Deadline: Same as Party Deadline

Sore Loser Law: Yes

Gubernatorial Term Limits: 2 Consecutive Terms

State Legislative Limits: None

Redistricting Authority

State Legislative Districts: State Legislature with Gubernatorial Veto

Congressional Districts: State Legislature with Gubernatorial Veto

Texas

Election Code Source:

Texas Election Code

Rules for Voters

Voter Registration: Yes Deadline: 30 Days Before Election

Absentee Voting: Excuse Required

Early Voting: In Person Early Voting

Felon Disenfranchisement: Disenfranchised until after sentence/parole/probation

Voter ID: Must present photo ID

Alternative ID Option: Those with an impediment can be exempted

Primary Participation: Semi-Open

Rules for Candidates

Independent Filing Deadline: After Primary

Sore Loser Law: Yes

Gubernatorial Term Limits: No Limits

State Legislative Limits: None

Redistricting Authority

State Legislative Districts: State Legislature with Veto—Backup Commission

Congressional Districts: State Legislature with Gubernatorial Veto

Utah

Election Code Source:

Utah Code Title 20A

Rules for Voters

Voter Registration: Yes Deadline: Election Day Registration

Absentee Voting: No Excuse Absentee

Early Voting: In Person Early Voting

Felon Disenfranchisement: Disenfranchised until completion of sentence

Voter ID: Must present ID—need not have a photo

Alternative ID Option: Voters without ID may cast provisional ballot

Primary Participation: Semi-Closed

Rules for Candidates

Independent Filing Deadline: Same as Party Deadline

Sore Loser Law: Yes

Gubernatorial Term Limits: No Limits

State Legislative Limits: None

Redistricting Authority

State Legislative Districts: State Legislature with Gubernatorial Veto

Congressional Districts: State Legislature with Gubernatorial Veto

Vermont

Election Code Source:

Vermont Statutes Title 17

Rules for Voters

Voter Registration: Auto Deadline: Election Day Registration

Absentee Voting: No Excuse Absentee

Early Voting: In Person Absentee

Felon Disenfranchisement: Not Disenfranchised

Voter ID: Non-Photo ID may be required for first time voters; No ID

Alternative ID Option: N/A—No ID Required

Primary Participation: Pure-Open

Rules for Candidates

Independent Filing Deadline: After Party Deadline, Before Primary

Sore Loser Law: Yes

Gubernatorial Term Limits: No Limits

State Legislative Limits: None

Redistricting Authority

State Legislative Districts: State Legislature with Gubernatorial Veto

Congressional Districts: At Large

Virginia

Election Code Source:

Code of Virginia Title 24.2

Rules for Voters

Voter Registration: Yes Deadline: 22 Days Before Election

Absentee Voting: Excuse Required

Early Voting: Absentee Mail Only

Felon Disenfranchisement: Disenfranchised longer than sentence/parole/probation

Voter ID: Must present photo ID

Alternative ID Option: Voters may cast provisional ballot, but must return with ID later

Primary Participation: Semi-Open

Rules for Candidates

Independent Filing Deadline: Day of Primary

Sore Loser Law: Yes

Gubernatorial Term Limits: 1 Consecutive Term

State Legislative Limits: None

Redistricting Authority

State Legislative Districts: State Legislature with Gubernatorial Veto

Congressional Districts: State Legislature with Gubernatorial Veto

Washington

Election Code Source:

Revised Code of Washington Title 29A

Rules for Voters

Voter Registration: Yes Deadline: Election Day Registration

Absentee Voting: N/A—All Mail Voting

Early Voting: N/A—All Mail Voting

Felon Disenfranchisement: Disenfranchised until after sentence/parole/probation

Voter ID: Must present ID—need not have a photo

Alternative ID Option: N/A—All Mail Elections

Primary Participation: Open—D, Closed—R for presidential; Top—Two Nonpartisan for others

Rules for Candidates

Independent Filing Deadline: Same as Party Deadline

Sore Loser Law: Yes

Gubernatorial Term Limits: No Limits

State Legislative Limits: None

Redistricting Authority

State Legislative Districts: Independent Commission

Congressional Districts: Independent Commission

West Virginia

Election Code Source:

West Virginia Code Chapter 3

Rules for Voters

Voter Registration: Auto Deadline: 21 Days Before Election

Absentee Voting: Excuse Required

Early Voting: In Person Early Voting

Felon Disenfranchisement: Disenfranchised until after sentence/parole/ probation

Voter ID: Must present ID—need not have a photo

Alternative ID Option: Voters may cast provisional ballot, but must return with ID later

Primary Participation: Semi-Closed

Rules for Candidates

Independent Filing Deadline: After Primary

Sore Loser Law: Yes

Gubernatorial Term Limits: 2 Consecutive Terms

State Legislative Limits: None

Redistricting Authority

State Legislative Districts: State Legislature with Gubernatorial Veto

Congressional Districts: State Legislature with Gubernatorial Veto

Wisconsin

Election Code Source:

Wisconsin Statutes Ch. 5–12

Rules for Voters

Voter Registration: Yes Deadline: Election Day Registration

Absentee Voting: No Excuse Absentee

Early Voting: In Person Absentee

Felon Disenfranchisement: Disenfranchised longer than sentence/parole/ probation

Voter ID: Must present photo ID

Alternative ID Option: Voters may cast provisional ballot, but must return with ID later

Primary Participation: Pure-Open

Rules for Candidates

Independent Filing Deadline: Same as Party Deadline

Sore Loser Law: Yes

Gubernatorial Term Limits: No Limits

State Legislative Limits: None

Redistricting Authority

State Legislative Districts: State Legislature with Gubernatorial Veto

Congressional Districts: State Legislature with Gubernatorial Veto

Wyoming

Election Code Source:

Wyoming Statutes Title 22; Wyoming Administrative Rules 002.0005

Rules for Voters

Voter Registration: Yes Deadline: Election Day Registration

Absentee Voting: No Excuse Absentee

Early Voting: In Person Absentee

Felon Disenfranchisement: Disenfranchised longer than sentence/parole/probation

Voter ID: Photo ID may be required for first time voters; No ID for

Alternative ID Option: N/A—No ID Required

Primary Participation: Semi-Open

Rules for Candidates

Independent Filing Deadline: After Primary

Sore Loser Law: Yes

Gubernatorial Term Limits: No more than 8 years in 16

State Legislative Limits: None

Redistricting Authority

State Legislative Districts: State Legislature with Gubernatorial Veto

Congressional Districts: At Large